CKS:

PACIFIST BISHOP AT WAR

EDWARD LEE HICKS:

PACIFIST BISHOP AT WAR

G. R. EVANS

LION

Published by Lion Books
an imprint of
Lion Hudson plc
Wilkinson House, Jordan Hill Road,
Oxford OX2 8DR, England
www.lionhudson.com/lion

ISBN 978 0 7459 5653 4
e-ISBN 978 0 7459 5655 7

First edition 2014

Acknowledgments
Cover images: Barbed wire © bulentgultek/iStock; Cross necklace © Hepp/iStock; British soldiers silhouetted along a ridge © Time & Life Pictures/Getty Images

A catalogue record for this book is available from the British Library

Printed and bound in the UK, September 2014, LH26

Contents

Acknowledgments

This is the place warmly to thank Alison Hull, commissioning editor at Lion, for expert editing and enjoyable discussions. The book owes a good deal, too, to bishops and clergy I have known down the years who have given me as a lay theologian some insight into the problems they faced. And anyone seeking to explore Edward Hicks's life owes an immense debt to Graham Neville's edition of the diaries for the Lincoln Record Society and his study of the radical politics of this likeable bishop.

Preface

W hat does a bishop who has declared himself to be against the use of military force do when his country goes to war? Britain was a great power and confident of her international importance and her right to respond to threats with all the force she could muster. The tide of the times was against a man who did not see things in that way during the First World War.

Edward Hicks kept frank and outspoken diaries of his time as Bishop of Lincoln before and during the war (1910–19). He often felt himself to be an outsider, perhaps partly because his background was not the usual one for such a senior churchman. But he was living through a succession of enormous changes in national life and attitudes and he was not a person to let that happen without doing what he could to influence the outcome.

The diaries – intimate, lively, full of risky remarks – offer glimpses of the scope being a bishop could give to an able and principled person willing to take some risks and work for unpopular or controversial causes. He sent one of his daughters to Oxford as one of its first women students and supported votes for women. He had long been a great campaigner for temperance because he saw the social and personal damage excess alcohol consumption was doing among the poor (and to some of the clergy too). When he was made a bishop he kept that up, and other campaigns, some of them growing unfashionable or looking very different in wartime.

But above all, he had to work out how to respond to the needs the war threw up in his diocese and beyond. The story of Edward Hicks and his family and their struggles to do the right thing in the Lincolnshire of the First World War throws new light in close-up on the problems of conscience the war created. He saw his own sons off to war. His views changed. He found he had to adapt to the surprising demands war made on his family, his diocese and his people. This book lets him add, partly in his own words, how he coped with the questions which arose among the people of the local churches – and the many local people who never went to church but found they wanted to be confirmed when war broke out.

The Man and the Job

Chapter 1

Beginnings

Soon after Edward Lee Hicks died, his children and his wife gave his first biographer, J. H. Fowler, descriptions of the husband and father they had known. It was Edward's wife, Agnes, who chose Fowler to write about her husband. Fowler had known him pretty well and he speaks warmly of the personal debt he felt after "a friendship of thirty years".

Christina, the younger daughter, one of the first generation of women to go to Oxford, described him for Fowler. She told him her father had made himself accessible to "any beggar, any poor woman, any broken-down man" who might appear, even at mealtimes. They would be "seen at once". "We seldom had an uninterrupted meal." She stressed that he was equally ready when his children needed him, though as a man of many interests he was not at home for much of the day. "He was always endlessly busy, and we saw, in point of time, little of him."

When he *was* at home, he made a point of spending time with his children; he treated them as intellectual equals: "Our raw opinions and uninstructed thoughts never seemed to be dull to him. We were never snubbed, and always encouraged to talk as to an equal in mind." He did not force the children to go to meetings they would not enjoy. But he would tell them "the things he had seen, noticed and thought during the day". He talked to them enthusiastically about music, painting and books:

When pictures were on a wall, my father looked at them. They were not to him as part of the wall-paper, though he saw them every day. … He really put his whole heart into whatever was on hand … He wanted to know all we were doing. He was always to us inspiration, zest of life.

He believed his children should follow their bent, girls and boys alike. "And we learnt, or ought to have learnt, to laugh at people without being unkind. My father was a first-rate mimic."

Before we meet this family of much-enjoyed children properly, there is a story to tell of Edward Hicks's own boyhood and his life before his marriage.

GROWING UP: THE SCHOOLBOY AND THE STUDENT

Edward Hicks was born on 18 December 1843 in Oxford, the elder son of a not very successful local tradesman. His father may not have been a leading businessman but that was not because he was idle or lacked ability. He had strong and varied interests. He was a great reader and a keen musician. He was politically active, supporting the Liberals locally. He campaigned against the Corn Laws, which were designed to protect the interests of great landowners but meant that the price of cereal crops rose and the poor went hungry. Edward described his father as "volatile, excitable, full of fun, industrious but unbusinesslike, dilatory and often irritable". On the other hand, he was "absolutely free from affectation or vanity, punctiliously neat, endlessly kind, generous, humble, but of unshrinking truth and courage". This second list, together with a sense of fun, were qualities in his father that Edward shared, and seems to have tried to cultivate in himself.

Edward's father's family came from Wolvercote, a few miles to the north of Oxford. For generations they had been tenant farmers of the Dukes of Marlborough at Blenheim Palace in nearby Woodstock. His mother, born Catherine Pugh (1812–97), was an Oxford girl, born in the working-class district of St Ebbe's, down the hill from Christ Church. She had little education but a sharp mind, a good deal of self-discipline and a strong sense of propriety. She allowed herself to read nothing but the Bible and books of a religiously improving sort in the daytime, but when evening came she read novels, poetry and biographies (especially of churchmen).

Edward's mother had been a Methodist as a child, but she became fed up with the squabbles among the Methodists. They seemed to her to be entangled in controversy and internal divisions, and she and her husband began to worship as members of the Church of England. Edward's parents brought him up as an evangelical Anglican as well as influencing him with their liberal political ideas, but he was left with an understanding of the Methodists which was going to be very useful to him when he became Bishop of the diocese of Lincoln, Wesley's birthplace.

Edward's parents – especially his mother – saw a good education as the way to climb the social ladder to an interesting life in which he would be able to have an impact for good. They sent him to school in St John Street, a handsome late-Regency street, then a relatively new speculative building venture of St John's College, Oxford. The 1851 census reveals that the houses were in multiple occupation and this little school would presumably have been one of the pioneering business ventures this new money-making project of the college was making possible. The schoolmaster was called Crapper and he taught the boys to be neat and learn assiduously, but he did not teach them Latin and Greek, without which no one could then hope to get a university degree.

From this small school, Edward went to Magdalen College School as a day boy. His mother took him there herself, and talked to the headmaster. She persuaded him to give Edward a scholarship, despite the fact that he was rather old to begin the classical languages he would need to succeed in such a school. (She later got a place for his younger brother too.)

At this school Edward turned out to be good at sport, especially swimming and rowing, and he famously beat a boy called Payne in a fight which went on for several days (with breaks for lessons). Here he had his first experience of the social distance between himself and many of the other boys. His lower middle-class home, and his family increasingly struggling with debt as his father's business failed, placed him at a social disadvantage. Perhaps this was where he first acquired skills in mixing with all classes in the class-ridden society of England in which he would one day become a bishop. He certainly became very good at it.

He turned out to be an extremely clever boy. Although he had begun Latin and Greek so late, he won the President's Medal for Greek and Latin Composition in his last year at the school. He had become something of a favourite of the headmaster too. He was able to win a scholarship to Brasenose College, Oxford.

BRASENOSE AND HENRY BAZELY

At Brasenose, Edward got a First Class degree in 1866. But he spent his time as an undergraduate talking as well as studying. Henry Bazely became Edward's close friend when they began as students together at the college in 1861. After Bazely's early death in 1886, Hicks published a "memoir" in the form of a book about him. It reveals Edward Hicks thinking through his opinions as a Christian for himself and it also shows him encountering a personality willing to take extreme risks with his own future, so as to awaken religious faith in ordinary people. Bazely was quite extreme. The French commentator Hippolyte Taine spoke (and Hicks put it) of his "intense conviction, which for lack of an outlet would degenerate into madness, melancholy or sedition".

Henry Bazely's extraordinary clerical adventures need to be seen against the background of some major upheavals in Oxford about the very nature and purpose of the church. Oxford had been the centre of the Tractarian Movement in the 1830s. This "movement" was named after a series of "Tracts" published between 1833 and 1841. It was led by individuals whose names would still have been familiar to Oxford's inhabitants when Edward Hicks was at the university as a student and later a don: Edward Pusey (after whom Pusey House was named in 1884); John Keble (who gave his name to Keble College, founded in 1870) and John Henry Newman of Oriel College, who had taken the Movement's concerns to what seemed to him the logical conclusion and become a Roman Catholic.

The Tractarians' *Tracts for the Times* had opened up a discussion about the fundamental position of the Church of England in the history of the Christian Church. The Tractarians said it should see itself as a "branch" of the universal church, like the Roman Catholic and Orthodox churches, its faith and order flowing from the early church as theirs could be shown to do. They did not consider that the Reformation of the sixteenth century had separated the Church of England from that tradition. They encouraged people to read early Christian writers and published translations in a *Library of the Fathers*.

Adherents of this "Oxford Movement" tended to favour ritual. They positioned themselves at the opposite end of the spectrum of churchmanship from the evangelicals. All this Henry Bazely resisted, and he was not alone. It was partly because of this particular "party preference" that the Oxford Movement created a controversy which continued to have an impact throughout the century.

The impact of the Tractarians led to some hard thinking about contemporary social needs and the foundation of the Christian Social Union (CSU). Edward Hicks was active in this organization as it evolved to attract a wider church, including people who were not themselves Tractarians.

Henry Bazely's father had been a Tractarian. His son reacted strongly against such an extreme high church position: "His father used to say to him, 'you are the most contradictious little chap I ever knew.'" Henry and Edward Hicks also had theological arguments, especially about the organization of the church and its ministry. Hicks says he was "surprised at his decided objections to Episcopacy, his strong Calvinism". These Calvinist sympathies took Bazely to Scotland to learn more about the way Presbyterianism worked in practice. He went to hear lectures in Aberdeen. But he expressed some disappointment:

> *The course of education for the ministry appears to be in itself very excellent and thorough, but I must confess I do not see any good effects of it in the students. They strike me as being a very worldly set of men, addicted ... to smoking and whiskey drinking ... I am very much disappointed.*

Hicks stresses that he himself was not persuaded by Bazely's arguments:

> *My own theological position is very different from that of my friend. Much of his conduct in relation to the Church of England ... I cannot approve, greatly as I admire his motives.*

But it is evident that he had given thought to the theology of episcopacy and remained sure in his own mind that bishops were good for the church, for he was not tempted to imitate what Bazely had done.

By 1875, Bazely had been ordained as a deacon in the Church of England, though holding strong puritanical and anti-ritualistic views. He wrote in 1876 to refuse an invitation from F. J. Jayne, a tutor at the new Tractarian-influenced foundation of Keble College, to give a Holy Week address. His reasons are clear: "I cannot but think [some] are (albeit unconsciously) preparing a way for the return to the errors of Rome, and hindering union between the Church of England and the sister Churches of the Reformation". Before he was ordained priest, Bazely withdrew from the Church of England, very possibly leaving Edward Hicks much less clear about his own position in the spectrum of Anglican opinion from high (Tractarian) to low (evangelical) than he had formerly been, but certainly having done a good deal of hard thinking on the subject. Hicks was one of nature's moderates and, though he was accused of holding opinions at either end of the spectrum, we shall see that as bishop he still wanted to hold the middle ground as far as he could.

Hicks begins his memoir of his friend by describing how familiar a sight Bazely became in Oxford as a street preacher. The Victorian period was an era of huge effort in overseas missionary work. Bazely opened Edward Hicks's eyes to the value of missionary work in England's own depressed communities. He was not the only experimenter in this sort of preaching, and not the only one to discover it unsettled him as a conventional member of the Church of England.

There was an obvious risk that the church hierarchy would seek to discourage this activity if it might breed uncertainties. However, open-air mission was allowed at Lambeth. So Bazely did this mission preaching in the open air with the approval of Tait, then Archbishop of Canterbury. Tait commented that:

It was impossible to pass through the streets of London without seeing unmistakeable signs on every side that there was a large population whom no church, and no chapel, and no ordinary religious arrangement were able to reach so as, even for a short time, to draw their minds to higher things.

In this way too a lifelong interest of Hicks's own in urban and rural local mission was kindled.

FELLOW OF A RADICAL OXFORD COLLEGE

What could Edward do next once he had his First Class degree? The careers open to him were limited by the family's lack of wealth and modest social status. There could be no family influence to help him. He had no independent private income. If he wanted to stay in the university and teach, he had to win a college Fellowship, which would provide room and board and some income (and plenty of interesting company and potential friendships with people of influence).

Corpus Christi College, Oxford, was in the process of reforming itself and was becoming a college of note in Oxford. It was one of only three Oxford colleges (Exeter and Lincoln Colleges were the others) to take advantage of the opportunity to revise their own statutes under the University of Oxford Act 1854. Open scholarships for students were created, the first awarded in 1857; there were also to be Open Fellowships. Hicks won one of these in 1866 when he was chosen to be a lay Fellow – the first the college had had – with responsibility for teaching Classics. There he stayed from 1866 to 1873.

Corpus offered him plenty of intellectual challenge. It would be hard to exaggerate how stimulating membership of one of the senior common rooms of the time could be. Their numbers tended to be small by present standards, so the Fellows knew one another well. They were usually engaged in pursuing their own lines of independent research at a time when "academic research" in the modern sense was quite new and experimental. It was not yet necessary to specialize and authors could and did write books on a range of subjects, as their interest took them.

Some of the sciences were being identified for the first time, as was Edward Hicks's own chosen "subject" of "classical inscriptions". Hicks had a serious accident while he was at Corpus. It does not seem to be known exactly what happened, but it left him lame and on crutches for a long time, so he spent his time on research into Greek inscriptions, which he could see were an important source of neglected information about ancient Greek history. During university vacations he could be found studying them in the British Museum, though it would be years before he could afford to go to Greece.

The choice of this enthusiasm fits with what we know of Hicks. While fully capable of wrestling with abstractions and theories, he tended to prefer the local, particular and tangible. It was a type of study Oxford classicists such as Benjamin Jowett (1817–93) were inclined to despise, in comparison with what they considered as the proper traditional study of the literature of the ancient world. Hicks admitted stoutly in his inaugural lecture as Lecturer in Classical Archaeology in Manchester in 1889, "We are still painfully afraid of anything unconventional".

Hicks never lost this interest, but, unlike some of his friends and colleagues, it became secondary for him to things he preferred to put first as a priest and later a bishop. In December 1906, he refused an invitation from James Hope Moulton (who had been working on Greek texts in papyri) to coedit a *New Testament Lexicon of Hellenistic Greek*. Moulton replied:

> *I must not press you … But while my Temperance, Citizen and Christian sympathies wholly agree with you, the student part of me insists on rebelling against the loss of expert knowledge which no one in England can rival.*

Hicks made a name for himself as a scholar just the same. The Imperial Archaeological Society of Berlin made him a Corresponding Member. In November 1917, after reading prayers at the House of Lords in the round of episcopal duties, he went eagerly to the British Museum "to see Hill about the Guthlac Inscription: it doubtless belongs to the middle 10th

Century: note how the *Roman* letters are just beginning to become 'Lombardic'".

ACADEMICS IN POLITICS

The Fellows of Corpus were often active in public life too, in comment through letters to newspapers and journals, in campaigning for causes, even in national politics. It was a time when a man (and occasionally a woman) could make a difference with his or her pen and speeches. England was a small world for intellectuals, movers, and shakers.

John Ruskin (1819–1900) appeared in the Corpus Common Room from time to time. While he was giving his lectures as the first Slade Professor of Art, Ruskin was elected an Honorary Fellow of Corpus in 1871 and given rooms to occupy when he needed them. Before Hicks encountered him there, Ruskin had been awakened to the need to question some of the assumptions of contemporary society. He had become both artist and social critic. In lectures given in Manchester in 1855 he had pointed to a choice between "two paths", to win peace for society "by resistance to evil" or to buy it "with base connivances".

To hear this compelling speaker and enthusiast ask "what our great world-duties are" was bound to fire young men's souls. By the time Ruskin came to Oxford to give his lectures, he was writing his *Fors Clavigera*, a collection of "letters" to "the workmen and labourers of Great Britain", which dealt with a variety of social and political problems. He exposed Hicks, like the other Fellows of Corpus, to radical ideas about improving the lot of the poor. He was against commercialism directed simply at making money. He deplored the way industrialization had deprived the working man of any personal satisfaction in his work or opportunity for creative endeavour. He wanted society reformed into a new kind of community. Hicks's later work and idealisms seem to bear the marks of some of Ruskin's urgings, particularly the belief that doing something practical and useful was often possible. Campaigning did not have to be all theory.

Hicks wrote about his impressions of Ruskin in some "Common-Room reminiscences" which were printed by his biographer Fowler in his memoir. He remembers something (but not as much as he would wish) of Ruskin's "talk in Common-Room". His recollections tell us perhaps as much about Edward Hicks as they do about John Ruskin:

> *He spoke much of social questions, but never with that dogmatism or vehemence that sometimes marked him in his occasional writings ... He told us how he had opened a little shop (I think in Paddington), where the poorest might buy any fraction of a pound of tea without abatement of quality or advance of price.*
>
> *Profound as was the impression made upon our minds by the ethical fervour of Ruskin's lectures – wherein his interchange of illustration reminded one of nothing less than the New Testament, – what most struck us, in living and conversing with him every day, was the astonishing genius of the man. ... He entered into everything with the keenest relish. ... When these marvellous powers of sympathy and observation were directed upon the facts of human life, no wonder that his language thrilled and confounded his hearers. ... He was the most wonderful and unselfish and tender-souled Prophet of his age.*

There are other accounts of the effect Ruskin had in Oxford, one in a description by Henry Scott Holland, who would be among Hicks's later allies in pressing for social reform. He was writing about

> *an odd little gathering which we called Pesec, because it was a tiny, political, ethical, social, economic sort of club, made up of a few dons and some favoured Under-grads, who met at*

*Arthur Lyttelton's, in his rooms over a chemist's shop in St
Giles (known therefore as "the Pill-Box") to talk about cities
and the Poor, and Social Problems, and all that we have heard
so much of since. We thought ourselves rather in "the forward
movement" in those far-away days. We were burning with
Ruskin and Carlyle: we read together "Unto this Last": we
discussed: we railed at the dry bones of the older Political
Economy: we clamoured for a Breath to come from the four
winds and blow upon these dry bones till they might live.*

At that stage of his life Edward was not planning to be ordained.
For one thing, it was positively unfashionable for a time in parts
of Oxford society. In any case, Corpus had distinctly secular
tendencies at the time. In November 1868 it abolished compulsory
attendance at chapel. To be ordained was, in that context, to break
out of the expected mould. But by 1870 Hicks had changed his
mind and was ordained as a deacon, then as a priest in 1871.

During his time in Oxford, Edward Hicks became familiar
with "bishop" as "character" and as "risk-taker". Samuel
Wilberforce (known as "soapy Sam" after Benjamin Disraeli had
called him "saponaceous" as well as "unctuous" and "oleaginous"),
had been Bishop of Oxford from 1845 to 1869. His period in
office covered Hicks's student life and his subsequent time as
an Oxford don at Corpus Christi College. Wilberforce had not
been reluctant to take a high-profile public stand, as his much-
misquoted contribution to the debate with Charles Darwin
about evolution in the brand-new Oxford University Museum
in June 1860 had demonstrated. He had written reviews and
commentary about evolution for some time and he could usually
command a large audience because he was well known to be an
exciting speaker.

At this meeting, at which a number of leading scientists
were present, it seems that Wilberforce may have alienated

his audience. He was said to have asked a question which he probably meant in jest. Did T. H. Huxley claim descent from an ape on his mother's or his father's side? That provoked T. H. Huxley to say that he himself would rather be descended from an ape than from a man like the bishop, who misused his gifts as an orator in this way.

Oxford was an unusual diocese in several ways. It is unique in having a cathedral which is also the college chapel of Christ Church – with the cathedral canons also acting as Fellows of the College (confusingly called "Students"). So Hicks's early experience of a diocese while he was in Oxford had been of diocesan life intimately entangled with that of the university.

Chapter 2

Parish Priest and Married Man

In 1873 Edward Hicks was offered the parish of Fenny Compton in Warwickshire, just north of Banbury and therefore within reach of Oxford. The Oxford and Cambridge colleges all had the "gift" of various "livings" as landowners, the wealthier colleges having huge estates across the country which included a number of livings because that patronage was tied to the land. Fenny Compton was one of the Corpus Christi livings.

A living meant an income which could vary a good deal in size, but which was historically tied to the parish. This living gave Hicks £600 a year. As a Fellow of Corpus Christi he had been on the stipend of a probationer Fellow, which was only £100 a year, though the college had raised that to £200 in 1868. (He got his meals and his rooms there too as a matter of course.)

Getting a living or "benefice" was essential for those who wanted to be ordained. It had long been a requirement to prevent the problem of "wandering" clergy (*vagantes*) which had arisen in the early centuries of Christianity, when disreputable characters sometimes turned up in places where they were not known, and pretended to be priests. So someone ordained to the priesthood would have to have a "title" or "entitlement" to be in charge of the souls in his new parish.

A living literally gave a priest a "living" for life. The patron of the living who had the right to nominate a particular priest might make the choice, but the living was actually granted by the local bishop. A priest who held such a living was called an "incumbent". He had a right to live in the parsonage house or vicarage and to take services in the church until he died, if he wished. We shall see that when he was bishop Edward Hicks often had reason to regret that it was simply impossible for him to remove some of the odder characters he found among his Lincolnshire clergy.

Perhaps as a result of this early awareness of the difficulties facing clergy who did not have private means, when he became a bishop Hicks was always sensitive to the problems of the poor clergy of his diocese, struggling to support their families on inadequate incomes. In his diaries he often mentions the poverty of a clergy family when he makes a visit in the diocese. On 20 February 1915, the diary records that he went

> *to N. Somercotes, where I had lunch with the Proudfoots. Close talk with them about the education of their children ... need a good school. I ... offer to pay their school expenses ... : they to pay for textbooks & travelling.*

(Samuel Proudfoot, who was one of Hicks's clergy in the diocese, was clearly a friend. He was invited to what Hicks calls a "Bird Dinner" to meet Warde Fowler the ornithologist on 9 February 1914. He also liaised actively with Samuel Proudfoot on temperance matters.)

Until the law changed in 1877, the Fellows of an Oxford or Cambridge college were all bachelors. Only the Masters of colleges were allowed to be married. If a Fellow wanted to marry he would have to give up his Fellowship and leave the college. It had as a result been a longstanding tradition of Oxford and Cambridge colleges to offer their vacant or available livings to young Fellows when they wanted to marry. Hicks did not leave Corpus Christi because he wanted to marry, but getting a living meant that now he could afford to support a wife.

Moving to parish work could come in useful too if a Fellow found he needed more time for his own work than he would have while he was teaching students. Hicks found he had a good few of these "scholar parsons" and parsons with time-consuming hobbies in his diocese when he became a bishop. It was an accepted thing that a rural ministry need not take too much of a man's time, or that he might have a curate if he could afford it. The requirement that these former Fellows should be ordained in order to become parish priests does not seem to have been regarded as much of a hurdle, and some of them used it as a stepping stone to the life of an independent scholar. Vocations could almost be taken for granted in the circumstances. Hicks was not like that. He turned out to be a dedicated cleric and he never treated his duties as a part-time occupation. But he too was a scholar who wanted to have some time for his work on deciphering classical inscriptions.

At first he took his sister Katherine with him to be his housekeeper. Kate shared the family interest in botany and music and had studied drawing to a level which brought her praise from John Ruskin. She trained to be a nurse and in due course became the matron at Wrexham Infirmary. That gave Edward an informed interest in nursing as a career for able women, and it must have provided a useful background during the war when women's nursing became important in a diocese full of wounded soldiers come home to convalesce.

Edward Hicks marries

Edward met his future wife through one of his friends from his time at Oxford. Edwin Palmer was Professor of Latin and a Fellow of Corpus Christi College, and in time he became Archdeacon of Oxford. Living in Palmer's household was his niece, Agnes. Hicks got to know her in that context. Agnes's father, the clergyman Edward Trevelyan Smith, had resigned his living in

1872 to become a Roman Catholic, dropped his surname, and gone to live in Bath. His wife, Agnes's mother, loyally became a Roman Catholic too. These events – with their potential for family estrangement – may explain why his daughter, who did not join them in their conversion, was living in Oxford. They are also a reminder that Anglicans, including the clergy, were still sometimes drawn to Rome in this post-Tractarian period as John Henry Newman had famously been.

In September 1876 Edward and Agnes were married in St Giles's Church in Oxford. She was married from her uncle's house. Hicks and Agnes were to watch one of their own sons become a Roman Catholic during the First World War, but there would be no estrangement in their own family.

Edward and Agnes had six children. The first was a son, John Edward, born in April 1880, but he died as an infant during the following cold winter. During the years at Fenny Compton, four more children were born: Mary, Bede, Edwin, Christina, and then the last one, Edward Rawle or "Ned", on 26 March 1892, during the years in Manchester.

Edward's sister Katherine often stayed with them, and Agnes treated Katherine as a member of her extended family. She writes about Hicks's sister joining them on "the early holidays with our small children":

> *His sister Katherine … was a welcome and cherished companion in many of our holidays. She was an accomplished musician and botanist, and helped to make our expeditions the more delightful.*

The whole holiday was designed to be educational, culturally and scientifically "enriching" for the children. "As soon as they were old enough to appreciate scenery, churches, flowers, ferns, shells, anything that came in their way was made a delight" to the children.

As the children grew older, we started as a whole family with luncheon packed and spent all the day out on the mountains ... The children learned to appreciate the old churches and villages around ... Their father's mind was stored with information on every conceivable subject.

Katherine was obviously able to contribute her share.

A RURAL PARISH: PLUNGING IN

When Edward Hicks became a bishop, he looked with an expert and experienced eye at the country parishes he visited, and took careful note of the state of the buildings, how the clergy were performing, local activities and whether the parish seemed to be prospering spiritually. He had the necessary experience in both a country and an urban parish. His country parish experience came in Fenny Compton.

He seems to have been thrown in at the deep end. It tended to be assumed that a Fellow of an Oxford or Cambridge college would know all he needed to know about theology, how to take services, and the other duties of the clergy. Preparation for ordination could in practice be vestigial for a man with an Oxford or Cambridge degree, as it probably was for Hicks himself.

This was a matter he was to comment on in 1912 when he made his first "Charge" (or formal pastoral guidance) to the diocese of Lincoln when he carried out his Primary Visitation there. We shall see Edward Lee Hicks the bishop shaking his head over the imperfect theological knowledge and general level of suitability of some of his clergy in the diocese of Lincoln. Many of them had been in their parishes for a long time. For those with some preparatory training, there had in recent generations been a chance of some postgraduate study at a college such as the relatively high church Cuddesdon, founded just outside Oxford in 1854 by Samuel Wilberforce while he was Bishop of Oxford. St Stephen's House was founded in Oxford in 1876; Westcott House in Cambridge in 1881. For evangelically inclined ordinands there was Wycliffe Hall in Oxford (1877) and Ridley Hall in Cambridge (1881).

In the era of the new "redbrick" universities it began to be realized that something would have to be done to ensure that there was a route by which non-"Oxbridge" men could get an adequate grounding to prepare them for ordination. Trinity College Dublin was favoured by some until the end of the 1860s. Durham University had been founded in 1832, but it took until the 1870s to become established as an acceptable alternative provider of training for men who wanted to be ordained, because of the dominance of the route taken by Oxford and Cambridge graduates.

Some of the candidates for ordination were not graduates at all. For them St David's College, Lampeter and other colleges founded by bishops to meet local needs had something to offer. They were producing about a quarter of the clergy by the 1890s, and these men sometimes entered the ministry from a working-class background and were not self-evidently "gentlemen". While he was teaching at St David's College, Lampeter, from 1883, Hastings Rashdall, another of the circle who shared Hicks's campaigning enthusiasms, had time to write his then definitive book on medieval universities. The college had been founded fifty years earlier for the education of the clergy in Wales. The standard expected was not high and Rashdall's teaching duties seem to have been patchy (Luke's Gospel, Cicero, Virgil, Sophocles) and not onerous.

GETTING THE FEEL OF THE PARISH

Hicks's predecessor as rector of Fenny Compton had been Dr Heurtley. He had been Oxford's Lady Margaret Professor and a canon of Christ Church Cathedral in Oxford from 1853. He seems to have got on comfortably with his parishioners though they were not his only concern. He was not exactly an absentee priest, but he did not live in the parish all the time because of his duties in the university. There were the usual debates among theologians at Oxford in his time and his own fairly evangelical opinions had been defended there with vigour.

Edward Hicks wanted to make some changes to the internal arrangements of the church itself, putting in a new altar and having lighted candles on it during services. It is hard to say what this tells us about his churchmanship. His proposed change at Fenny Compton may merely suggest that he wanted to move the parish away from too strong an evangelical emphasis towards a more middle position, but it was naturally a sensitive thing to do, especially in times when these questions were highly controversial in the Church of England.

The parish was not universally happy at this evidence that he might be more "high church" than their old vicar. One parishioner was so indignant that she said she would not come to church again. Hicks suggested a compromise in which we can glimpse the peacemaking, witty and sometimes ironical future bishop. If she would tell him when she wanted to come to Communion he would make sure the candles were placed on the floor. This seems to have satisfied her.

The study of ancient Greek inscriptions had the virtue for a busy parish priest that it could be picked up and put down and did not require the long hours of sustained concentration that writing on theological topics would have needed. Hicks used what leisure he had to publish the results of this scholarly work, but parish life definitely came first for him. He stirred the parish up and set about engaging everyone who lived there in the life of the church. He held prayer meetings each week, and started mothers' meetings. He got the parish interested in supporting missions to Africa and elsewhere.

Discovering causes to fight for

It was at Fenny Compton that Hicks developed some of his lifelong campaigning concerns. They were connected with the heartfelt wish to better the lives of his fellow human beings, which was natural to him, but also probably sharpened by his encounters with Ruskin's ideas.

He found agriculture locally in depression and the agricultural workers in trouble. He did what he could to help. The system of land tenure was part of the problem. A clergyman was in an unavoidably compromising position because of recent changes to the charges on land which were affecting the profitability of farming and the income of farmers and labourers.

In the Middle Ages "rent" for land took the form of tithes, or "tenths" of the produce of the land. Monasteries as landlords were major recipients of these tithes and some went to parish clergy, where the church was landlord. The Tithe Commutation Act of 1836 had replaced this ancient payment in kind with a money payment. Elements of this payment still came to the parish clergy and the income formed the basis of the living. Clergy, like secular landowners, could waive their rights. The Act was put into effect quite speedily, but a survey was required and there had been disputes about the sums of money said to be due. In any case, in a year of poor harvest agricultural tenants might find it difficult to pay what they owed. Some resentment of the local clergy was to be expected.

During this battle over the conditions of agricultural workers, the atmosphere within the church's congregation at Fenny

Compton was affected. Employer and employed were less happy to worship together; there was tension and discomfort in many parishes. Edward Hicks, a boy from an ordinary lower middle-class family, was now recipient of "tithe" income on behalf of the church and counted as "gentry". But he was finding that he was not altogether on the side of the gentry in his sympathies.

Hicks began to realize from observation of what was going on in his own parish that the poverty was often exacerbated or even caused by heavy drinking. The agricultural workers themselves had set up a parish temperance society to try to deal with the drinking problems which were making a bad situation worse. In 1877 he joined in with their efforts and gave up alcohol himself, becoming a member of the United Kingdom Alliance for the Total Suppression of the Liquor Traffic. He met Richard Grier, a missionary preacher and an activist on the question of the disestablishment of the Church of England and the "sale" of livings. Grier was a leading member, who set about converting Hicks to the view that total abstention was the right way.

> *Under his tuition, during those happy ten days, I became a decided abstainer (I was more than half convinced before) and a Prohibitionist, and joined the U.K.A.*

Temperance became a lifelong campaign.

The Elementary Education Act of 1870 was followed by the Elementary Education Act 1880. The result was to make education compulsory for children from five to ten years old. That was a financial blow for poor families, because children compulsorily at school could not earn so as to contribute to the family income. As an *ex officio* manager of the village school where he "almost daily taught", Hicks saw two sides of this change. Pragmatically, he "perpetually said it would be far more sensible to teach Botany than Grammar". Looking back on the village school from the distance of two years' experience of urban ministry, he later commented with an almost Wordsworthian nostalgia:

> *certain is it that the rustic child – even apart from school – is a far more civilized creature than the gutter-boy of the slums. The peasant lad has his thought and memory full of the facts of natural life – he has conned the book of nature and has learnt to live by employment of nature. Observation, memory, skill of hand, alertness of mind and body, – all these are necessitated by the life of the peasant. I never came across a labourer in the village who could be called "unskilled".*

But such a boy still had to be got to school if he was to be able to read and write and do elementary arithmetic or have the slightest chance of the sort of "social mobility" Hicks himself had enjoyed.

In the face of the impossibility of making ends meet, some families simply emigrated. In 1873 a group of thirty-five from Fenny Compton and Mollington left Liverpool with their children for New York. For those who chose to stay in the village, the ever-practical Hicks did what he could to ease the financial constraints of their lives. He organized a "cooperative" shop in the village and arranged for "allotments" to be provided out of seventeen acres of land belonging to his landowner churchwarden and friend E. P. R. Knott, and farmed by one of his tenants.

The idea was to help families grow their own food. He showed persistence over this. Christ Church, Oxford, was one of the major landowners in his parish. Ten years on, he wrote to Dean Liddell of Christ Church – the father of the Alice of Charles Dodson's (Lewis Carroll's) "Alice" books – to ask the college to make more land available for allotments. He gave examples of other leading landowners who had such grants to their credit and whose reputations had been enhanced as a result. Hicks's letter to the dean set out a typically pragmatic argument:

Here are numbers of labourers, thrifty, sober, intelligent and resolute men, who are the pick of the agricultural class; and they see the land going to ruin. They hear the farmers' endless complaints, and one after another they are sent adrift by the masters, who say, "I have got plenty of work for you, but no money to pay you with." These labourers say, Very well: if you can neither pay rent, nor employ labour, and are leaving both landlord and labourer penniless, and the land to ruin, why may we not have a chance of trying?

The college did not respond at once, but in 1894 it eventually gave a few acres for use as allotments.

The mid-nineteenth century marked the beginning of the modern trade union movement in England. Those who favoured social reform, as Hicks now increasingly did, often took an optimistic view of the good trade unionism could achieve. The movement began among factory workers, but agricultural workers caught on to the idea that collective action could work for them too. A National Agricultural Labourers' Union was founded in Warwickshire in 1872, led by Joseph Arch (1826–1919), who was a Methodist preacher as well as a political and social activist. It began to set up branches in villages nearby, one of which was Fenny Compton. The movement had some success and agricultural wages rose a little, but the energy died out of it. One difficulty was that it was much harder for agricultural workers than factory workers to hold meetings or confront a particular employer because they were more widely scattered and each employer had comparatively few employees.

Henry Bazely had thoroughly awakened Edward Hicks to the realization that mission was needed as badly in England as in Africa. Hicks wrote to his mother to describe a visit to Birmingham to hear three American evangelists preach. That had made him very dissatisfied with the size of his own congregations. Two miles away, there was a cluster of housing known as the "tunnel houses" from their association with the digging of the adjacent canal tunnel. Navvies were now working on the building of the railway nearby. Hicks took services to them, to try to reach those who would not come into the church to worship. In 1877 he invited R. M. Grier, a cleric from Lincoln who was his wife's family friend, to come and preach in a mission for ten days in the parish of Fenny Compton. This was potentially dangerous because it took the church's work outside the safe and lawful boundaries of familiar liturgy and order. Edward Hicks was having to decide how far to follow in the steps of a Henry Bazely.

Reflecting on what he had learned, he spoke at a Church Congress in Manchester in 1888, on "How to Supply the Defects of the Parochial System by Means of Evangelizing Work". He approved of flexibility, including the approach of the Salvation Army, though that too was controversial among the leaders of opinion on social reform. Like Edward Hicks, William Booth (1829–1912), founder of the Salvation Army, had been moved by the problem of poverty and influenced by Methodism. In 1890 Booth published *In Darkest England and the Way Out*, a book possibly ghostwritten by William Thomas Stead, the editor of the *Pall Mall Gazette*. It made proposals for "cooperative" solutions to the problems of poverty. Not everyone agreed: T. H. Huxley (1825–95) wrote a series of letters to *The Times* in which he attacked Booth for self-aggrandizement. So Hicks was reaching out, beginning to experiment, becoming more and more involved in fostering social reform as far as he could in his own parish, and also beyond. But he was having to consider carefully how far to go and in which directions.

EXPERIENCE OF ANOTHER DIOCESE: WORCESTER AND A RURAL
PARISH

At Fenny Compton in his first parish, Hicks had been in the
diocese of Worcester. The bishop at the time was Henry Philpott
(1807–92). Here was another prominent public figure. In
Cambridge he had risen to be Master of St Catherine's College.
He became vice-chancellor (a rotating office in those days) in
1846 and in 1856–57, and when Cambridge needed a chairman
for the Cambridge University Commission, after the passing of
the Oxford and Cambridge Act in 1877, he seemed an obvious
choice and a safe pair of hands and was called from Worcester to
take on the role. He proved to be a much less exciting bishop for
young Edward Hicks than Wilberforce, and probably not much
of a support for a young priest learning his job, but august and
eminent as a model for the future Bishop of Lincoln. Philpott
was a rather quiet though assiduous Bishop of Worcester from
1860 to 1890. He did not hold diocesan conferences or play
much if any part in the national meetings of bishops.

But all was not dignity in the Philpott family. Hicks noted with
apparent amusement in his diary for 6 February 1916 that Henry
Philpott's brother had been a notorious "seceder" from the Church
of England in the diocese of Lincoln. Hicks had been visiting St
James Deeping that day, where he had celebrated the Eucharist.
The patroness of the living was the Dowager Lady Exeter, who
lived in the village – "v. Low Church", comments Hicks:

> *The Vicars have of late all been v. protestant: notably Mr.*
> *Tryon, who actually seceded from the Church in the 90s, with*
> *others of the local Clergy who differed from the Church on*
> *other grounds than Baptismal Regeneration, & with them*
> *built in St. James Deeping a "Cave of Adullam" (Calvinistic*
> *Methodist) so named on its front!*

The other "seceders" included the Bishop of Worcester's brother and William Tiptaft, founder of the Baptist church in Abingdon. The interior wrestlings which led to these leaving the Church of England are a reminder that Edward Hicks reveals nothing comparable by way of theological or spiritual struggles of his own.

Chapter 3

New Directions

In due course, in the mid-1880s, Hicks began to look for a new post. This was probably prompted by the expense of his growing family, perhaps by the desire for new challenges. "I had kept up my reading and was beginning to desire some work in which I might once again serve both education and the church," he commented in 1912. Perhaps he might succeed as a schoolmaster? He applied for a post at Haileybury in Hertfordshire, which was then as now a leading public school.

The experience must have sharpened his awareness of the disadvantages of not having financial independence and an influential family behind him. Applying for jobs suitable for a gentleman in that period involved the provision of open testimonials from persons whose opinion could carry weight. This was an earlier form of the modern use of "referees" and it depended heavily on having the right "contacts". His rival for the Haileybury job had eighty pages of testimonials, printed as a book. Hicks's own testimonials included recommendations from contacts he had made through his time at Oxford, the headmaster of Eton, the President of Corpus Christi College, Oxford, the High Master of St Paul's, the Dean of Christ Church and other leading Oxford figures, Mark Pattison of Lincoln College, Benjamin Jowett of Balliol, the Provost of Oriel, professors Nettleship and Jebb, the Warden of Keble. His testimonials also included one from the French ambassador to the English court and one from the Professor of Archaeology at Strasbourg. Without those allies his application could not have been taken seriously. But still Hicks did not get the job.

He was, however, offered another post in 1886, as principal of Hulme Hall. His new job was something quite different and a real novelty in English higher education. After centuries of monopoly of university education in England, Oxford and Cambridge now had rivals. New universities were being established in the rising industrial cities. The first was the Victoria University of Manchester (1880), which brought together the well-established experiment at Owens College, Manchester (dating from 1851), the Leeds School of Medicine (founded in 1831) and University College Liverpool (added to Manchester in 1882). Other new "civic" universities followed during Hicks's lifetime, in Birmingham in 1900, in Liverpool (in its own right) in 1903; in Leeds (in its own right) in 1904; in Sheffield in 1905; in Bristol in 1909. But Manchester was a pioneering venture, and Hicks now had the chance to take part in the experiment.

One of the practical problems which had to be solved in the new universities was where students were going to live. There was no college system, with its built-in food, shelter, pastoral care and student discipline, as there had been at Oxford and Cambridge for several centuries. The Society of Friends had provided a hostel for Owens College students, Dalton Hall, which asked no questions about residents' religious beliefs or denomination. An old trust set up in 1691 to support "four poor bachelors" at Brasenose College, Oxford, was one of a number of such trusts whose terms were able to be adapted under recent legislation affecting Oxford and Cambridge college trusts. The Hulme trustees bought a house in Plymouth Grove, Manchester, big enough to house thirty-two Owens College students. It was to be a Church of England hostel but it was not to restrict itself to Anglican students only.

MANCHESTER AND AN URBAN PARISH

Manchester was a very different diocese and it exposed Edward Hicks to another face of the Church of England. The Industrial Revolution had created new needs for the church to meet because of the immense movements of population which brought large numbers of people into the towns to work in the factories. That was one of the reasons for the creation of new dioceses, like the one for Manchester which was freshly created in 1847, from part of the old diocese of Chester, and placed in the province of York.

The Bishop of Manchester when he arrived in the diocese was James Moorhouse (1826–1915, Bishop of Manchester from 1886–1903). Moorhouse had had an unusual beginning as a clergyman. Born into a family of cutlers, he went to Cambridge with a view to ordination only after a few years in the family business and some educational catching-up to equip him in Latin and Greek. After his ordination in 1854 he started an educational institute for working men and he continued this kind of work as he moved on to new parishes. There were stories that he was a popular footballer and played the game with his students.

By 1867 he was vicar of Paddington and a well-known London preacher, and in 1874 he was given a prebendary canonry (a canonry granted to a local parish priest) at St Paul's Cathedral. Then he was called to Melbourne, to be bishop there from 1877. Moorhouse found there was plenty to do in Australia. He needed to set up proper academic and training expectations for local ordinands, get a cathedral built, and deal with some quite extreme inter-denominational hostilities among Australian Christians, particularly the hatred of Rome he found there. He returned to England to the bishopric of Manchester in 1885. There he went on being energetic, conscientiously visiting his parishes, and he found he had to deal with controversy about ritual and "Roman" tendencies in Manchester as he had in Melbourne.

But Hicks's close links were with Moorhouse's successor Edward Knox, who was Bishop of Manchester from 1903–21. Hicks and his family became very friendly with the Knox family. Knox (1847–1937) was an evangelical, born in India but educated at Corpus Christi College, Oxford in the period when Edward Hicks was there. When Knox wrote his *Reminiscences of an Octogenarian* he included an account of his time in the parish of Knibworth (1885–91). He knew, as Edward Hicks did at first hand, how the agricultural depression had affected churchgoing in rural parishes:

> *Visits to my father's parish in Rutland had shown me that*
> *Joseph Arch's Agricultural Labourers' Union had created since*
> *1874 a strong prejudice against the Church, and acted very*
> *unfavourably on the labourers' churchgoing. I had witnessed*
> *my father's perplexities arising out of the terrible agricultural*
> *depression of the later '70's.*

He also shared Hicks's sensitivity on the fierce questions about "ritual" which could divide parishes. His precedessor had been a Tractarian and "a rumour had gone about that [he] was intending to wreck all his work, and to hand the parish over to the Dissenters". Hicks could have written the sentence with which Knox sums up what he learned in a country parish:

> *I found there an education which Oxford could never have*
> *supplied; for lack whereof my subsequent experiences would*
> *have been considerably marred.*

Knox also described his family in his reminiscences. His wife was the eldest daughter of the Bishop of Lahore, one of the English missionary bishops of the age. He praised her for "finished scholarship" and "artistic culture', from which her children had benefited:

> *All her boys [his sons] won entrance Scholarships, two at Rugby and two at Eton, three of the four being first in their elections. Her eldest and favourite son is known to a wide public as the Editor of Punch. The literary productions of her four sons and one of her daughters fill several pages of the Catalogue in the British Museum.*

The friendship between the two families was to endure and have important consequences. It led to the marriage of Hicks's daughter Christina to the Bishop's son Edmund George Valpy Knox (1881–1971), the one who was to be future editor of *Punch*. It also led to Ned Hicks becoming a Roman Catholic under the influence of another of the Bishop's sons, Ronald Knox.

PRINCIPAL OF HULME HALL

Hicks was elected first principal of Hulme Hall. Many of the students came from a different social background to the Oxford and Cambridge students Hicks had known, and Hulme Hall itself lacked the experience and back-up he could have relied on in an Oxford college. But he did have his family and the home environment their presence helped to provide for the students. His mother, now in her seventies, lived with them. There the Hicks family lived out the belief he described in a letter to his argumentative correspondent Horsfall: "The claim of Christianity is that it can appeal to the individual and offer him miraculous power, through the means of grace, to break through the force of his surroundings." (Thomas Coglan Horsfall was one of the strongest supporters of the creation of the Manchester Art Museum and Ancoats.) But as his first sermon as bishop suggests, Hicks characteristically saw some tension in deciding between the pursuit of beauty and helping others.

There were only two students when he got to Hulme Hall. That may have been a good thing to begin with, because the Manchester students tended to be younger than the Oxford ones and enforcing student discipline in the "Oxford way" was not going to be easy. Oxford itself (Cambridge had its own concerns) was a little nervous that it might be forced to change, as Benjamin Jowett of Balliol College had commented in the late 1840s:

> *There is nothing I wish less than to see Oxford turned into a German or a London University. On the other hand, is it at all probable that we shall be allowed to remain as we are for twenty years longer, the one solitary, exclusive, unnational Corporation – our enormous wealth without any manifest utilitarian purpose; a place, the studies of which belong to the past … so exclusive.*

The Church of England had not yet thought through its duties to students in these new universities. Edward Hicks had to find his own way.

Fowler collected some partly anonymous recollections from those who had lived in Hulme Hall while Hicks was in charge. These tell us that he was universally kind and accepting. One old student said:

> *During the whole of my five years at Hulme Hall I was, so far as I know, the only Unitarian in the place, but I never found that this made the slightest difference to the great kindness, sympathy, and helpfulness with which Canon Hicks treated me.*

Hicks made an effort to create an environment which would be both socially and intellectually satisfactory. He wrote prologues and charades for the students to perform on various occasions.

One, H. Stones, who became a clergyman, described how "weekly Shakespearian readings in the drawing room, in which at first one took part shyly, were soon looked forward to"; these "gave the touch of home and made us feel all of one family". He commented that "no father could have taken a greater interest in the well-being of those under his care; it was manifest no less in their recreations than in their studies". This was unsentimental. "The careless were never allowed to go unwarned, and the word of encouragement was never wanting."

Hicks's own experience as a college Fellow in Oxford and in the village school at Fenny Compton left him with the urge to teach, as well as supervise behaviour and provide an appropriate environment to encourage serious study. He offered lectures at Owens College on classical archaeology and he got on with his own research work on Greek inscriptions. There was no museum but he had a collection of coins and slides and photographs to use in teaching.

He tried to provide Manchester's science students with some background in the classics and a notion of the discoveries of contemporary biblical criticism:

No student ever had a more sympathetic or brilliant tutor than Dr Hicks. His lecture was the event of the week ... The fifteen poor men before him inspired him to his best work just as much as a brilliant company of Oxford undergraduates would have done – nay, some of us imagined that of the two he preferred to teach us. His lectures were like the man, full of vitality, thought, suggestiveness and power ... The Bible, under treatment of this master mind, became to us a revelation indeed, but a revelation of personality. Evolution, Modernism, German Criticism, all had been assimilated by the lecturer, and these only served to illuminate that which the Bible stood for: the supreme expression of the way of life. Verbal inspiration and all other literalisms passed away from us as the mist before the sun. He made us realize that God's interest was the human interest, and we learned to love the Bible by loving Canon Hicks.

The young Unitarian wrote that he had lived at Hulme Hall for five years from 1887, in preparation for an intended move to the Unitarian foundation and old dissenting academy of Manchester College, which was moving back to Oxford, where he intended to study theology and become a Unitarian minister. Hicks read the Greek New Testament with him and "when he came to passages around which theological controversy had raged, he made no effort to bias my judgement, or to prejudice me in favour of the views or renderings which he himself accepted". He simply explained the differing views of leading scholars. "His desire was always that we should seek the truth – not that we should be forced to accept certain opinions."

Another former student who was later ordained describes Hicks as a tutor who exposed his pupil to the excitement of research and scholarship. He was reading for the Honours Course in Classics:

Our lessons were often interrupted by the arrival of a parcel of pressings from inscriptions. I can see him yet, eagerly opening these parcels, and, forgetting all about my shocking prose and translation, he would invite me to join him in deciphering and in supplying the missing portions where they occurred. His eager excitement over the task was like that of a schoolboy.

Nevertheless, Edward Hicks understood that it was neither possible nor perhaps desirable to try to recreate Oxford in Manchester. For one thing, the resources were not there. He recognized that the Manchester students could scarcely hope for exposure to the scholarly world he had learned about at Oxford. When Owens

College made him Lecturer in Classical Archaeology in 1889, he gave an inaugural lecture in which, regretfully but with alarming frankness, he realistically warned the students they must "pursue an unambitious course" because there was no chance of their doing research. While "as an epigraphist I know what it is to spend whole days deciphering a line or two", as Manchester students "you will be spared its labour, but you will lose its advantages".

SALFORD AND MANCHESTER CATHEDRAL

The principalship of Hulme Hall turned out to be just a bridging post. Hicks stayed for only a few years, but this was long enough to bring him (it seems) to the notice of James Moorhouse as a promising local cleric, partly perhaps because of his paper at the meeting of the Church Congress which was held in Manchester in 1888. In it he had made a number of points which show he had been thinking about the role of bishops. In reality the freeholds of parish priests gave so much freedom and security that it was easy for incumbents to get away with letting things slip, neglecting their parishioners, being wildly eccentric or even giving rise to scandal. The remedy, he thought, lay partly in improving episcopal oversight – as well as encouraging the expression of public criticism where it was appropriate.

In 1892, Hicks was made a canon of Manchester Cathedral. This canonry went with responsibility for a slum parish with a large population, St Philip's in Salford. Just as he had at the very different rural parish of Fenny Compton, Hicks set about providing appropriately for the needs of local people. He was concerned about the level of poverty and the resultant poor health, as well as about their spiritual welfare. He became a public critic of the behaviour of exploitative landlords in the slums.

A pamphlet was published in 1904 entitled *Five Days and Five Nights as a Tramp among Tramps: Social Investigation by a*

Lady, published through the Women Guardians and Local Government Association. The "lady" and her companion "dressed very shabbily" and set out to discover what it was really like to be poor and homeless. Seeking refuge in a hostel for the night, they took a cubicle amongst numerous beds crowded together in a room, some occupied by men, many beds with bedbugs, with a single bucket as the only sanitary arrangement; there they were able to listen to the "often profane" talk of their fellow lodgers.

They discovered that when they walked about the streets not dressed as ladies, men called disrespectfully after them. Women, on the other hand, talked to them trustingly as in a similar position to their own, told them of domestic violence and their fears of testifying against a violent husband. They learned at first hand how debilitating is lack of sleep and days spent wandering about to pass the time, with nothing to eat. They had to pawn clothing to buy a little food. They became cold and wet and then ill.

Edward Hicks wrote a preface for this account in which he said that he had insisted that the author and her associate "pilgrim" keep in "certain revolting particulars" because they were "essential to her case". The facts she found "are a terrible indictment of our present arrangements" and he hoped they would "quicken the conscience of many more women to offer themselves for election" as Poor Law Guardians.

This was the world of local need in which Hicks set about doing what he could. Following the same logic as had taken him out of the church building to find the local people in Fenny Compton, he took the church to his reluctant parishioners by holding meetings in the open air in the parts of the parish where there was the worst deprivation. He supported missions conducted by the Church Army to try to bring the gospel to those who, even in a churchgoing age, never went near their parish church.

His interest in the rights and special difficulties of the women among the poor had him starting a club for the millworkers at which they could be offered support in resisting temptations to sexual involvements outside marriage. There was "temperance" work to be done too. It was the habit in local factories to require new employees to pay "footing-ale", that is, pay for drinks for the other employees. This encouraged drunkenness so Hicks supported an Anti-Footing League which was campaigning to end this practice. He became president of the local children's temperance organization, the Lancashire and Cheshire Band of Hope Union. Patterns of lifelong interest and involvement were set here which we shall see again when he was Bishop of Lincoln.

THE MANCHESTER SOCIAL CIRCLE: NEW LASTING FRIENDSHIPS

Life in Manchester offered him a cultured circle not quite the same as that at Oxford but satisfying in its way. The novelist Mrs Gaskell, who had a house a few doors down from Hulme Hall, ran a literary "salon". Hicks and his wife were visitors at the house even after her death when her daughters went on living in Plymouth Grove. J. H. Fowler, Hicks's future biographer, was at Manchester Grammar School and so was the local historian F. A. Bruton, who was a master there and with whom Hicks shared scholarly interests. Another important name for Hicks's campaigning future amongst those Hicks encountered again in Manchester was C. P. Scott, who had been a Corpus Christi undergraduate when Hicks was a Fellow. Scott was going to be an important ally in years to come.

Scott became editor of the *Manchester Guardian* from 1872, and that gave Edward Hicks an entrée into journalism. He did some regular writing as a columnist for the *Manchester Guardian* from 1904 to 1910, calling himself "Quartus". This could be controversial work and would have not have been so easy to get away with once he became a bishop. In *The Tablet* of 26 December 1908, Canon Richardson wrote to criticize

Hicks's views on education, describing them as tending to make the poor dependent on society's support. This was, he argued, "a false philanthropy" by which "we have robbed the present generation of every particle of their independence and made them spongers":

> is not our business, then, to set up homes more than schools and strict cleanliness more than school extravagance? The amount of money wasted on our elementary education system is dreadful, but like the horse-leech it cries for more.

Scott was also a useful ally on temperance. Hicks visited his home and kept up the friendship after he left Manchester. Scott became a Liberal MP in 1895 after unsuccessful earlier attempts. The Manchester "Oxford" circle also included W. T. Arnold, a Liberal and a grandson of Dr Arnold of Rugby.

THE TEMPERANCE MOVEMENT IN MANCHESTER

In deciding to become teetotal as a relatively young man, Hicks was doing something unusual, which would be noticed at every social gathering among members of what had become his own class. Why did he do it? He was always clear that his interest and concern had been triggered because he had learned to see temperance reform as the essential starting point for social reform. At Fenny Compton, Hicks had become convinced that the excessive consumption of alcohol – particularly beer – among the working classes was a primary cause of poverty. It affected working life and ate up wages, leaving the drinker's family poor and needy.

He perceived similar problems among the urban poor when he moved to Manchester, where he saw different faces of the alcohol problem. In late Victorian and Edwardian society, the upper classes drank alcohol as a regular part of a normal social life. The lower classes drank too, but not necessarily at home. The brewing industry supported an extensive network of public houses, where working men typically drank beer, though Victorian London had its "gin palaces".

One way of avoiding the dangers of alcohol was to keep away from any social contexts in which drinking was normal and drinking to excess commonplace. Temperance enthusiasts gradually set about finding themselves premises. These could provide a base and a permanent local presence to work from, where it might be possible to offer non-drinkers an alternative to a public house. For this purpose the *Advocate* listed several

> *objects which should be sought to be accomplished ... A respectable eating house ... a respectable lodging house, to accommodate persons who object to stopping at public houses ... a place of casual accommodation, where persons can come to transact business, read the papers, or enjoy social intercourse, or where parties, societies and committees can meet for similar purposes.*

Teetotal catering should be provided. "Rather than let people go to the public-houses ... it is also recommended to supply various liquids which are pleasant to the taste ... Coffee, tea, milk, ginger beer, lemonade, peppermint water and raspberry vinegar" are suggested. "The latter are much in use, diluted with hot water, and sweetened."

By the 1850s most large towns had a temperance hotel, though they were not all very comfortable. Hicks and his wife used temperance hotels if they could when they travelled. During his time as Bishop of Lincoln, Hicks regularly stayed at the Thackeray temperance hotel near the British Museum when he was in London, as his diaries note.

On 12 December 1888, Hicks wrote to Thomas Horsfall, founder of the local art museum in Ancoats, a venture inspired by John Ruskin, "You will not blame me. For social reformers so realize their difficulties that they are very tolerant of each other – if I think you have assigned less than its importance to the Drink question." He was clear in his own mind about the pathway from drink to poverty. Hicks had argued in his correspondence with Horsfall that the problem was not simply that there was poverty in the slums:

> *Slums that can build up the fortunes of men like Sir W------ X----------, or Mr. K---------. Slums that can support all the drinking dens in Ancoats, are not full of poor people. They earn, and they have, and they throw away; or rather, they employ their earnings ... in procuring their own degradation and destruction.*

This was not the only long and sometimes disputatious correspondence Hicks enjoyed. He wrote a cover note for a collection of the politician Sir Wilfred Lawson's letters to him, which he had bound in 1907, a year after Lawson's death. This was to be one of several contacts his temperance work brought him into, with men whose opinions differed from his own; however, he approved most fundamentally of the way Lawson "always approached the question from the point of view of the people, and their right to improve their own social condition". Lawson (1829–1906) who became a radically inclined MP and a lifelong politician, had been brought up by his baronet father, who was a Liberal and an active campaigner for peace (and for free trade as well as for temperance). Wilfred was educated at home by a tutor hired from a dissenting academy and later a Congregationalist minister. These were the choices of a well-to-do family for a son who was barred from Oxford and Cambridge as a student who was not a practising Anglican. The dissenting academies were not necessarily a second-rate choice. There was an excellent higher education to be had at some of them.

So Wilfred Lawson was reared in a climate of unfashionable ideas and Edward Hicks approved of him because "he felt keenly the sin and sorrow of the world, and was pained above all by the folly of his fellows" and because Lawson "always approached the question from the point of view of the people, and their right to improve their own social condition".

He did not approve when Sir Wilfred heaped unfair blame on the clergy:

> *From the first I read diligently the articles in the Alliance*
> *News, and especially the clear, humorous, but always*
> *argumentative speeches of Sir Wilfred himself. In reading*
> *these I was often annoyed by the sarcasms and jokes that he*
> *loved to hurl at the Bishops and the Clergy. Very soon I found*
> *myself so much vexed, that I wrote from my country rectory to*
> *remonstrate with him.*

So the correspondence began. "His letters to me became very frequent from about 1890–5." He even helped in Lawson's election campaign when he became an MP in 1906. Lawson favoured a policy of "Local Veto" of liquor shops, which appealed to Hicks as a simple practical device for ensuring that there was less drinking by making it more difficult to buy drink.

Hicks believed that, practically speaking, temperance was the first thing to tackle in social reform, and was confirmed in his view of the importance of temperance campaigning at Salford. It was nationally recognized that the influence of manufacturers of alcoholic drinks remained powerful. There were strong commercial brewing interests there, and in neighbouring Manchester. Hicks was to remain very conscious of the problem of lobbying by the drinks industry.

CHRISTINA GOES TO OXFORD

Edward and Agnes Hicks were unusual Victorian parents who believed their children should follow their bent, girls and boys alike. At Owens College, Manchester, in a brave new world of civic universities, higher education for women had already seemed an acceptable innovation. A separate college for women had been provided in 1877, and a Department for Women became part of Owens College in 1883.

Mary, the elder daughter, seems to have been quite content with family life. She was married in January 1908 to a local clergyman in the Manchester diocese, Henry John Lockett. Mary seems to have had some periods of poor health on which her father worriedly comments, or perhaps difficult pregnancies. At intervals through the diaries her father mentions his delight in her and her family, but there is no suggestion that she was another Christina from the point of view of a desire for higher education.

The Hickses' sons seem to have had limited academic ambitions. Ned was to go as a boarder to his father's old school. His father had had the pleasure of seeing him get a school prize when he was invited to do the prize-giving at Magdalen College School in 1910. He went on to the University. There he did not do very well. On 1 August 1914, Hicks notes tersely in his diary that "Ned has a 3rd in History". We hear little of the educational achievements of the other children, with the exception of Christina. Christina was sent to Withington Girls' School in Manchester. This was a pioneering school which began in 1890, like other girls' schools in cities and major towns, at the instigation of local families who wanted their daughters to be educated on the same lines as their sons, and to the same standards.

In June 1878 an Association for the Higher Education of Women had been formed in Oxford. It attracted some very senior supporters, including the Master of University College, G. G. Bardley and T. H. Green of Balliol. Its supporters soon divided into two camps. Edward Talbot, Warden of Keble College, said any proposed college for women must be restricted to members of the Church of England. It was only in 1871 that the Universities Tests Act had removed that as a general requirement for admission to Oxford or Cambridge and the subject was still highly sensitive. Talbot's party eventually founded Lady Margaret Hall, and the rest, including Mrs Humphrey Ward (1851–1920) – a novelist Hicks enjoyed – set about starting the venture which became Somerville College, where "no distinction will be made between students on the ground of their belonging to different religious denominations". Somerville Hall, Oxford, dated from 1879. By 1894 it was called Somerville College.

The Hickses may have favoured the idea of a university education for Christina and encouraged her to be intellectually ambitious partly because at Fenny Compton they had got to know a family with two daughters who had done the same. Mr E. P. R. Knott, a gentleman farmer with clergy in the family, was Rector's Churchwarden, as will be remembered, and Mrs Knott was the organist (there was also a son). The family became lasting friends and great supporters of some of Hicks's "causes". Knott did not become a teetotaller himself, but he joined the local temperance society Hicks began in 1879, and came to the initial meeting of local people which also drew the local Wesleyan minister.

Vera Brittain describes in the first volume of her autobiography, *Testament of Youth*, the family resistance she herself encountered when she wanted to go to Oxford just before the First World War. Edward Hicks's younger daughter faced no such battle. When Christina went to Somerville in 1904, she was nineteen. She went as a Scholar, read English literature and won the Coombs Prize in 1906, though she graduated with only a second class degree.

The College was at an important stage of its development, "growing up" from the rather cosy family atmosphere of its beginning with a few young women, to the full dignity of a significant institution. It had provided itself with a proper library building only in 1903, though not without a good deal of authentically "academic" argument about what it should look like. During Christina's time there the principal, Miss Maitland, was in her final illness. She died of cancer in 1906 at the age of fifty-seven, to be replaced by Mary Penrose, who was to see the college through towards full recognition as a college by the university and the decision to allow women to take degrees, and preside over its work in wartime and its temporary exile to Oriel while its buildings (next door to the Radcliffe Infirmary) were requisitioned by the War Office for hospital purposes.

One rather bad-tempered impression survives of life at Somerville in 1904. It was written by Lady Rhondda (Margaret Haig, then Margaret Thomas), who did not stay long but soon left and got married. She said:

> *Somerville smelt frousty [sic] to me … I disliked the dowdiness of the dons, and still more of the other girls … I could not bear the cloisterishness of the place; and felt irritated by the cautious way in which we were shut off from contact with men, the air of forced brightness and virtue that hung about the cocoa-cum-missionary-party-hymn-singing girls, and still more the self-conscious would-be naughtiness of those who reacted from this into smoking cigarettes and feeling wicked. And I disliked the … atmosphere of ladylike culture that hung about the dons at play.*

Miss Penrose sent a standard welcome letter to those who arrived in 1907, warning freshers not to go for walks or long bicycle rides alone and never to go into colleges unaccompanied. If they went to lectures in other colleges they must go in twos and threes and sit together. Female virtue must be protected and chaperonage was still the norm when the young women and the young men met.

It was not easy for a highly educated woman to begin a career. For those of wealthy background there was no need to earn a living. Margaret Haig's wish for an Oxford education included no long-term purpose: "I had no notion of making any further use of my education when I had got it ... The 'done' thing was to live at home and do nothing but amuse oneself indefinitely."

When her parents went to Lincoln, their younger daughter, Christina, was in her twenties. She had left Somerville having passed the same examinations as the men, though until 1920 women students were not allowed to graduate so she did not actually get a degree. Three or four years later when Edward Hicks became a bishop, she was still living at home in the role of the unmarried daughter who would be expected to look after her parents as they aged. She says they

> offered me the choice of going away to make a career for myself or of being a "home daughter," whichever I pleased; they never thought of taking this for granted as a right. I have never known another daughter so treated, and I have asked many.

THE SUFFRAGETTES IN MANCHESTER

Manchester had a Women Suffrage Committee from the 1860s, so Hicks will have encountered the cause before he went to Lincoln. Christian Social Union members certainly discussed "women suffrage". There were mixed views among them. Henry Scott Holland declared himself in favour of suffrage for women but against the suffragettes' methods. Not all Christians in positions of leadership in the church warmed to the idea of "votes for women". In 1908 a Committee for Opposing Female Suffrage commanded the support of the Bishop of Peterborough, Hilaire Belloc, G. K. Chesterton, M. R. James, Rudyard Kipling and Charles Oman. This became the National League for Opposing Female Suffrage, with Lord Curzon as president. In 1909 a Church League for Women's Suffrage was founded in opposition to this, chaired by A. S. Duncan-Jones, with the redoubtable Maude Royden as a lead speaker.

Chapter 4

Passions and Preferment

THE CHURCH ARMY

Edward Hicks did not hesitate to make use of the organizations which were willing to allow him to talk or preach to them, especially when they helped him to reach out to a "constituency" of the laity. One of the most useful of these, he already knew, was the Church Army. A year after he began work in Salford, he had called for contributions of money and effort from others to help with the programme of active outreach to local people:

> *Street preaching, assiduous visiting, Church Army Services every evening, Band of Hope and other meetings – these (in addition to ordinary parochial ministrations) are some of the methods we employ. We hope by degrees to create a better public opinion among the people themselves: this can only be done by constant converse with them.*

He also stressed the importance of people's need for beauty when they had to live in grimy and depressing surroundings. This was to be a theme of his first sermon as Bishop.

The Church Army had been a creation of the early 1880s, the idea of a Church of England curate called Wilson Carlile.

He wanted to draw the servant and working classes into active membership and even into working for the church as lay helpers, (with appropriate training). He attracted huge numbers to "witness" meetings. He realized that this new "Church Army" was unlikely to meet with ecclesiastical approval without some careful diplomacy on his part. He moved fast to take the idea to the Church of England Congress which met in 1883. Disapproval there was and it was strong. There was talk of "dragging the church into the gutter". But by 1885 he had gained the support of the bishops who formed the Upper Convocation of Canterbury, and the Church Army became an accepted and respected part of the Establishment.

It proceeded carefully, publishing restrained descriptions of what it was offering so as not to alarm the parish clergy. The fear of big open meetings whipping up "Enthusiasm" recalled disquiet over early Methodism and still earlier worries of the sort which had led to the Conventicle Act of 1664 (which had been passed to prevent religious meetings of more than five people) and the Conventicles Act of 1670 which fined anyone attending or holding a religious assembly other than a proper Church of England Prayer Book act of worship. It was promised that Church Army meetings would be conducted on "earnest, discreet Church lines, introducing evangelistic adaptation of the Prayer Book" and "Lantern services, with magnificent art pictures, both in the open-air and inside". As a result, the Church Army got away with holding tent missions and beach missions and even meetings held at the factory gates for the workers within.

Hicks had joined in with the work of the Church Army while he was at St Philip's and he and his colleague Captain Rowlands went into the slums of Salford, risking their personal safety in what could be a violent area.

THE PEACE CAMPAIGNER

It is during the Manchester period that we can begin to glimpse the shaping of Edward Hicks's attitude to war. Their continuing correspondence revealed that Thomas Horsfall and Edward Hicks did not see eye to eye on military matters. Horsfall, who had his own agenda, was writing in strong advocacy of compulsory military service long before the First World War broke out, in *The Improvements of the Dwellings and Surroundings of the People: The Example of Germany* (London, 1904) and *National Service and the Welfare of the Community* (London, 1906). He recognized that some saw it as a concomitant of the need for "retaining and extending our already vast Empire". But for him it was perhaps better to see it as beneficial to the community, an aspect of education.

In Germany, he explains, a boy may qualify for a shorter period of required military service by passing an examination, and that is a great incentive to work hard at school. He passes through discussion of urban life and the needs of towns, the poor physique of town-dwellers and their higher death rate, to consider and compare "drunkenness" in England and Germany. The Germans are great beer drinkers but they do not seem to produce the communities of "drink-sodden, dirty, miserable men and women, such as we have". His chief arguments in favour of introducing National Service are that it would reveal the physically poor state of the urban working classes and create a desire for social reform. He cited the Boer Wars as a revelation that change was needed. He rejects the arguments commonly put against introducing National Service. Above all, it is not true that it encourages war and makes boys violent.

Edward Hicks explained in a paper he read to a Peace Conference late in his time in Manchester that he remembered hearing of the Crimean War as a boy and what he called "the war-fever of the time". It was "war-fever" which troubled him. He saw how easily people were led into war or stirred up to support it by government propaganda and the heightening of fear of an enemy when it was painted in alarmingly strong colours.

This conference was held in the Friends Meeting House, in November 1904, and what he said was published in *Commonwealth (the journal of the CSU)* (January, 1905), pp. 8–11. The next time when Hicks may have had to think out his attitude to war, following the Crimea, concerned British behaviour in South Africa. There was a history of all this by the time he became concerned. Britain had annexed the Transvaal in 1877, although it had recognized that it was independent. The first Boer War followed in 1880–81. Now another was afoot.

Some of the temperance campaign supporters who were Hicks's allies in that cause – including Henry Scott Holland and C. P. Scott – had supported the Transvaal Independence Committee. Theirs were not the only voices, some with intimate knowledge of South Africa and its tribes, tracing what they described as a "selfish and discreditable course of conduct" on the part of the British government going back more than twenty years. There were calls for the publication of suppressed documents. Those who protested were called unpatriotic and worse. The *Manchester Guardian's* circulation suffered. That committee had lapsed after 1884, during the period when Hicks was still at Fenny Compton.

The second Boer War (1899–1902) found him in Manchester. He had not been entirely silent on the subject of war in the intervening period. In 1897 he wrote in the *Manchester Guardian* in favour of mass meetings which protested against the government policy of using British ships for Turkey against the Cretan liberation movement.

The second Boer War was in part a continuation of the struggle which had been going on for more than a century between the "Boer" Dutch settlers and the expanding British

Empire, for control of southern Africa. The discovery of diamonds and gold made the territory commercially valuable. The pretext for war this time was the claim that Britain needed to protect the voting rights of British settlers in Boer-controlled territories. After a stand-off and failed negotiations, the Boers declared war on Britain in 1899. It soon became clear that if Britain was to win it needed to send more troops. It did so. Once the British forces were dominant, the Boers moved to guerrilla ("insurgent") tactics. Boers were imprisoned by the British in the first-ever concentration camps. These became infamous, holding civilian Afrikaaners including women and children as the British set about clearing the farms and destroying crops in a "scorched earth" policy.

With modern hindsight, the policy mistakes made by the British government were serious. It also became clear that British recruits to the army tended to be in poor physical condition, and that indicated that there were serious poverty problems in the country which were not being addressed by governments. There was plenty for a conscientious clergyman to speak out about.

At the time Hicks was still a residentiary canon in Manchester Cathedral. That required him to preach but it raised the question of choosing a "proper" subject and the suitability of expressing his personal views on such matters as the Boer Wars. He took the risk and preached on South Africa on 27 August 1899, taking as his text 1 Kings 22:6, "Shall I go into battle?"

His arguments were characteristic. He regretted the way reason and common sense and moderation had been lost sight of. "Prejudice and passion have prevailed instead of calm and collected reasoning ... Statements of the wildest sort, pleas wholly groundless, have taken hold of the popular mind". It was a process which may prompt echoes in a modern reader's mind of the way the Iraq War began in 2003. The "capitalists of South Africa" have been lying in order to mislead, claimed Hicks.

Outside London, opposition to the Boer War was concentrated in Manchester. A Manchester Transvaal Peace Committee was started in November 1899. It was chaired at its first meeting by Hicks. In late August he tried to get his friend Charles Gore, then a canon of Westminster Abbey, onside, offering to preach a strong sermon in Manchester if Gore would do the same in London; but Gore was not sure of his own position. He had heard differing views on both sides of the question. Hicks preached a further sermon in January 1900 which the Manchester Transvaal Peace Committee published under the title *The Mistakes of Militarism*.

This was a war in which it was not always clear, at least at the beginning, which side was in the right and whether Britain was behaving well or badly, and the misleading propaganda made it difficult to be sure. The Bishop of Hereford, John Percival, was more confident that he understood the position. He wrote to *The Times* on 22 October 1901, about this "holocaust of child-life … We who ask these questions ask them in no spirit of political controversy; no man would seek to make any political gain out of the sad fate of these little ones".

Hicks seems to have opposed the Boer Wars because he thought the motives for them were corrupt and mistaken, rather than because he believed that war was *always* wrong. His public utterances on peace and war were nuanced. Generally it seems he thought it right to try to stop war beginning. The church, he thought, should not glorify war but stress its damaging effects and costs. But once war began, he took the characteristically pragmatic view that the aim was to conduct it as morally as possible. He supported military action from Europe to stop Turkish massacres in Armenia in 1896 and had preached in support.

Accused, like other opponents of the war, of supporting the Boers and being unpatriotic, he learned some useful lessons about the result of taking a view which went against the Establishment position.

THE RADICAL SOCIAL CAMPAIGNER AND THE MODERATE CHURCHMAN

During this Manchester period, Hicks became increasingly outspoken on a variety of subjects, sometimes from the pulpit. But these tended to be calls for social reform. Doctrinally he remained orthodox and he thought orthodoxy important. Though he kept up with the emerging and sometimes challenging trends in biblical scholarship they do not seem to have disturbed his beliefs.

His parents had brought Hicks up as an evangelical but his churchmanship seems to have become much more moderate. It had to, during his time in Salford. Salford was a very mixed community. At one extreme of opinion stood the legacy of the Oxford Movement, with its delight in ritual and imagery, and at the other, evangelical and Nonconformist insistence on avoiding anything which could smack of idolatry or Romanism. As Bishop of Manchester from 1870, James Fraser (1818–85) had tried to suppress what he considered to be the excesses of one of his clergy (the Reverend S. F. Green who was vicar of Miles Platting), by applying the Public Worship Regulation Act of 1874. The accused priest was eventually imprisoned but released on government insistence when W. E. Gladstone intervened.

Hicks took care not to inflame either extreme and to focus on providing practical pastoral support to the people of his parish of St Philip in Salford. He worked with the local Roman Catholics to improve local schools. He worked with Nonconformists in his temperance campaigning. He made use of tent meetings and other mission experiments outside the actual churches of the Church of England.

Hicks's reluctance to be associated with any particular group, in terms of churchmanship, became clearer as he grew older and more experienced in ministry, despite his evangelical upbringing.

His diaries when he was bishop hint at some strong views, but there seem to have been especially a dislike of extremes. He also disliked persecutions. He was not unduly troubled by ritual, and he defended the relatively "high church" forms of worship in Manchester Cathedral against those who criticized them. What he seems to have minded most was that the life of the church should be orderly and peaceful and dignified. Above all, he favoured "undogmatic and humanitarian religion".

ME, A BISHOP?

This was the man who became Bishop of Lincoln in 1910. His mother said in 1886 that she was disappointed that Hicks did not yet have a bishopric, when his contemporary John Wordsworth, who had got only a second class Oxford degree in 1865, had been made Bishop of Salisbury at the age of forty-two in 1885, and F. J. Jayne, ordained with Hicks, had the important benefice at Leeds and confidently expected to be a bishop soon.

Some felt that Hicks might have been entrusted with a diocese sooner if he had not been so outspoken. Politicians were sensitive about him until Asquith offered him Lincoln in 1910. Even then he was the Prime Minister's second choice for a diocese which had, as Asquith noted in his letter, "a large Nonconformist population" and special difficulties. But Asquith rightly attributed to Hicks the necessary "large and broad-minded conception of the true functions of a chief pastor of the Church". And Edward himself recognized that although contemporaries who had got there sooner had done so without giving up their college Fellowships for college livings, he now saw that the years at Fenny Compton, in comparative obscurity, had been of "golden preciousness" as preparation for the pastoral work of a bishop.

Hicks did not disappoint the King once he had given the necessary royal approval to the appointment. He tackled a task which some of the bishops before him seem to have neglected, going round his parishes and meeting the clergy on their home turf, inspecting the church buildings, assessing how well the local people were being cared for pastorally and spiritually. His impressions he noted in his diary, with a sharp eye and considerable frankness. The resulting picture of the life of the church in this great northern diocese in the years immediately before the First World War and during the war itself is a mine of information about aspects of life going far beyond the strictly ecclesiastical.

But before we join him on the journey we need to look first at what he understood to be the role of a bishop, and then at the kind of fist some of his notable predecessors in Lincoln had made of the job.

Chapter 5

What is a Bishop For?

W hat did Edward Hicks think a bishop was for? We need to set his new job in its context, as he had to do himself. The "Episcopal Charge", *Building in Troublous Times*, was the detailed encouragement to his clergy which he made in a series of twelve short addresses given at key places round the diocese over two weeks in June 1912. This was a task all bishops were expected to carry out every few years. It began with a Visitation, in which the bishop asked all the clergy to answer a list of questions (Articles of Enquiry). That enabled the bishop to discover various diocesan statistics and judge the strengths and weaknesses of what the clergy were doing. Edward Lee Hicks's Charge became his most important statement of his ideas about the church and a bishop's task within it. He published it and it adds greatly to what he says in his diaries, giving the sweep of his thinking. It also contains many indicators of his personal convictions, such as: "It is difficult to rescue the drunkard without abstaining oneself."

He might have answered the question "What is a bishop for?" in two ways, as he reflected on his new task. One way was practical. He had been a clergyman in the Church of England long enough to have seen what a bishop actually did. He mentions that several times in the Charge. He was well aware that he was going to have a range of pastoral responsibilities which reached into every part of the diocese and potentially touched the lives of everyone who lived there.

Some of the work would be the kind of thing he had always done. There would be "mission". He would have to do his best to bring the gospel to the people who – even in an England where a high proportion of the population went to church – could be apathetic even though they counted as "practising" Christians. He would go on with his social work, but should that include his campaigning? Now he would have authority over many parishes and over their parish priests. He knew he would have to be tactful but firm with the clergy and that the problems he had learned to cope with in one parish would be multiplied. He must have been well aware by this time how various and eccentric Anglican clergymen could be.

CONFIRMATIONS

There was one special new task for him. Hicks knew that the most likely time for a Christian to come face to face with a bishop in person was at a confirmation. In churches which practised infant baptism, as most of the West had done since the late fourth century, it was found to be important to have a further ceremony at which children could accept with real understanding the promises made on their behalf at baptism in infancy. The tradition was long established and accepted in the Church of England that only a bishop could "confirm". So a confirmation usually meant a visit to the parish or the district. That offered a bishop a chance to see how well a parish was doing without appearing to arrive for an "inspection".

Those coming to be confirmed might be numerous and of various ages, if there had not been an opportunity for a local confirmation for some years. Here would be a chance to meet some of the people of the diocese as individuals. In fact, Hicks found himself doing a great deal of confirming, especially once the war began. Wartime produced a surprising number of young men who wanted to be confirmed when they joined the army and young women involved in war work too. The *Lincoln Diocesan Magazine* for February 1921 records that the number confirmed in the diocese in 1920 was 4,270, in 1919, 3,580, in 1918, 3,880 – "The average for the preceding five years was 4,067". In 1913 the number was 4,431 and in 1912, 4,844: "We have apparently therefore somewhat recovered from the dislocation of parochial and pastoral work occasioned by the War, but have not yet recovered the pre-war standard." Even this was a standard Hicks had thought not good enough in his Charge of 1912, because it represented less than half of those who were baptized, and in a growing population too.

DOES THE CHURCH NEED BISHOPS?

But there was also the theory. Here the Charge is a constant reminder that he was a scholar who knew the historical background to the life of the church and the history of theology. The other answer Edward Hicks would have given if you had asked him about his new responsibilities was theological and ecclesiological. He had been an Oxford don and he always remained a scholar with academic knowledge at his fingertips. Although his great interest lay in deciphering ancient inscriptions, he was an informed theologian who could deal perfectly well with abstract ideas when he needed to. He had spent a good deal of time as a young man discussing technical questions of theology and the doctrine of the church. He had a fairly comprehensive knowledge of the history of the great controversies down the centuries. He kept up to date with current controversies too. There are appearances in the diaries by old Oxford friends and colleagues and visits to Cambridge, where Hicks knew many of the theologians who were shaping Anglican debate. He could usually join in any academic discussion as an equal.

That knowledge breaks the surface from time to time in the record of his work, when he was confronted with a theological question which needed an immediate answer. For example, on 6 July 1916, he caught the early train to London, where "the majority of Bps. met, *quite privately*, to discuss 'Reservation'." "Reservation", or keeping of the bread and wine consecrated at the Holy Communion instead of ensuring that it was consumed at the end of the service by the celebrant if there was any left, was a practice in the Roman Catholic Church, where the doctrine of transubstantiation was accepted. This is the belief that the bread and wine become the actual body and blood of Christ, so that it seems fitting for them to be the object of prayer or devotion if a portion is kept in a vessel for the faithful to contemplate. Protestants had rejected this practice because they felt this to be a form of idolatry.

On this occasion, the bishops held a debate. The Church of England accepted the practice of keeping a portion of the consecrated elements to take to the sick who could then share the Eucharist with the congregation in that way. The Bishop of Oxford had been strict in forbidding any form of Reservation used to allow "prayer or devotion". The Bishop of London said he was not prepared to be so strict, but the other bishops, except the Bishop of Birmingham, did not share his view. "I think this day well spent" commented Hicks at the end of the discussion.

ARE BISHOPS NECESSARY?

Whether the church should have bishops at all was a controversy of very long standing. It was still a chief point of difference between Anglicans and Nonconformists in Edward Hicks's lifetime. He met and worked with Nonconformist ministers and the members of a variety of churches without this difference getting in the way very much when there was a common cause to unite them. The common cause was usually practical and pastoral, involving one of Hicks's favourite campaigns to improve the lot of his fellow men. But the fact remained that the Bishop of Lincoln had no real counterpart in the leadership of the Methodists or other Nonconformists in Lincolnshire or the diocese. Nor could he, strictly, "recognize" their ministries.

The Church of England remained the established church. It had not stopped having bishops at the Reformation. It had continued to accept most of the doctrine of ministry which the Middle Ages had inherited from the early church. This included the belief that a bishop (*episcopos* or "overseer") had a responsibility for "overseeing" the pastoral care (*cura* or "cure") of the people in a geographical area. That was why in a diocese all the people were members of the bishop's flock.

Within that "diocese" were parishes, smaller local areas, each with a priest in charge. The bishop remained the shepherd of the diocesan flock, and the priests who served the parishes and looked after local communities of "sheep" were simply the bishop's "vicars" (deputies or representatives). He was therefore responsible for ensuring that they did their work well – because they did it on his behalf – and that they too had pastoral support when they needed it.

Historically, this division of a bishop's area of pastoral responsibility had become a necessary arrangement throughout Christendom because once the numbers of early Christians multiplied, a single local church could no longer serve the needs of all the Christian population in each area. In times when the fastest mode of transport was the horse, believers would simply not be able to get to church very often unless churches were more numerous and dotted about the diocese. In England a parochial system to meet this need was emerging by Anglo-Saxon times and the parish boundaries fixed then became resistant to change. The parish system survived events of huge political and ecclesiastical importance, the Norman Conquest and the Reformation. Throughout the centuries and beyond the Reformation the ancient concept of the diocese headed by a bishop persisted in the Church in England which became the "Church *of* England".

That did not happen without some dispute and disagreement. Although the need for bishops was never seriously challenged in the Greek Orthodox Eastern half of Christendom, it was fiercely objected to during the Reformation in Western Europe by groups of reformers who claimed that this system was a corruption of the New Testament. In the Bible, it was argued – particularly by the "Calvinist" Presbyterians – that "presbyters" and "bishops" are two words for the same thing. The Presbyterians said that in allowing the "pyramid" structure of bishop, with priests and deacons "under" him to evolve for more than a thousand years, the church had taken a wrong turning.

The three-stage ladder to the episcopate, climbed by Edward Hicks and all other bishops in the modern Church of England and in the medieval church from which it emerged, involved first being ordained as a deacon. The deacon could not celebrate Holy Communion or give people the assurance that their sins were forgiven when they repented. In due course, usually once he had served as a curate to a parish priest, the new cleric was ordained a priest, and then he was able to preside at the Eucharist and pronounce absolution. Finally, the few who became bishops were consecrated for that higher office by at least three other bishops. Then they had powers to ordain deacons and priests and to join with other bishops in the consecration of other bishops.

Presbyterians held that the deacons of the New Testament were intended to have a different sort of role from the presbyters. They were to look after the practical needs of the community, making sure that its widows and orphans were cared for. They believed that the presbyters had responsibility for teaching and preaching (the ministry of the Word) and should govern the church by committee. There should, they considered, be no superior form of ministry with additional powers, such as the power to ordain attributed only to bishops. In Scotland, a form of Presbyterianism triumphed and in England too adherents of this view continued as Nonconformists and dissidents after the Church of England got its settlement and its position as the established church under Elizabeth I.

This claim to an episcopal "power to ordain" offended other Nonconformist reformers too, who emerged as the "Congregationalists" and are now part of the United Reformed Church which united Congregationalists and Presbyterians. They argued that it was for the people in the local "gathered church" or worshipping community to choose their ministers. Top-down ordination had no biblical warrant, they insisted.

These adherents of alternative structures pressed their case in sixteenth-century England and beyond, but the Church of England had kept its bishops and a series of Acts of Parliament down the centuries had tried to ensure that Nonconformists or dissidents were disadvantaged as citizens and thus discouraged.

Edwards Hicks grew up in mid-Victorian English society where the Church of England was still the established church and, until the University Tests Act of 1871, no one was allowed to become a student at Oxford or Cambridge unless he was a practising Anglican. These were the practical structural arrangements Hicks was familiar with and his conversations with the challenging Henry Bazely and the more anticlerical of the dons at Corpus do not seem to have made him think otherwise.

But he was well aware that when he found himself working with Nonconformists in his diocese he would have to tread carefully. His family background had originally been Methodist, as we have seen. Lincolnshire was John Wesley's birthplace, and the Methodists still had strong support in Lincolnshire. American Methodists had bishops, so Methodism did not entirely rule them out in the way Presbyterianism did, but the English Methodists organized themselves differently, in Connexions, divided into geographical Circuits in Districts. Methodists had ministers and deacons, but these were appointed to the Circuits, so they lacked the close local pastoral responsibility of Anglican priests with their enduring attachment to specific parishes.

SUFFRAGAN BISHOPS

The process of evolution of the idea of the bishop had included the realization that sometimes a bishop needed an assistant bishop or "suffragan". A suffragan could share the tasks which were special to bishops; for example, by conducting confirmations. A suffragan bishop might be given an area of his own within the diocese or he might just act as a reserve bishop and give assistance when the bishop needed it.

The diocese of Lincoln had recently acquired a suffragan bishop because Edward Hicks's predecessor, Edward King, had begun to feel that he needed help as he grew older. A suffragan bishopric of Grantham came into being from 1905, held by Welbore MacCarthy (1840–1925) from 1905 to 1920. It would be 1935 before another suffragan bishopric was added, this time for Grimsby.

Welbore MacCarthy had spent most of his career as a missionary in India, where he had been ordained bishop. *The Times* obituary of 24 March 1925 notes that he had returned to England in 1898. He had been appointed by Edward King to a living in the diocese of Lincoln. King had made him a rural dean and he became a prebendary of the cathedral in 1901. He must have seemed a natural choice when King asked for a suffragan to help him.

Edward Hicks inherited this arrangement. He seems to have seen the role of the bishop in very personal terms. He was not good at delegation. He does not appear to have worked very closely with his suffragan, though they were such near contemporaries. He notes briefly on 8 September 1910 that he has been instituting the Bishop of Grantham as the rector of Stoke Rochford. He describes a pleasant social visit to Grantham with his wife in November 1913.

BISHOPS IN COUNCILS

From the early Christian centuries, bishops traditionally had "shared" responsibilities, sometimes carried out individually and sometimes in councils or synods, which met to approve collective decisions about the defence of the faith or problems about order and discipline in the church. These could be taken on behalf of the church as a whole, especially when it was necessary to protect the faith against heresy. Or they could be taken more locally, for example to make sure worship was conducted in an orderly and appropriate way in a province of the church, and to ensure that there was discipline of the clergy where it was needed.

Edward Hicks had to do all these things. The Church of England had two provinces, the Province of York and the Province of Canterbury, each with its archbishop. Lincoln fell into the province of Canterbury. We shall see Hicks going to London for meetings of Convocation and discussing all sorts of problems arising in the Church of England (many of them arising afresh in wartime) with his fellow bishops. He could be quite caustic in his diary comments about these meetings, but then he admitted that he always felt a bit of an outsider.

THE BISHOP AS A PUBLIC FIGURE

A bishop was supposed to set a good example to his clergy and his people. No one ever seems to have suggested that Edward Hicks was not a good man. No shadow of scandal ever touched him. But he did take a public stand on matters of social reform, the position of women and the rights and wrongs of the war, all of which placed him in an exposed position. The question whether a bishop should speak out on political and social questions often arises today. It is nothing new.

Of all Hicks's personal enthusiasms, his temperance campaigning was the most controversial for a bishop. But there was one temperance organization in the Church of England Hicks could uncontroversially give his name to as bishop. He headed the diocesan branch of the Church of England Temperance Society (CETS; founded 1862) in succession to his predecessor, Edward King. The CETS published strong enough warnings to satisfy even Hicks's powerful concerns: "The train of physical wreckage that lies in the wake of drunkenness is, unfortunately, a matter of only too common knowledge." It stressed that "medical men had more experience of the home and social life of the people than any other professions (excepting possibly the Church), and it was the duty of the profession to influence public opinion". It claimed that "the industrial drinker" was the one who "stands most in need of our help as Temperance reformers". Even so, Hicks sometimes felt he had gone too far. On 8 November 1911, there was a "great CETS meeting in Town Hall" at Grimsby. The "outgoing Mayor, Mr. Wilkins – Wesleyan teetotal Liberal in chair. I spoke with too little care & reserve – *Deus misereatur* [may God have mercy]."

Chapter 6

A Hard Act to Follow

W hen he wrote his Charge, *Building in Troublous Times* for his Primary Visitation of the diocese in 1912, Hicks described his illustrious predecessors with respect and affection:

> *There is nothing, probably, in the world so likely to humble a man, and divest him of self-importance, as to be promoted to high and responsible office. ... If any spark of self-confidence survived in me, unquenched by the sense of my vast responsibilities, it would be effectually damped by the remembrance of that great line of bishops whom I am called to succeed, and whose memories hover about me in my daily tasks and travels.*

Hover they did, to judge from the frequency with which he mentioned one or another of them in his diaries. As a new bishop, Edward Lee Hicks regarded his medieval predecessor Hugh of Lincoln (1135/40–1200) as something of a hero. St Hugh, "the nobleman brought up as a Cistercian monk", caught his imagination from reading his chaplain's *Life*, "so that we seem to know him and love him today almost as if he were a contemporary". On 29 January 1913, Hicks gave what would now be a lecture with slides to the Girls' High School on St Hugh. (At that date, the slides had to be shown "with Lantern".) On 13 November 1913, he went by the 5.55 train to Skegness to lecture on St Hugh but he was tired and says it fell rather flat. On 23 March 1914, he went to Burgh College in the rain again to lecture on St Hugh, where it "seemed to go well". He found he could even make use of his lecture on St Hugh as part of an educational visit with a wider purpose. On 2 December 1914, he

> *Addressed the girls of Miss Stotherd's school [in Spalding] at 9.30 on the changed edn & training of girls, & its perils which can only be safeguarded by true Religion.*

Then, perhaps as a treat after the moral lesson about "perils", he gave them a talk "on the Life and Character of St Hugh". He does not say how this went down.

Perhaps what appealed most to Edward Hicks was the evidence that Hugh had been a bishop with a social conscience. Unlike the many "absentee" bishops of the period, he spent most of his time in his diocese. Hugh had been bishop from 1186 when the diocese was still almost the enormous size decreed by William the Conqueror when he reorganized England after his victory over the English in 1066. It had shrunk a little in 1109, when it lost Cambridge – with its brand new university composed of refugees from Oxford – to the diocese of Ely. Hugh travelled about the diocese, overseeing the clergy and trying to ensure that the people got the pastoral care they needed, just as Hicks tried to do more than seven hundred years later. Hugh protected vulnerable people from persecution. He resisted being controlled by the King and being "bought" by royal patronage, and preserved his independence as far as he could.

The cathedral at Lincoln had been damaged by an earthquake the year before Hugh became bishop. He put a great deal of energy into getting it rebuilt in what was then a modern (Gothic) style, and enlarged. Hicks had fellow-feeling with him here, too, because he loved the church's buildings and especially the cathedral Hugh built, and he also shared with Hugh an active concern to preserve and improve the church buildings of the diocese.

Any medieval Bishop of Lincoln also had links with Oxford, which then lay within the medieval diocese. It was Hugh who consecrated St Giles's church there in 1200 and enlarged the church of St Mary Magdalen, churches which stand today at either end of the broad thoroughfare of St Giles in Oxford, round the corner from Hicks's first little school. Here was another living link to his own childhood and youth.

On 22 September 1912, Hicks paid a "longish call" on "the daughters of old Bp. Mackenzie once Bp. Suffragan of Nottingham, & (earlier) Subdean of Lincoln". They entertained him with "much talk of old Lincoln people & times". The elder Miss Mackenzie showed him her watercolours, including one of the statue of St Hugh on the south-west pinnacle of the cathedral which had been taken down for repair. She had made her drawing of the unrepaired statue when she had the opportunity to see in close-up. She followed up this interesting conversation with a letter giving the details she had been able to add from talking to another sister, and a new drawing taken from what she believed to be the only surviving copy of a pre-repair photograph. Edward Hicks stuck this letter into the diary.

Robert Grosseteste

The other historically especially memorable medieval Bishop of Lincoln had been Robert Grosseteste (bishop 1235–53). Hicks had less to say about him in the diary. Perhaps he did not catch his imagination in the same way as Hugh had done. Certainly less was known about him in Hicks's lifetime than has emerged through recent research. In the Charge he is briefly "the son of a village peasant", an "Oxford scholar" and "the greatest mind of his age in Western Europe".

On 22 April 1916, Hicks visited the cathedral cloisters

where, at the foot of the Library Stairs, we examined the slabs & fragments which remained of Grosseteste's tomb. C. [Canon Cole] told me that a drawing of the tomb before its demolition by the soldiers exists in the Library, made very roughly by Sanderson & Dugdale. Rough as it is, it might enable us from the fragments to recover the appearance of the Latin monument. The figure was of bronze. I must look into this.

The destroying "soldiers" were part of the Puritan anti-royalist Roundhead army in the Civil War of the mid-seventeenth century. They had been going about their appointed Puritan task of destroying anything which looked like an "image" in England's churches and cathedrals.

Here his interest was evidently in the historical remains more than the work of the intellectually ambitious Grosseteste who had been Oxford University's chancellor in his time, and a pioneering academic researcher in his day.

BISHOP KAYE AND HIS LETTERS

Among the records left by Hicks's more immediate predecessors as Bishop of Lincoln is the correspondence of John Kaye (Bishop of Lincoln 1827–53). Kaye gets a mention in the Charge as "the statesman bishop, and resolute reformer of abuses". Kaye was a much less natural writer of readable prose than Hicks, more pompous in his tone, less anecdotal. Versions of the problems Hicks was going to encounter over the decay and sometimes now inappropriate sizes of churches which could not always accommodate the contemporary numbers of local people, arose for Kaye too. But while Hicks's diaries read as though robust exchanges were uncommon and readily dealt with by his gentle peacemaking and tact, Kaye's letter collection gives the full flavour of the knockabout vigour of a nineteenth-century bishop's correspondence.

One correspondent wrote:

> *Be so kind as to peruse in the enclosed documents for your private amusement – and then throw them into the fire, and pray don't trouble yourself to answer this letter.*
>
> *It appears that our cock, the curate of Nettleham, shews a white feather. These little, round, fat, oily men of God will not fight – and no archdeacon, not even Bishop Bonner, can make them ... I expect, in the course of a day or two, to meet some of the principal parishioners of Belton about the repairs of their church – when I shall get a further insight into Bricks's misdoings.*
>
> *It is my opinion that I shall be able to lay before your lordship such authenticated statements as will enable your lordship to give him a good sound reprimand.*

This letter comes towards the end of a lengthy correspondence with the Bishop about Nettleham started by William Clayworth, a churchwarden. A dispute had arisen about a plot of land which had been allocated under the Enclosure Act for 1776 which covered parts of Lincolnshire. It was intended to yield rent or benefits "for the use of the parish church of Nettleham". A dispute followed in which the appointment of churchwardens became part of the argument, and this explosion gives a flavour of the resulting atmosphere. Hicks was going to face his share of heated local arguments in his parishes, though by the time this parish is mentioned in his diaries, he was near the end of his life and that old squabble seems to have faded. But we learn that this was by now a living yielding its priest only a very small income.

Elsewhere among the letters of Kaye's episcopate, we read that there are not enough seats in a church building. If the church is too small people complain, it is alleged, and some go off to worship with the Methodists. Here was a problem Hicks was going to encounter too, where a church building had become the wrong size for its congregations, sometimes too large, sometimes too small.

Another letter, sent on 3 January 1842, came from Wainfleet. It informed Bishop Kaye that "our rector who is fond, *between ourselves,* of making innovations, intends converting 100 of these free sittings into pews, and appropriating them to certain persons". This was a church built only twenty years previously, with a donation of £40, with the condition there should be "400 sittings free and unappropriated". In fact Cholmely, the rector, had written to the Society for Building Churches to get leave to "appropriate" 200 sittings. There was much anger in the parish, with that special fierceness historically peculiar to arguments among Christians in local churches.

Alongside these local irritants, evidently generating much ire and intrigue in the parishes affected, Kaye had to deal with points of propriety, good order and theology. Possible simony (buying ecclesiastical preferment) was drawn to his attention (a rector who had succeeded his father and expected to be succeeded by his son, "the emoluments of the living" suiting "the convenience of the man"). Hicks would have to deal with a case of alleged simony too. There was an allegation that a churchwarden was a "promoter of schism" and theological questions arising in a parish which had been referred to the bishop. The bishop was consulted about what to do if local people object to an incumbent and the setting up of local schools (a matter close to this bishop's heart). Hicks would encounter a similar range of problems being brought to him as bishop.

There seems to have been little diocesan "ecumenism" under Kaye. There was controversy over the burial of Dissenters: "Whole nests of houses have been entirely unprofitable which have before yielded something". This is all put down to "Methodist antagonism" (January 1852).

Edward King

Hicks's immediate predecessor, Edward King (1829–1910), had been Bishop of Lincoln from 1885. The "sanctity" of Edward King became something of a cult in his diocese in the quarter of a century during which he was its bishop. "Not, technically, a saint, it is true, since the Anglican Church does not canonise, but very evidently a saint in the estimation of his flock", said the author of a distinctly hagiographical biography. Hicks describes him tactfully in the Charge as a bishop "who by sheer beauty of character added a fresh lustre to the Anglican Episcopate".

This reputation, whether deserved or not, was going to make King a hard act to follow. He had been prominent in high places in his earlier career, and stood higher in the ecclesiastical constellation of influence than Edward Hicks. He was described as "a Bishop who was constantly to be seen in the remotest parishes, a Bishop who enjoyed nothing better than confirming ploughboys". This was "indeed a novelty". But Hicks commented that when he set about his own round of systematic visiting of the parishes of the diocese, he often found that no bishop had visited for a very long time. And Edward King, like Hicks, had the advantage of the building of the railways to get about a large diocese comparatively quickly.

Edward King was no ecumenist and no moderate. He had been an undergraduate at Oriel, John Henry Newman's Oxford College. He had been a close friend of Edward Bouverie Pusey and a founder of St Stephen's House in Oxford, a notably "high church" theological college. In March 1854 he told Samuel Wilberforce, the Bishop of Oxford that he wanted to be ordained.

King's ordination as deacon followed in June, so his formal training must have been negligible. He learned on the job, as a curate at Wheatley, where he served under the priest who was grandfather to his future biographer, Lord Elton. Elton evidently felt that he demonstrated strong pastoral skills and a saintly nature there.

Bishop Wilberforce recognized his gifts and in 1858 he made King chaplain to Cuddesdon College, which also had high church leanings in its training of the clergy. By 1863 the still youthful King was Principal and parish priest of Cuddesdon. In 1873 he became Regius Professor of Pastoral Theology at Oxford, a chair created in 1842 and in the gift of the Crown, but in practice requiring the backing of high politics. W. E. Gladstone evidently approved. King took this post seriously and remained a leading intellectual to a degree Hicks chose not to do. Though Hicks kept up his work on classical inscriptions where he could, it seems he consciously gave it a lower priority.

King was a campaigner for mission in the slums and social improvement. He made some activist friends, including Hicks's own friend and ally Henry Scott Holland, who spoke of his appointment to the See of Lincoln with "surprise and delight". He did his best to foster the work of mission, both internationally (especially in Calcutta) and the ventures going out from Oxford, which included the settlement in Bethnal Green and the Christ Church Mission. Gladstone's further approval secured for him the See of Lincoln.

There King's interest in improving the training of clergy continued. The Bishop's Hostel was the theological college for the diocese, and he took a real interest in it. He organized reading societies and annual retreats for the clergy at which they could keep up their studies. These were all activities Hicks would continue and develop.

Towards Protestant Dissenters Edward King declared friendly feelings:

I need hardly say that I have never had any harsh feelings against Nonconformists, and, I might add, especially not towards Wesleyans and Primitive Methodists, because I have always felt that it was the want of spiritual life in the Church and brotherly love which led them to separate. The more we can draw near to Christ ourselves and fill ourselves with His Spirit, the greater power we shall have for unity. What we want is more Christlike.

However, despite this benign and impressive record, King made enemies, especially as a bishop. He wore a mitre, which was a great provocation to those who feared he had Romanizing tendencies. In June 1888 the Church Association petitioned the Archbishop of Canterbury, accusing King of illegal ritualistic acts such as making the sign of the cross and having lighted candles on the altar. Benson, the archbishop, was unsure what to do. The trial, eventually held, went to appeal before the Judicial Committee of the Privy Council.

Edward Hicks is chosen to follow Edward King

Hicks got his bishopric late in life. The *Church Times* discussed his appointment. It thought he was too old; that the church needed younger men. In any case, the beloved shadow of Edward King hung over the process. He did not get the job because he had any knowledge of the needs of the diocese of Lincoln, though he had grappled with some comparable rural problems at Fenny Compton. He knew something of northern England and its needs from his time at Salford and in Manchester, but Lincoln was in the province of Canterbury, not that of York. Instead, he was appointed for "political" reasons, the sort which so often lie behind "top" appointments and may reflect an inability of the decision-makers to agree on the choice of more popular or obviously suitable candidates. The Prime Minister, Asquith, made the recommendation to the King, although the Archbishop of Canterbury, Randall Davidson, was apparently not enthusiastic.

Learning to Be a Bishop

Chapter 7

Enthronement and Getting Started

On 24 June 1910, Edward Lee Hicks, already sixty-seven years old, was consecrated Bishop of Lincoln in Westminster Abbey, and began to keep a diary. The first entry in the diary on this date – which was John the Baptist's day – gives the names of the three bishops who made him a bishop. (Three bishops are required by canon law.) One was Randall Davidson, the Archbishop of Canterbury. The archbishop had the formal "assistance" of Edmund Knox, Hicks's old friend the Bishop of Manchester, and another close friend, Charles Gore, who was now Bishop of Birmingham.

This brief diary entry does not mention the immense events taking place in the country or their consequences for the church. The King had died in early May and in the background of the day of consecration, the archbishop was much involved in the formalities surrounding the accession of King George V. Edward Hicks could not have been left in any doubt that becoming a bishop was going to draw him into politics at the highest level and in new ways. His own opinions would now have to be thought about afresh because they would be taken as the opinions of a member of the Establishment, the Bishop of Lincoln.

The problem which was probably exercising the archbishop most on the day of the consecration arose in the territory of churchmanship where Hicks had already run into trouble when he was accused of being too sympathetic to "ritual" over those candles on the altar at Fenny Compton. Since 1689 when William and Mary succeeded the Roman Catholic James II, a new king was required to make a declaration with a strong refutation of Roman Catholic doctrines on the first day when Parliament met after his accession to the throne, or else at his coronation. Its tone and language now caused offence to Roman Catholics, and members of the House of Lords had written to the Archbishop of Canterbury to say so. So the archbishop was busy with redrafting and consulting interested parties. On 28 June, only four days after Hicks's consecration, a new version was tried out on Parliament but rejected because it did not go far enough. It was not until 27 July that a version was arrived at that began to command general acceptance.

Would Hicks have to give up some of his favourite causes now he was a bishop? Or could he simply throw himself into the new job in a new part of the country, combining as best he could the knowledge he had gained from the rural and the urban parish ministries he had previously experienced in the dioceses of Oxford, Worcester, Manchester? Would he have to learn new skills to cope with new responsibilities? His diary is full of clues, especially as he gained confidence and began to treat it as a place for his frank opinions rather than a cautious record. He had had, after all, plenty of opportunity over the years to see what being a bishop meant.

It was not long before Edward Lee Hicks, the tradesman's son, found himself – briefly – at the centre of power. The next day, 25 June, he went to do "homage" to the new king at Marlborough House. This was a tradition left over from the Middle Ages, when a bishop was technically one of the King's "barons" and the lands which went with the see or diocese were entrusted to him in return for an act of formal homage to the monarch, designed to ensure loyalty. The medieval requirement to provide the King with men to do days of military service when needed had lapsed. Hicks was not going to have to send men from his diocese to fight.

In 1910, a bishop would be "brought" to the King by officers of church and state. Winston Churchill, who was home secretary at the time, and the Bishop of Ripon (Clerk of the Closet) took Hicks to the King. He knelt in the traditional way to do homage. That meant placing his hands together as though he was praying, between the hands of the King, as a symbol that he was the King's subject and servant. Then he took the Oath of Fealty (faithful service) and "kissed the King's Hand" (he gives the word a capital H in the diary entry). There is an air of the ordinary boy from an Oxford home slightly surprised to find himself in high places about the way he describes the exchange with the King. He got up to go and the King politely took the initiative and made a little conversation: "I understand that you are going at once, to Lincoln to your work, & therefore wished to do Homage today." Hicks said he was "and that I was grateful to his Majesty for making arrangements for me".

He and Agnes went to Lincoln the same afternoon and "slept in the Palace". The Old Palace was traditionally home to the Bishop of Lincoln. It really was a palace, though that day the workmen were still there "in possession, & things were in an unfinished state". It had been built on a lavish scale in the Middle Ages as befitted the bishop of such an enormous and important diocese. It had to serve as an administrative centre as well as an impressive episcopal residence. The Victorians added a chapel for the bishop's own use, dedicated to St Hugh, seating about seventy. The Palace was a historic building, but cold and uncomfortable and expensive to maintain by the early twentieth century. Servants were not a luxury but a necessity.

On 26 June, which was a Sunday, Hicks was up in time to celebrate at the 8 a.m. service of Holy Communion in the cathedral and he notes that he managed to arrive in his robes, so some thoughtful packing and planning must have been done before they left the ceremonial occasions in London.

On 27 June he was complaining to his diary that he was being "pestered with Photographers". The previous bishop's private secretary, William Smith, was an immense help, "full of information ... he knows all the people & traditions of the Diocese, & is a careful man of business". Hicks found him rather slow and "verbose" compared with his counterpart at Manchester, but his "thoroughness" was evidently very reassuring.

The enthronement followed on 30 June. Hicks did his best to give the townsfolk a good show. He decided to dress as "I believe Bp. King would have done", in the best robes the diocese had for its bishop – "We got out of the bank the lovely jewelled gloves". His new ("just secured") domestic chaplain, the Reverend W. Rowland Rhys, went first with the "best" pastoral staff, and behind him walked the Reverend. A. S. Duncan-Jones, a Fellow of Caius College, Cambridge, who was to serve as one of his examining chaplains. The bells rang and the mayor and various civic officials and councillors from Lincoln and other towns read an Address of Welcome. A lot of photographs were taken "with the Kodak en route, snap-shotting".

Then, in the traditional way, he approached the cathedral's Great West Door and took the pastoral staff from his chaplain, and "knocked loudly seven times with its butt end". The doors were opened, the Mandate was read and he was admitted.

This was his first opportunity to tell the people what kind of bishop he was going to be. His address, he says, "was intended to do two things especially". The first was "to indicate that my sympathies lay with the friends of democratic reform". The second was "to explain the meaning of the ceremony, as indicating the important place religion ought to have in a community of civilized man, and also the dignity & beauty of religion". These two may seem odd choices, unlikely to be well aimed in their general appeal. He risked offending powerful interests with the first; he risked appearing remote from the practical daily concerns of ordinary people with the second. But they were evidently his own genuine priorities.

Hicks was not a man who found he enjoyed publicity or secular ceremonial on those occasions where the bishop's presence was expected. His first days were full of such ceremonies and official engagements, one of which prompted the first of his frank exclamations about "a speech of fulsome & wearisome rhetoric".

THE DIARY

Who arranged the events and activities for the new bishop we can now read about in the diary? Edward Hicks had to get used to having a (male) secretary, who had served under previous bishops. The secretary was careful and punctilious and will have reined back any incipient follies in the new bishop with courtesy. Hicks could frame a general plan of what he was going to do and what his priorities were going to be, but the secretary was going to be the source of advice on many daily details.

It is in those daily details that the picture emerges of the way Hicks got to grips with the job and his reactions to the stream of new people and things he encountered each day. The first few pages of his diaries show him engaging for the first time in a huge variety of new activities, and trying to get into his hands, without entangling them, the many strings of his responsibilities. He was not going to be the sort of new broom that arrives with a grand plan and sweeps clean. We can follow him in some detail through the diary pages, and the daily journeys and meetings and activities look as though they have come up for his attention rather than being systematically planned ahead.

At the beginning, the diary seems to have been kept as a semi-official record rather than primarily as a personal record or memorandum for Hicks's own use. He even began by leaving alternate pages blank. For more informal recording, he carried a notebook about with him in which he jotted down odd thoughts, ideas for sermons – anything which struck him. On 8 August 1910, the classical scholar had his moment. He went "To the Museum: to present my coin of Nero, found in our drainage works at the Old Palace." This was of course also an opportunity to get to know the people who staffed the museum.

He wrote the diary episodically, sometimes covering several recent days at a time and admitting that he might have misremembered a date. He did not try to cover every day or every event, but chose what had struck him as worth including. It was physically a big and "official"-looking record, though it grew more free and casual and risky as the years went on. These first diary entries turned out to note starting points for areas of work and interest which became of much greater importance in wartime.

The dean

One of the first matters for the new bishop to attend to was getting to know the clergy at the cathedral. Formally speaking, the cathedral canons and its staff were none of a bishop's business. They were the responsibility of the dean and governed by their own Chapter, which met to make decisions about cathedral affairs. The cathedral clergy were also canons, by virtue of the permanent posts they held on the cathedral staff. These were "residentiary" canons, who had a particular role connected with the running of the cathedral, such as the Precentor who looked after the services. Others were "prepentary canons" who held livings in the diocese and had their own parishes but whose "stalls" in the cathedral were theirs by right because they held livings whose income originally came from the diocesan estates. Some prebendary canons were given their canonries as a mark of honour or for other reasons. A question arose for Edward Hicks when the prebendaries of Lincoln Cathedral presented him with a problem about the right to preach in the cathedral. This could be sensitive. The residentiaries sometimes tended to regard the prebendaries as an inferior class of canons. It was not all rivalry and internal disputes. Some cooperative effort had recently been made by the Chapter to tackle the need for repairs to the cathedral fabric. But Hicks will have known from Manchester experience that he would have to exercise a good deal of diplomacy.

From the uncomfortable position of not being in charge of the cathedral, the bishop had to work with them all, and he had certain responsibilities for troubleshooting when things went wrong, as sometimes they did. There is no surviving sketch of Chapter meetings at Lincoln but the flavour of the notorious quarrelsomeness of such bodies is all there with satirical exaggeration in Anthony Trollope's mid-nineteenth-century *Barchester Towers*. Edward Hicks and his wife were no Dr and Mrs Proudie and none of his chaplains appears to have been a Mr Slope. But even in the comparatively small Lincoln Chapter of his time, Hicks had his share of difficult characters to deal with.

Edward Hicks had an old friend in the dean of the cathedral, Edward Wickham, who had made him welcome "very warmly" the moment he was "nominated Bishop in April 1910". He had invited him and Agnes to stay "and gave ... every possible assistance". In the Charge, Hicks made special mention of him and his immense knowledge of the diocese. When he arrived to be Bishop, he said: "I found his counsel invaluable, the more so because he carefully abstained from offering me advice; he left me always to take my own line." Dean and bishop can be a difficult relationship, because although the cathedral is named after the *cathedra*, or seat from which the bishop preaches when he is present, it is the dean's cathedral, not the bishop's. In the early Christian world, the bishop's throne was the symbol of the authority of the local bishop to teach and his duty to protect the one true Christian faith. But the dean is in charge of the building and it is only with his permission that the bishop may enter to preach from his throne. This is why a new bishop at his "enthronement" must ceremonially knock on the cathedral door and ask to be admitted.

Dean Wickham had known the new bishop since Hicks was an undergraduate. Wickham had been a tutor at New College and Hicks's examiner when he was taking his degree; later they had examined students together as fellow dons. Wickham had then been headmaster of Wellington College and he had invited Hicks to be an examiner for his Sixth Form boys. The diary lists all this in the second entry, in an odd little note beginning, "NB. It was an immense advantage to me…" which suggests that Hicks felt he was writing for posterity at the beginning of keeping a diary as bishop, for he would scarcely have needed to remind himself of the details of this long acquaintance.

A review of a *Memoir* of Wickham's life, published by Lonsdale Ragg in 1911, summed him up: "Quiet and unobtrusive as he was, in matters of principle he was inflexible." The *Memoir* praised him for his "patience", "courtesy", "fairness" and "firmness of judgement". In his quiet way, Wickham was an "activist" dean, outside the cathedral as well as within. He tidied up the Chapter's financial and accounting difficulties and got electricity installed in the building. He took a lively interest in local educational provision, as a governor and chair of a management committee, and after the passing of the 1902 Education Act he drew up a syllabus for religious instruction in schools. He served on a Convocation committee which was exploring Prayer Book revision.

SOME BUSINESS IN OTHER PLACES

Despite having apparently put the King to some inconvenience so that he could do the obligatory homage to the Sovereign and get to Lincoln as speedily as possible after his consecration, Edward Hicks was off again to Manchester the day after his enthronement and he spent the first week of July in Manchester, London and Liverpool. On 1 July they were given a reception "at the Lord Mayor's Parlour ... The Bp. of M. & heaps of people present. Many kind things were said", the remarks of his friend the Bishop of Manchester were "overmuch". The Hickses were given a useful cheque for £1,850. That earned one of Hicks's not infrequent exclamation marks in the diaries. He did not explain where this money came from but it has all the marks of a collection made in the diocese to give him a good send-off. And the lack of inherited family money still mattered. "This will help me get in with comparative ease", he wrote, thinking no doubt of the expenses of moving house.

The next day, Saturday 2 July, was degree day at Manchester University. Edward Lee Hicks was to be given the honorary degree of LittD. He would have been familiar with the way this is done in Oxford at Encaenia, with the speeches in praise of the recipients in Latin in the old rhetorical tradition. In Manchester, he wrote, he was introduced by Dr. Conway. This was to be "the speech of fulsome & wearisome rhetoric". Another of the honorands, Guilmant, who was to be made a Doctor of Music, had an even more elaborate panegyric. "Why not put these speeches in brief Latin?" he asked the diary.

On Monday 4 July Hicks set off for London, for his first meeting of Convocation as Bishop of Lincoln. Convocation, the "Parliament" of the Church of England, had its two "Houses" of bishops and clergy, just as the secular Parliament had its Lords and its Commons. There were separate Convocations for the provinces of Canterbury and York, and Lincoln was in the southern province. (Bishops, of course, were also eligible to sit in the House of Lords as Hicks was to do later in his episcopate.)

In later years he always liked to stay at the Thackeray Temperance Hotel when he was in London, but on this occasion he was offered hospitality by Edward Talbot, the Bishop of Southwark. This was an old friend. He had been Warden of Keble when Hicks was in Oxford and he had preached at Hicks's ordination when he was made priest in 1870. The friendship remained strong enough for him to stay with the Hickses when they moved to Manchester. It was an irony that Talbot had been the first choice for Lincoln and had turned it down, so that a few weeks later it was offered to Edward Hicks.

Talbot may even have been instrumental in that. He was a close friend of the Archbishop of Canterbury too and he had written to him in April 1910 to say that he thought Edward Hicks "very able ... A churchman of good tradition ... A man of most fearless & virile morals: keen for things of liberty – &, of course, temperance". Hicks was perhaps to realize the next day at Convocation how close-textured was the network of the leading figures of the Establishment and of the Church of England within it. He found he had "much talk with the Archbishop", who evidently wanted to get to know the new bishop better. He has, noted Hicks, "an extraordinary acquaintance with all political & court doings".

There was a decision to be arrived at about how much to say at this first Convocation. But he was among men he already knew well and who were familiar with his views. Hicks allowed himself "a few words" in the discussion of the Poor Law Commission Report, enough to dissociate himself "as a Social Reformer from the undue pessimism of the Bp. of Birmingham", his friend Charles Gore.

On 7 July, the Church Council met at Church House and he was evidently stimulated by the quality of some of the speeches he heard on topics of current policy importance for both church and state. He mentions those by Sir Alfred Cripps "on the Education Question", Hensley Henson, Lord Hugh Cecil, Lord Salisbury and Lord Halifax (on divorce).

The next day he was back in the north of England, to attend a service in the Lady Chapel and be shown over the new building which was to become Liverpool Cathedral, a "mediaeval & gothic edifice".

Chapter 8

Diocesan Business

Back in Lincoln, Edward Hicks began in earnest on the daily work of a diocesan bishop. From affairs of state and high-level discussions about social issues he moved in a few days to preaching at St Paul's in Lincoln on 10 July, a "small Church", for "the opening of the new organ". Even here he was confronted with the effect of being a bishop, and a new one who would naturally be the subject of local curiosity. The church overflowed and "hundreds" had to go elsewhere to worship that day. Now he was a bishop, he would be responsible for confirmations in the diocese, an activity which was to take on a new frequency and urgency in wartime, he would find. His very first confirmation took place at Habrough on 14 July. "About 20, very mixed in age & quality. Three or four young engineers from Immingham among them", he noted in his diary.

On 16 July he experienced his first encounter with one of his more difficult clergy. Here was another new role and new set of duties, for he had to get used to the fact that all his clergy were his "vicars", serving their parishes in the diocese on behalf of their bishop. He wrote a frank comment in his diary, which was already turning from a formal into a more personal record – "Revd. G. W. Hunt to see me: his use of incense. A foolish ill-tempered man".

The use of incense was a highly sensitive matter in the warfare between high and low churchmen, Tractarians and evangelicals. We cannot really be sure how far Edward's own preferences had moved from his Methodist early childhood after all those conversations with Henry Bazely and others in Oxford. His comments in his diaries while he was bishop suggest that what was always uppermost in his mind was avoiding adversarial extremes. On 17 July he was invited to preach at a church he found was "evangelical" and "the following Sunday at a 'High' Church, down hill. When I accepted, I knew nothing of the topography of these Churches, nor of their ecclesiastical bearings". But this was clearly a good signal to send the diocese, that their new Bishop was not of any "party ... I thank God for his guidance, & take courage", he added.

Almost at once he was travelling again, to perform a task as a symbolic figure. On 23 July he set off for Grimsby by train, to dedicate "the new Mayor's pew and mace-rest" (he allowed himself an exclamation mark at this) at a "Corporation service". While he was in the area he preached at St Andrews, noting the name of the vicar, Mr Lenton, for he had to learn names as soon as he could. St Andrews needed a new "side Altar" consecrated. Scenting excessive high churchmanship, Hicks asked the vicar "not to put up an Ober-Ammergau crucifix" (a cross with the dying Christ upon it) and notes approvingly that "he most readily assented". The following day offered a *large* garden party at the vicarage. The new bishop was evidently still an attraction.

On 28 July, he was driven to Grainthorpe to reopen the church which had been closed for repairs. Agnes or Christina often accompanied him on his travels to more distant parts of the diocese, though he does not as a rule tell the diary which. At Grainthorpe he quietly took the opportunity to take stock of the parish and its incumbent. This was to become a habit.

Here

> *the state of the parish is bad, the Vicar, a Cambridge honours man, not having the least idea of being a pastor, & being parted from his (2nd) wife.*

Hicks had time to form a fuller view about what he had found. He slept that night at the vicarage, where the priest "entertained" him with a gramophone, explaining that he could not get to concerts but liked music, especially Wagner.

So ended the first month since his enthronement. The pattern of his ministry was beginning to be set: visiting his parishes as occasion offered and meeting his vicars; being a distinguished presence at important local events; meeting the people rather less, except where there was a confirmation, or perhaps a garden party. Another area of his responsibilities presented itself on 2 August when he was able to "admit" a new intake of students to the local theological college, the Hostel. They had been waiting for "admission" since his predecessor fell ill. The Hostel and its problems were to run as a repeating theme through his episcopate.

Another church had to be reopened after restoration on 3 August in Thetford near Horncastle. There was another "odd Vicar":

> *Mr Wood – a sort of hermit scholar, who lives in his garden. He has all the modern books on Bible study. I fear the Parish is not wisely or thoroughly handled.*

Hicks kept an eye on this situation. The "mad but good" Mr Wood would become a continuing problem. These eccentric clergy and the difficulties they could present became a reason for taking the running of the Hostel seriously, for it could help to prepare a more reliably educated future clergy.

When the laity came to see him they could be demanding. On Saturday 6 August 1910, Bishop Hicks held "interviews". There appeared an example of a type still familiar to Anglican clergy as the novels of Barbara Pym mischievously confirm, the notorious "Miss Hughes – in consequence of my sermon on defective faith: she is rather a crank". The persistent laywoman with religious questions was perhaps something he had met before. He acted quickly. "I handed her over to the Rev. C. E. Lambert of the Hostel, who saw her repeatedly." This was a wise move. A bishop could easily find a lot of his time taken up by a very few insistent individuals of this kind. The same interview session brought a visit from "the Churchwardens of New Bolingbroke", who wanted "to pour out their woes about Dr. Hunt", their vicar. "Such good, honest, *stubborn* Lincolnshire farmers! Alas, what can I do with a lunatic – for such he virtually is!"

The following day, Sunday 7 August, took him to reopen another church which had been repaired, at Cherry Willingham, and to meet another vicar, the Reverend H. Hall. Hicks was humane, surprisingly charitable about some of the clerical behaviour he uncovered, and tolerant of the more harmless of the eccentricities he found. He notes that "Rev. H. W. Hall, Vicar … is somewhat of an antiquary & his hobby is iron-work and smith's work". In mid-August the density of dates in his diary seems to have eased a little, though he had an appointment to speak to the men at Ruston's works, one of a series of talks to factory workers.

All this, the encounters with the great business of state and the small affairs of the diocese was evidently setting him thinking. The result appears in the first addresses he was to give in his Charge in June 1912. It is worth setting his ideas out here in outline, although he was not going to give the addresses for nearly two more years, because it makes sense of the decisions we can see him making day by day in these first months. At Sleaford, Tuesday 11 June 1912, Hicks began by speaking of "troublous times for Christianity and the Church". He took a grand overview of the state of the nation and the church's opportunities and responsibilities within it. It is "drifting into materialism", with the rich affluent because of "their needless and enervating comforts", the poor oppressed because of their "grinding poverty". But he was always positive. This could be the beginning of "a great religious revival", he suggested.

His clergy needed to be conscious, as he had become, that some "quite new problems" were emerging, prompting questions such as "How are we to mix with non-Christian peoples on terms of equality and brotherhood? How are we to maintain peace, and prevent war, between the Christian nations of the West?" How was social order to change, now England was an "Industrial Democracy"? Furthermore, how were the clergy "to feel and act in respect of the enfranchisement of women, the restriction and suppression of the liquor traffic, the prevention of the State-regulation of vice, the peace movement, and other forms of social and moral agitation?"

At Grantham on the Wednesday he took as his subject "the problems before the Church". He spoke of the danger that the spiritually minded might "deem the organization of the forces of righteousness against the social evils of the time as outside the province of true religion". Such people thought it "sheer worldliness" for Christians to take arms alongside "other citizens for the redress of political wrongs and the remedy of economic evils". Hicks called this "pietism". The question was what should be the "practical programme" for the church. Self-discipline, he suggested, and trying to "enlarge and enrich the opportunities of others". And thirdly, "we must believe in freedom: freedom of thought, of enquiry; freedom of speech, and of action", as long as "our liberty does not infringe upon our neighbour's comfort".

There was much more in the addresses which followed, but we shall come to those in the story of 1912.

THE SUDDEN DEATH OF THE DEAN

Edward Hicks did not have the benefit of Wickham's familiar and supportive presence for long. On 13 August he went to York with "dear Agnes" intending to have a short holiday. He noted in his diary for 13 August 1910 that he had been at a service at All Saints' Church, York; of this he had some caustic things to say in his diary:

> *Very "High". Much incense. Sermon on the "Assumption of our Lady" etc. Not Anglican! Revd. Patrick John Shaw, Vicar. (I subsequently spoke to the Archbp of him. Appointed by his uncle the late Archbp. Hopeless to deal with him: wishes to be a martyr).*

Then suddenly on 18 August came the shocking news of the death of "our beloved Dean" in Switzerland. As he often did when he had to express strong feeling, he broke into Latin and calls him *Decanus noster dilectissimus* ("our most beloved Dean"). He went back to Lincoln alone on the 20th, leaving Agnes at Chollerton, and we find him preaching on the dean's death in the nave of the cathedral on the Sunday. Describing the loss of Wickham, he said, "His sudden removal I felt to be a calamity."

He asked for and got a successor he thought would be to his taste, T. C. Fry. Thomas Fry (1846–1930) remained dean throughout Hicks's episcopate. Fry was a Cambridge man, an Old Testament scholar and active in movements for reform of the church. He had been a headmaster. His wife was a Greene who came from a leading family of brewers which might have boded ill, but Fry himself was a total abstainer and shared Hicks's enthusiasms for the temperance movement and for Christian socialism. He was also a Liberal in politics. He belonged to the Christian Social Union and had been one of the authors in a collection of essays on the reform of the church edited by Hicks's friend and ally Charles Gore. His interest in education endured in the form of active support for the Workers' Educational Association movement. So there was plenty of common ground and shared interest.

MEETING THE FACTORY WORKERS

By now the new bishop was feeling less of a beginner. Many of the tasks he had done for the first time he was now doing regularly, though there were still some "firsts". On 7 September of his first year in office, he went to talk to the men at Clayton and Shuttleworth's, an engineering firm in Lincoln. This factory was making tractors of advanced design and decades earlier it had been employing over a thousand men. It had been exporting its products to Eastern Europe and it had branches in Austria, Hungary, Czechoslovakia, Poland and Ukraine. Two days later he was in Grimsby on another visit to workers, where he encountered the press and learned something about the publicity which was going to attend his activities. He and the mayor and others "went over the Docks & the Fish Pontoon". Then they were escorted to "the top of the Water-tower, & over the net-making & Ice Factory". He was impressed. "Quite wonderful, all of it." He seems to have committed a faux pas when he was presented with a sou'wester "which I admired & wanted to purchase ... The 'Daily Mail' & other papers made a good deal of the business!" he notes wryly.

A new experience on 8 September was the institution of Welbore MacCarthy, who had been made the Bishop of Grantham and Hicks's suffragan bishop, as rector of Stoke Rochford. That provided the suffragan with a living and an income.

Hicks was sometimes meeting his clergy in multiples now. He spoke to the clergy of the Rural Deanery of Aveland on 21

September, first in the beautiful church at 11 a.m., then at the Chapter meeting which followed. After luncheon he spent time in the garden for talk, where he found he had opportunities to meet "many men". There was the "eccentric" T. A. Stoodly, rector of Dowsby. He was in poor health and asked for permission to be non-resident. Hicks said yes. He had provided the parish with a good temporary substitute and Hicks notes that his eccentricity is so extreme that it may be better for the parish to have him go away for a while. He also met the Reverend Arthur Howard Galton, the vicar of Edenham. He realized too late that this was the author of works he had read "on the Church in France". This must be Galton's *Church and State in France* (London, 1907), which begins with an apologia in which Galton claims no special expertise. He has relied on the work of others. But he explains at length in his preface how his interest has been engaged by his own experience of encounters with Roman Catholicism in England and the relevance to Anglican clergy of the principle of separation of church and state.

A week later, Hicks encountered at first hand the problems which could arise from the system of patronage of livings. In many of the Lincoln parishes the hereditary patron was a local landowner. During the twentieth century this pattern was to change as dioceses acquired the patronage and brought the whole process of choice and appointment into the hands of the bishop, but in the period when Edward Hicks was Bishop of Lincoln patrons could still be a problem. We shall see Hicks wrestling with various difficulties about having to square patrons of livings who wanted their own way, and deal with unsuitable clergy previously appointed on their say-so. On 29 September 1910 he wrote: "After reopening Church at S. Willoughby I lunched with the Vicar & his wife … & his nice, but nearly blind, very eccentric patron Lord Dysart – Lord D. is a Liberal, a Freetrader *and* an AngloIsraelite!" The "Anglo-Israelites", while mostly remaining members of the Church of England, held the view that the Anglo-Saxons were the descendants of the lost ten tribes of Israel.

THE AUTUMN OF 1910: MISSION, WOMEN WORKERS, TEMPERANCE

With the autumn of 1910 came introductions to more of the areas of Hicks's new responsibilities.

Hospital visiting by the clergy was a duty which was to change with wartime and the arrival in the diocese of wounded soldiers, but Hicks took it seriously as bishop even before he had wounded soldiers in the diocese to try to comfort. On 2 October 1910, after preaching at the harvest festival at Lincoln County Hospital, Hicks "went round all the wards, & spoke to *every patient* & every nurse! On 25 August 1911, he "Visited injured Policeman ... *Riot & looting* in Lincoln on Saturday midnight".

On 3 October he seems to have had his first encounter with the determined Mrs Weigall, would-be well-known presence in the diocese, at the annual meeting of the local Church House. Here was a different sort of ambitious woman of the time from those he came to respect, one who used social connections and wealth rather than intellect and campaigning to make her mark, and whose "cause" was mainly her own advancement. Edward Hicks makes it pretty clear what he thought when "Mrs Weigall arrived (late) in a Motor with her Highness Princess Louise of Schleswig Holstein. There was a large attendance, & this arrival caused rather a flutter: but I kept my head & went right on".

Grace Weigall was the only daughter of the founder of Maple furniture, and she had inherited a great deal of money when her father died in 1903. Having obtained planning consent for a "bungalow", she set about building a mansion, Petwood, "Tudor to Jacobean", as its architect described it, and filling it with Maple furniture. She had divorced her first husband, a German diplomat, who had made her Baroness von Echardstein. In 1910 she married Sir Archibald Weigall and set about making a social impact. He was a professional soldier who had served in the Second Boer War and risen to the rank of major. In 1910 he stood for Parliament as a Conservative candidate, but it was not until 1911 that he got in, by a by-election, for Horncastle in Lincolnshire. Meanwhile, his wife was busy climbing socially.

The Church House meeting was not the only thing in Edward Hicks's diary that day. He had to preside again at 5 p.m. When he became a bishop, Edward Hicks already had considerable experience of mission in both rural and urban environments, and he was to encounter a number of oversees missionary bishop "returners". In Lincoln he found the Novate Novale, the Lincoln Diocesan Society of Mission Clergy. This had been in existence since the late nineteenth century. He thought it needed shaking up. On 3 October 1910 he presided at an "important meeting" of Novate Novale. He says he "tried to lead them to something like light". On 23 November 1910 he attended a committee meeting of Novate Novale: "I fear it will be difficult to reorganize this Society, & make it really efficient."

The evening of 3 October was the beginning of the Diocesan Retreat. These clergy "retreats" continued a provision fostered by Edward King when he was bishop. On 3 October one of these was led by the Tractarian Bishop of Stepney, Henry Paget. This was perhaps an arrangement and a choice of leader for the retreat made by Hicks's predecessor, because on 18 October 1912, Hicks mentions that he had been at a service in Grimsby where Paget preached "on dear Bp. King, & Oxford memories". But it seems to have been a good choice for the diocesan clergy in 1910: "His addresses were marvels of felicitous and playful criticism. ... helping us to examine ourselves, & full of love & sympathy." The Old Palace was "full of Clergy up for the Retreat".

There was still a surprising variety of demands. On 9 October, the Bishop preached at a "*Football* Service": "A big affair, but not so impressive or multitudinous as I had expected. But my words were widely reported." But then along would come one of his main interests, a first occasion with great implications for his future ministry. On the 10th arrived the delegates of the National Union of Women Workers, a trade union organization for women. Hicks, like others of his time who were interested in social reform, tended to be enthusiastic about such collective movements for the workers and even about "collective action".

That day, he addressed a "public meeting" of the NUWW. He gives no details; he just says, "I spoke." But he must have approved, because the next day the Women Workers were given a "Reception" at the Old Palace. There was "a big crush". He notes some names: Mrs Waterhouse, Miss Margaret Robertson, Miss Edith Lawson, Miss Henty, Miss Burstall. (These suggest that it was the "ladies" and the educated women who were leading the endeavour, rather than the ordinary women working as domestic servants or in the factories.) The Bishop was sending a very strong signal that he approved of them and their campaign. Was this wise? Were they respectable? We can only speculate whether he was urged to countenance their activities by his wife and daughter Christina. His sermon in the cathedral on Sunday 14 October was addressed to the "Women Workers".

These women's organizations trying to make themselves felt in politics had some successes. A NUWW Resolution of 1901 had pressed for compulsory registration of midwives and that was achieved quite quickly. But the sophistications of the world of political manoeuvring had to be mastered, and women, unlike male trade unionists, lacked the leverage of withdrawing labour in key industries.

The Common Cause, 28 October 1909, carried an article about the NUWW's annual meeting of the previous year, which had been held at Southsea, and the hopes for this one at Lincoln at which Hicks was to speak. The account reveals how much such organizations had to learn about the mechanics of running a meeting. It had been realized at Southsea that it was unwise to try to tackle enormous subjects such as "the poor law reports" in a short conference ("too vast to be crammed into one day"):

> *It is perhaps reckless to generalize from so small an experience,*
> *but it was at least noteworthy that the two men who read*
> *papers – Dr. Macnamara on "Poor Law Children" and*
> *the Rev. Charles Matthews on "Women in Australia" –*
> *were very ready with their advice, very sweeping in their*
> *generalizations and very sure they knew a great deal more*
> *than their hearers.*

Women had some way to go in mastering the skills of making themselves felt in public meetings so as to make their mark equally with experienced male speakers – "the women speakers were for the most part diffident and inconclusive in spite of their intimate acquaintance with facts".

On 17 October he went to a meeting of the United Kingdom Alliance (UKA), an organization with support from quarters which would not have been approved by many Church of England members. Edward Hicks had made a decision not to end his temperance activities when he became bishop, even those which were not related to the Church of England. By the first decade of the twentieth century, the temperance campaigners among whom Edward Hicks certainly counted himself prominent and committed were not regarded as merely individuals with bees in their bonnets. There was widespread unease about the effects of the national "drinking culture". Misuse of alcohol was a problem which was coming to exercise the nation, despite the hostile lobbying of the brewing industry.

That opposition made Parliamentary debates on the subject of possible restriction highly contentious. The "Balfour Act" of 1904 sought to ensure that breweries would be compensated for enforced closure of pub premises which would affect their sales. It was expected that more than two thousand licences a year would be withdrawn. The Liberals accused the Tories of giving in to lobbying by the brewing trade designed to limit the damage to their profits.

This method of controlling the nation's drinking proved ineffective. In February 1908, Asquith, then Chancellor of the Exchequer, made a speech in the House of Commons calling for the rate of suppression of licences to be sped up, with the intention of bringing about the closure of a third of the public houses in England and Wales. The Licensing Bill then being discussed included a shortening of opening hours on Sundays and a ban to prevent women being employed in pubs. The Bill was unpopular with ordinary drinkers as well as the liquor trade. The Liberals began to lose in by-elections. The upper classes did not like it either. The Bill was defeated in the Lords.

The Lloyd George government tried another tactic in the 1909 People's Budget. This provided for heavier duties on public houses and breweries. The Lords defeated that proposal too and the ensuing fury led in the end to the 1911 Parliament Act which restricted the power of veto of the House of Lords where budgets and money bills were concerned. The 1910 Licensing Consolidation Act comprehensively repealed and revised legislation on alcohol made in the last two generations, but it spared the drinks industry a good deal of the restriction imposed on it so far by the efforts of campaigners and the will of Parliament.

On 19 and 20 October came the first Diocesan Conference of Hicks's episcopate. Within the diocese, the bishop presided *ex officio* at these conferences. The Diocesan Conference also included lay people, and it too was a forum in which politically contentious matters could be aired. At the conference in 1907, when Edward King was still bishop, in an invited speech, T. C. Fry (later to become dean) had addressed the conditions of workers and the attitude of the church. He called the trade unions "a dyke to resist the flood of unmoralised capital".

Diocesan Conference gamesmanship required a bishop to be a politician, not in the party sense, but so that he was able to make his point among the lay leaders of the community in ways they would respect. Some sympathized with Hicks in any case. Herbert Torr was a would-be Liberal MP and activist in the Christian Social Union and the Church Reform League. Other leading Liberals (especially C. H. Roberts MP) in the county became his allies. Charles Roberts seems to have become a great friend of Hicks. C. H. Roberts's wife was the daughter of the Countess of Carlisle who was a force to be reckoned with in the temperance movement, and an active supporter of the UKA.

Another local Liberal figure, Lord Heneage, had his quarrels with the politician and great landowner, Christopher Turnor (1873–1940). Turnor was observed to be acting as host in his great house to slum children, working men and women, noblemen and women, teachers, squires "and a succession of those whom he was helping over stiles". He famously welcomed all social classes into his house, making no distinctions: "There were no rules, the whole house was open and free." Members of all social classes could be seen in conversation as equals. The house hosted post-war efforts too; the Archbishops' Committee on Industry, for example.

Getting to know important people in the diocese, beyond those who came his way through work for causes and organizations and through the Diocesan Conferences, was something Hicks seems to have tackled piecemeal rather than systematically. Conspiring was not his natural way. His diaries do not suggest that he made it a priority. In his parish visits he does not usually mention the local lay bigwigs at all, though his predecessor Edward King had apparently made a habit of dining with the local gentry on a visit and on a separate occasion with the local clergy.

Hicks was pleased with the way his first Diocesan Conference went. It "went off very well", he wrote in his diary. "All was crisp & lively, without heat, but not without humour & wit. Lord Wm Cecil was the hero of the Conference. He surprised us by his depth of feeling & his breadth of view." William Cecil (1863–1936), who was to become Bishop of Exeter in 1916, was the son of a Tory Prime Minister, Lord Salisbury and Chaplain to the King, as well as Rural Dean of Hertford. So he was well-connected in both church and state.

Hicks was delighted to find himself "regarded as a good chairman – decided, humorous & good-tempered. This is wonderful". But it turned out that he had annoyed some of his listeners by avoiding the usual bland conference "resolutions" and trying to stimulate serious concern about inroads by trade and commercial interests into the expectation that Sunday would be a day of rest. He was still learning to balance on the tightrope of expectations when he wanted to offer a reforming lead as bishop.

LATE AUTUMN, A CROWDED DIARY

On 24 October Hicks visited Immingham docks, commenting that he could see that the "miles & miles of docks" and the "25 miles of Ry. Sidings for coal" promised that it was "soon to spring up into a busy centre". He was to mention this in his Charge in 1912. Two years later, Immingham was to become important to the war effort. Of more immediate concern was the unsatisfactory local vicar. He gave Hicks a lengthy and "portentous luncheon … I wish the Church had a wiser head & bigger heart to represent it here!"

That evening, after a train journey back to Lincoln, came the annual meeting of the Lincoln Temperance Society. He had been unenthusiastic about a Conversazione, the currently fashionable "social networking event", held in the Central Hall by the Temperance Society, at which he was "received" on 11 September 1910: "Very kind, but very buttery, & *very* long-winded. Oh dear, how ungrateful I am." But this meeting was much more enjoyable. Charles Roberts, as Liberal MP for Lincoln and fellow enthusiast, came to stay at the palace with Will Crooks, one of the first Labour MPs (though briefly out of Parliament; he was to be re-elected at the General Election in December). The annual meeting went off splendidly with Hicks in the chair and the other two as principal speakers. (Crooks was a eugenicist who described the disabled as "human vermin", but there is no indication that Edward Hicks agreed with him on that.)

The 26 and 27 October were spent on a visit to Oxford with Agnes. Hicks had been invited back to his old school to present the prizes. The president of Magdalen College was their host and, confessing to some emotion, Hicks "distributed the prizes, at my old school, in the fine schoolroom". He was especially pleased when his son Ned who was at school there "got his prize". "It was a soul-stirring time!"

THE CHRISTIAN SOCIAL UNION

Two days later, his mind was on the Christian Social Union. On 29 October, he wrote in his diary that there had been an "Annual Meeting of Local CSU at the Hostel. I spoke & presided". His previous history with the Christian Social Union was already quite a long one and, like his enthusiasm for the UKA, his support for its work was heartfelt.

The CSU was started in Oxford in 1889, with a London branch developing from 1890. By the time Edward Hicks became Bishop of Lincoln, the organization had spread throughout the country and it had about five thousand members and sixty or so branches. Its purpose was to foster a Christian citizenship in both theory and practice, which would include improving social conditions. This chimed well enough with Edward Hicks's view that "it would seem that no small part of the duty of a Christian gathers round his status as a free citizen of a Christian democracy".

His contemporary biographer, Fowler, suggests that Hicks saw social reform as a kind of "war of good and evil". This was thinking which came naturally in the circle of activists among the clergy of the day. "Socialism", a word of nineteenth-century invention, did not have quite its modern meaning, though it soon acquired connotations of an ideal of regulating society for the common benefit.

DUTIES IN LINCOLN AND LONDON

The very next evening, Hicks was preaching on behalf of the Society for the Propagation of the Gospel, again with energy and feeling: "I begged for a worthy collection, i.e. worthy of our convictions & the object, & of the heroism of our missionaries. I gave £4 myself, & asked everybody to unloose their heart and purses. We collected £21." He realized that fund-raising on this scale was exceptional. "Of course this must not be done every time."

At the beginning of November he set off with Agnes for the meeting of the East Anglian bishops, and a week later on 8 November he was off to London to go to Convocation for a meeting due to last from the 8th to the 11th. But he travelled back to Lincoln in the late afternoon on 9 November for a dinner with the Lord Mayor, before returning to London by the 7:23 a.m. train the next morning. Charles Roberts, the Liberal MP, was present too. Hicks made the effort because, as he says, "Bp. King had made a great point of being present *always*" on such civic occasions "& had cultivated good relations with the civic authorities". Hicks wanted to continue this and he allows himself an "I *was there!*"

He evidently felt it important to get back to London because there was to be a meeting of the Church of England Temperance Society on "Inebriate clergy". He had some of his own in the diocese. Clergy as well as laity could trouble him because he thought they drank too much or took a permissive attitude to excessive drinking.

"HOME REUNION" AND ECUMENISM

Hicks comments on 29 November 1910 that he had "consecrated [a] new burial ground: thus ended a long feud between Ch. & dissent, Vicar & Burial Board of the Parish Council". In Wesley's birthplace diocese, Hicks was going to have to establish good relations with the Methodists and other Nonconformists for practical as well as theological reasons. There had been late nineteenth-century moves throughout the Anglican Communion to mend the breaches between Protestant churches, some of which dated back to the Reformation. "Home Reunion" was a repeating theme of the early Lambeth Conferences, including Resolution 75 of the Fifth Lambeth Conference of 1908. In 1910 the World Council of Churches launched what became the modern ecumenical movement at its meeting in Edinburgh.

With the – to him painful – exception of Roman Catholicism, Edward Hicks's general policy when dealing with Christians of other denominations was to try to avoid divisiveness. That does not make him an ecumenist, but it certainly makes him a peacemaker. Hicks's approach to working with "Nonconformists", the Protestant Dissenters, was typically humane and practical, though it shows some occasional flashes of his personal prejudices.

THE BISHOP BECOMES EXHAUSTED

This travelling and crowded sequence of important engagements – often in areas of activity about which he cared very much personally – would have tired a much younger man. There followed more crowded weeks in the approach to Christmas as Hicks went about the diocese meeting clergy, consecrating a new burial ground, holding another unencouraging meeting of the Novate Novale missionary project, holding his first ordination.

There are hints of growing fatigue. The diary entries become terse. The newly formed Lincoln Record Society, under the guidance of Charles Foster, felt entitled to ask the Bishop to be its head, even though he could not be expected to do much by way of helping with the editing. However, he could provide a venue and help to make a meeting a pleasant social occasion as well as a business meeting. He notes in his diary that the Lincoln Record Society met at 2 p.m. on 25 November 1910 – "Six to luncheon". But he had difficulty with the names of these guests without Canon Foster's help: "Foster absent! I didn't know who was who! alas!"

On 29 December he completely forgot that he was supposed to be addressing the Policemen's Bible Class at the YMCA. He was fetched "just in time". The YMCA, founded in 1844, had set up one of its first branches in Manchester, and Hicks evidently thought well of its efforts to reach out to "unchurched" young people. It had become an international organization.

There was a realization that he must avoid being seen to take a "party political" position. Just before a poll at Boston, due on Monday 5 December 1910, he noted in his diary:

> *Everybody excited about politics. At 6.30 I preached in the great Parish Church for S.P.G. [Society for the Propagation of the Gospel in Foreign Parts] to an immense congregation. I did my best to avoid anything which could be twisted into a*

political allusion, and yet be earnest about the Kingdom of God. How I succeeded I know not.

He ended "a momentous year" with a diary note of surprise to find himself where he was. "I wonder at my spiritual unworthiness," he wrote. "But God employs very imperfect instruments." This personal humility was sincere enough, and it set the tone for the Charge to the diocese in his first Visitation in June 1912. But it went with a quiet competence.

Chapter 9

Overwork and its Consequences

"I have been rushing all over the Diocese, & have got to know people far better outside than in the City itself," wrote Edward Hicks on 4 January 1911. The "people" he had been meeting included the laity as well as the clergy. Hicks took trouble over getting to know his sheep. Preaching in sometimes surprising contexts, outside the walls of a church and the context of its regular worship, was something he had done since the days in Fenny Compton. As we have seen, Henry Bazely had set him an example in his Oxford days, and he had found the method effective in his rural parish and also in Manchester.

What was he trying to achieve in this first year as bishop, beyond meeting as many of his people, clergy and lay, as he could? Above all, perhaps, he wanted to reach people who did not go to church, make them realize that the church might have something to offer them: comfort, support, spirituality. He often spoke at meetings where his words might not be taken as "preaching" exactly, though the line between a sermon and a talk or lecture could be fine and those listening to a bishop might well assume he was preaching to them.

In his Charge, Hicks was to be startlingly open-minded about unorthodox preaching. On Wednesday 19 June at Horncastle his theme was the work of the laity and lay readers. His theme was the need "to call in the assistance of laymen" to support the clergy, especially in villages of "vast area" and with a scattered population. Hicks favoured calling in "without fear or hesitation the help of our lay folk in evangelization". He thought they should not be restricted to using only the Prayer Book forms – "My own practice, in managing the Church Army Missioners" in Salford "was to forbid the use of any prayer-book in their services". Extempore prayers and hymns known by heart were the thing. "All was to be as informal, as unconventional as possible – reverent of course, but informal." The object was "to rough-hew stones for God's temple. Then we sent them on to the parish church to be shaped and built properly in". The Methodists had done much "effective work" in evangelizing "our parishes ... Surely we could have done all this ourselves, had we tried".

He continued the unremitting pace of work during January. One of his duties as bishop was to appoint the chancellor of the diocese's Consistory Court. This kind of court had become, since some Victorian transfers of powers to the secular courts, a somewhat vestigial ecclesiastical local court of the Church of England. On 5 January 1911, the court's proctors were elected. Hicks could already see that, ironically, the minority candidates "had with them the wisest and most judicious of the Clergy".

Edward Hicks managed another month into the New Year before his health gave way, and there is a gap in the diary from February to late May while he recovered. On 6 January he and Agnes went to Colwyn Bay "for a week's complete rest", but that was evidently not enough to hold off an episode of prolonged illness. As soon as they were back he was greeting a Manchester colleague, Bishop Welldon, who had come to stay. He had returned from Calcutta in 1902 and was now serving as Dean of Manchester Cathedral. He was "full of good stories – e.g. Dean (Robinson) of Westminster and Lady Agatha Thynne, & her stay at the Deanery to qualify for being married at the Abbey ...

D[itto] & the Actress [story] to be confirmed". On 17 January he was at last "caught" to be photographed by the Lafayette's man (the photographers), so that official photographs might be available. There was a dinner at the Old Palace for forty-three of the mayor and corporation. Hicks had taken the precaution of arranging for there to be "3 boxes of excellent cigars" which the diners "appreciated". There were speeches. And then the men retired to join the ladies, as was customary in the Edwardian period, and were "received" by Agnes and Christina and the new dean's wife, Mrs Fry.

THE CHURCH OF ENGLAND PEACE LEAGUE

The following day, after this demanding late night, he was at work again early in a cause close to his heart. He was to remain president of the new Church of England Peace League from 1910 until he died. The CEPL had little more than a hundred members in 1911, and had formulated its objectives before war broke out or was seriously feared. It looked back to the Boer Wars in its thinking as much as forward to any future war. The first of its aims was "to keep prominently before the members of the Church of England the duty of combating the war-spirit as contrary to the spirit of Christianity, and of working for peace as part of the divine ideal of human society". The second was "to promote universal and permanent peace among nations". This was to be attempted "by encouraging the growth of international friendship" and "by working for the adoption of arbitration and conciliation in place of war and for other peaceful means of settling international disputes".

In presiding over the League, Hicks had some heavyweight support from within the Church of England. Hastings Rashdall and Thomas Fry, Lincoln's own recently appointed dean, were impressive names to have as vice-presidents because they were deans of cathedrals. Rashdall approved of Hicks. He wrote a letter of thanks to his mother at the end of December 1922 for a copy of the *Life* of Hicks written by Fowler soon after his death (which she had perhaps given him for Christmas): "He is a man after my own heart. He ought to have been a bishop 20 years before. If he had been Bishop of London all these years, it might have made a vast difference to the Church." Hicks reciprocated his regard. In May 1913 he had been reading Hastings Rashdall, and found his collected essays with others such as Charles Gore, "excellent, but revolutionary". It was a balance he liked.

As well as "big names" to lead the group, prominent speakers were persuaded to address the League, including Gore and C. H. Roberts. As a church organization it was important that the new Peace League should be seen to be politically as well as ecclesiastically "broad church". So on 18 January, Hicks met Mr and Mrs Luddington from Downham Market, who came to see him "early about the draft Manifesto of the Ch of E Peace League to be settled at the Committee tomorrow. I am President of the Society. Nice people: though Tories!" Activists in the new Peace League could be seen to be not all "left wing".

The pressure continues

More travelling followed on the 19th, to Billingborough, where the last incumbent had just resigned. Hicks had "a long close talk" in the station waiting room with the rural dean and Dr Richards, who was "in charge of Dowsby", before he and the rural dean went on to Billingsborough. His policy of working amicably with Nonconformists where he could did not mean he thought it unimportant if local people preferred chapel to church. He notes quite sharply that Richards's predecessor "had emptied the Chapels & filled the Church to overflowing". This one "has emptied the Church, filled the Chapels, & helped the Wesleyans to build a big new one!" While he was in the area, Hicks went to call on the vicar of Horbling. This was a living with a low income and although the vicar's wife looked consumptive it did not seem that they could afford for her to have a fire in her bedroom. The vicar looked "hungry & gaunt". Hicks "sent him £5 with a kindly note".

His weekend was not to be uninterrupted, but the interruption which came was welcome. On Saturday evening "at 6.30 found Captain Rowlands (of Salford) waiting for me, & the Captain from St Andrew's, Grimsby, where R is conducting a Pioneer Mission". Rowlands was his old Church Army colleague from Salford. They all "had tea together, & they told me of the horrible & shameless immorality of Grimsby. Then we went into the Chapel, & had prayer together".

G. B. Wilson was one of Hicks's great allies in the UKA. Hicks "declared himself" a supporter within the diocese according to the diary on 23 January 1911, when "George B. Wilson ... came to stay a night ... to help me in our meeting of protest against a 'Trust' Public House which it is proposed to open in Monks Road ... We held a *crowded* meeting". A group at the back "led by one resentful man ... wanted a public house *simpliciter* [they just wanted a pub], as being a working man's privilege ... They have never had any Temperance teaching, & are as opposed to the Ch. & religion as to Temperance". The question to be addressed was what kind of public house it should be, but Hicks found that the crowd which came was divided along quite different lines, "between those who wanted more drink shops & those who did not".

This was his first real "outing" in the diocese as an active temperance campaigner. Leading local clerics, some of them senior, had lent their support and "they are surprised at my opposition", says Hicks. On 26 January he was still in fighting mood. At a "capital" meeting of the Prison Gate Mission he was afraid that he had perhaps "harped overmuch on the Drink".

On 30 January 1911, there was "A capital Ch.A 'Conference'" when the founder of the movement, Carlile himself, was "with us". Then Hicks's health gave way, and no more diary anecdotes and asides were confided to the diary until the end of May.

Chapter 10

Return to the Fray

WOMEN'S SUFFRAGE

Women's suffrage was again on the political agenda and it was becoming a cause close to Hicks's heart. The Women's Enfranchisement Bill was debated on 5 May 1911. Mr Goulding MP spoke indignantly about the scandal of the low level of women's wages. The government could get away with reducing them, he claimed, because it was not afraid of the consequences in the ballot box. Women could not express their sense of unfairness through their votes because they had no votes:

> *Is there a single Member who thinks that a Government, except under great financial pressure, would dare to reduce the wages of their male employees by 25 per cent? Yet Lord Haldane and this Government, with an overflowing Exchequer, did not hesitate last year to reduce the wages of the female machinists at Pimlico by this amount on service trousers – namely, from 3d. to 2¼d. per pair.*

The narrative of events in the diaries picks up again, but for a time in less detail, beginning with a meeting of the bishops at Lambeth which Hicks attended for its second day on 24 May.

Most of the main threads of the Bishop's activities had begun before his illness so there are fewer "firsts" in the next diary entries and more opportunities to watch him developing his skills as a bishop. But there is a first hint of war to come. On the evening of 27 May, Hicks moved the first Resolution at a meeting convened by the mayor in support of the Arbitration Treaty which was being negotiated with the USA. The plan was to ensure that there should be arbitration not war if there were disputes between nations, a scheme strongly favoured by Hicks. A form of the treaty was signed in August.

The problem of what to do about difficult and eccentric clergy arose again on 3 June. Hicks wrote to the vicar of Gedney about "His 2 *mad* letters to the Supt of Heswall Nautical School" near Birkenhead. He added in brackets to this entry: "(Mr. G. wrote & promised me June 5 to send a frank apology to the Sup.)"

On 11 June came Edward Hicks's second ordination. His concern for the welfare of the newly ordained is clear. With a restraint he would not have shown perhaps in later diary entries, he commented on an ordination sermon given before he and Agnes had the "*Ordinati* & their friends to tea". "If I might privately record two criticisms" of the preacher (Canon J. G. Simpson), he begins...

The first criticism was that Simpson was "so full of the power & work of the Holy Spirit, & of our need for spiritual fire, that he is over-harsh in his contempt for Anglican primness & convention". This may reveal as much about Hicks, who was rarely extreme or emotional in his expression, as it does about Simpson. Hicks was always most comfortable on the middle ground. It worried him to hear Simpson so comprehensively "depreciate forms & rites & ceremonies" in a sermon preached to the newly ordained. "He is virtually a Jansenist v. Anglican 'Catholics', a Pietist, almost a Quaker ... The revolt may be natural, the remonstrance needed & wholesome: but his language is one-sided."

His second criticism expresses fears that success may be bad for a rousing preacher such as Simpson. He may be "injured – morally & spiritually – by success, & a sense of power, & by studying every thing from a theoretical & rhetorical point of view". Here is Hicks the practical man, uneasy with flourish and too much colour. The *ordinati* shared their tea with "Mr & Mrs Scull" and their fourteen-year-old daughter who were visiting Lincoln from Pennsylvania. Mr Scull had been confirmed by Edward King and he seems to have brought his family to see the Bishop of Lincoln, not realizing that there was a new one.

By 15 June Hicks was back to problem clergy. The next one was an absentee. Absentee clergy holding livings and drawing the income while living somewhere else, and perhaps paying a proportion of the income of the living to a curate to take services, had been a considerable problem in earlier centuries. This was a practice with a number of factors. One was the use of curates to do the job of a parish priest when they had not had a period of induction into the realities of the job, as deacons. Hicks mentioned the history of this problem in the first week of his Charge. On the Thursday he spoke at Louth, about "the character of the clergy". For ordination early in the nineteenth century

> *practically the only necessary document was a man's College testimonial, in addition to his Arts degree. There was hardly any Ordination examination … Beside this, most deacons were sent at once, as soon as they were ordained, to take charge of the parishes of non-resident incumbents.*

Things began to improve from the 1830s, he says, but he wanted his own clergy to think hard about the importance of proper training.

Here was a contemporary example of a partial absentee. The Reverend W. Osborne was vicar of Stainton with Newball but he preferred to live in Lincoln. Edward Hicks had found out only by calling at the vicarage where he "found only care-takers". Osborn said he was "in Stainton most days" and that counted as "residing". That brought the Bishop up short. What could he do about it? "What *is* legal 'residence'? And what am I to do with this incompetent, pious old shuffler?" He does not say exactly, but in a week he had a letter from "old Mr. Osborne *gratefully* accepting my conditions" so he evidently – and typically – found a diplomatic solution.

AN INVITATION TO THE CORONATION

The end of June brought the Coronation of the new king, and one of the perks of being a bishop. Hicks and his family had seats in the Abbey for the coronation of George V on 22 June as one of the leaders of the established church. His diary entry for the day is a characteristic mixture of awe at the dignity of the occasion and the homeliness of the pleasure of getting home for tea at last:

> *Bkfast at 6. Carriage at 7 for the Abbey ... In our places by 9. Service at 11–1.40. Immense, beautiful, orderly concourse: exquisitely arranged & planned ... We did not leave the Abbey before 4: home at 4.30. tired but not overtired, hungry & glad of tea.*

THE END OF THE FIRST YEAR AND THE ANNIVERSARY OF CONSECRATION AS BISHOP

At the end of the first year, on the anniversary of his consecration, Edward Lee Hicks took stock of what he had achieved so far. He admitted to his diary that he was finding it difficult to strike the right balance of attitude and behaviour in dealing with his people. He was not finding it easy to be severe or even dignified:

I have worked hard, & tried to be kind and charitable always
… I must be dignified, without pride or self-consciousness: for
some men need keeping in place: all this is not easy for me.

On the practical side, he thought he was "gradually perceiving the difficulties & problems of the Diocese". "It does not need fresh organizations," he wrote, "but rather fresh zeal & spirit." But there was going be a need for a thorough review of the provision of churches in the diocese. "A good many new churches will be needed, & there will be many to be raised." This was to be another theme of his Charge in 1912, in his analysis of the statistics he had gathered through his Articles of Enquiry.

The illness seems to have left its mark on his confidence about the amount of work he could do and still stay fit. Remarks about being tired began to appear in his diaries sometimes. He could still be cheerful and optimistic, as he was about a county Band of Hope committee meeting on 24 June. The Band of Hope, the children's arm of the temperance movement, was something he wholeheartedly supported. But on 28 June he went to bed after supper at 8:30 p.m. *"very tired!"* and the next day, despite the pleasure of seeing not only Boy Scouts but also *Girl Guides* lining the road when he arrived to preach at a patronal festival, he "felt somehow, very tired, & rather crushed".

His clergy sometimes had problems with their curates too. On 30 June, one of his priests had come to lunch to complain that his curate, whose name was Morton, was "restless & disobedient". He was a returning colonial clergyman. Hicks allowed himself some biting remarks; he "has been lay reader in charge of Kangaroo I. or some such place, in Australia, & has come to England full of himself: he needs reducing to his proper dimensions".

At the other end of the scale were the "deserving poor clergy", struggling to manage on inadequate incomes from their livings. Clergy poverty was to be another of Hicks's themes in his Charge in 1912. At Boston on Tuesday 8 June he spoke about clergy poverty, the smallness of many endowments, the fact that "many of the clergy are in sore pecuniary need". That was bad enough, but it was if anything worse that the selection of a priest for a parish often depended on whether the candidate had private means to supplement the income from the living. On Thursday 20 June Hicks spoke at Spilsby about "Church Finance". The archbishops had proposed a scheme under which the dioceses would become the units of voluntary contribution: "The next step will be to find out how much – roughly speaking – every Deanery and every Parish may fairly be expected to contribute towards the Diocesan Fund. It is this process which alarms the parishes." It "savours of taxation, and not of voluntary giving".

As he made his round of visits to the parishes in 1911, Hicks found many excellent clergy doing a good job. He liked to see a happy family in the vicarage, a supportive vicar's wife. But even the best could be struggling financially. On 2 July, after a visit to Winthorpe, where he saw the "little Church" and met the curate, Hicks "Gave him £1: very poor: clean, nice wife & 6 dear little children. They live in a tumble-down cottage close to the Church. Everything clean, tidy & religious. Deserve help". The value of livings varied greatly in terms of their annual income, as he spelt out in his Charge. He had found by then that there were thirty-seven benefices in the diocese with less than £100 income to pay their vicars, forty-one with less than £150 and fifty-seven with less than £200. A labourer could expect to earn not much less than £100 in a year.

Diary entries such as that for 16 July 1911 show Hicks realizing as he went visiting round the diocese that this question of providing adequate incomes for the clergy was connected with the problems being caused by the growing population and the need for new churches.

*NB A new Church will soon be wanted at Sutton. Send a good,
pious, & rather well-to-do man there, who will draw & keep
the people together, & seize the right moment to build a new
church when the population has grown so as to need it.*

This was to replace the "awful 18th century barn called the Church".

On 2 July 1911, the Bishop "opened" a Church Army mission "on the sands" at Skegness, where he preached. On 31 July 1911, an HM Inspector of Schools had come to see Hicks "about the lack of open spaces in this city, & the need of some general town-planning, to avoid slums in the near future". There was a pervasive view that slums bred bad behaviour, and the lower classes were possessed of a weaker moral fibre by virtue of their lowlier station. That was Hicks's view, too, with the addition of his great conviction that drinking among the working classes made poverty worse. He had long held that the temperance movement was implicitly and at base a movement for general social reform.

Bishops varied in the ways they responded to such calls. Charles Gore liked to be in contact with ordinary working men. He was Midland president of the Workers Educational Association. Hicks's natural way was simply to respond to the problems he met in a pastoral context first as a priest then as a bishop without distinction of class. But most of those he met as a bishop seem to have been of his own new "adopted" class.

BETTER EDUCATION FOR GIRLS: THE LINCOLN HIGH SCHOOL

On 3 July, the Bishop was present at the opening of new buildings for the "girls' High School" by Miss Susan Wordsworth. This was the Lincoln Christ's Hospital Girls' High School. The school, opened in 1893 on the Christ's Hospital foundation, was one of the rash of girls' high schools which had their beginning in the late nineteenth century. This was not the only one to benefit from the charitable intentions of King Edward VI, who had founded Christ's Hospital in the sixteenth century with an endowment now worth a great deal of money. King Edward's schools in Birmingham included a King Edward VI High School for Girls from 1883 and that too had been funded from their ancient royal endowment.

The Lincoln high school enrolled about thirty girls when it opened. It had little equipment and very few books; the question of standards to be set remained open. But although women who went to Oxford, like Christina Hicks, or to Cambridge could not yet gain degrees even if they passed all the same examinations as men, London university was different. There a girl could get a degree. So the girls' high schools had something to aspire to academically. Lucie Savill (1878–1970) had been appointed as headmistress by the governors of the school, in March 1910, so Edward Hicks had had no hand in her appointment. Nevertheless he was going to encounter her in his work as bishop.

CONVOCATION, LONDON AND OXFORD

From the high school it was back to London to stay with the Bishop of London, Arthur Winnington-Ingram, for the meeting of Convocation which ran from 4 to 7 July. Hicks may often have felt an outsider at these meetings but he could join in with gusto when it was time for an academic debate. For 4 July to 7 there is a single diary entry. At Convocation there had been "desultory debates on Burial Service for Suicides", on "poor Law Reform", "and especially Revision of Pbk [Book of Common Prayer]. " Various reports were before the bishops and these were supposed to form the basis of the discussion. Contemporary controversies often engaged the bishops when they met, and the publication of a high-profile book on a key subject could set them twittering with anxiety and urging a clamping down. Hicks was evidently effective when he tried. For instance, he persuaded them to decide not to ban priests who agreed with W. H. Frere, who was sceptical about miracles in the New Testament, because, he says, "this book could only be dealt with by *argument*".

Hicks has quite a bit to say on the liturgical issues raised by the attempt to revise the sixteenth-century Prayer Book. "The Bishops are getting tired of this subject", but he could see its importance. A liturgy embodies a theology. Every word of the Elizabethan text had been weighed in a time of high controversy when the choice of a term could start a new battle, with new cries of "heretic". Hicks got his fellow bishops to take seriously the idea of getting in some "Liturgical experts".

Then it was time for a night in Oxford. Traditions lingered on from centuries earlier. Lincoln College, Oxford, still had the Bishop of Lincoln as its Visitor when Hicks was bishop and we see him doing his Visitorial duties there. On the evening of 7 July he went to the Lincoln College Gaudy. (The "Gaudy" – derived from the Latin *gaudium*, "rejoicing" or celebration – is an annual feast held in each college.)

He mentions that he met various friends and academic acquaintances there – "Harry Lockett there: also Prof Lloyd of Bangor, & Kirsopp Lake of Leiden, & many others". Kirsopp Lake (1872–1946), then coming towards the end of his decade at Leiden University (1904–14), was a New Testament scholar who had discovered his specialist interest while cataloguing Greek manuscripts in the Bodleian Library in Oxford; Hicks mentions later that he has been reading him on the epistles of St Paul.

July showed Hicks in mixed moods, exasperated and tenderly affectionate. Rearranging his library with the "children's help" (he does not say which ones), separating off the books he expected to leave to the diocese, and those which belonged to it anyway; describing the vicar of Mablethorpe as "tall, dreary, ineffective, with ridiculous utterance of the service", reading sometimes much too fast and sometimes much too slowly, with an organ-playing daughter reasonably competent but "too *slow*"; preaching to a Sunday School Teachers' Association at Caistor which had been founded in 1808 and was still going strong, and finding a crowded congregation of children, teachers, and friends.

The "Council of the Lincolnshire Record Society" met in his study on 21 July, followed by a visit from someone called Torrey who only wanted to talk about himself, then a Garden Party given by a Mrs Wright of Brattleby, then back to write a sermon "for dear life … A bit of fish was brought to my side. Thus I finished it off. *Laus Deo* [praise be to God]".

The sermon was for a visit to Oxford. He stayed at Keble College, and preached in the cathedral at Christ Church at 10 a.m. Even here people kept wanting to see him. The young don James Thompson of Magdalen College, who had stayed at the Old Palace in January 1911, came to call, worried about the reception of his book (a contribution to the current Oxford debate with its challenges to orthodoxy) and pleased to hear that Hicks "had strongly deprecated ecclesiastical censures". He was worried that he was going to be "censured" for what he had written and then other young Oxford theologians might be censured too, "& so might come a grave schism". Edward Hicks had another day in Oxford including a visit to Radley where he watched "their grand Four-oar races".

Back in Lincoln midweek he noted a meeting on the Wednesday at which he felt he had been quite successful in a potentially difficult situation: "At 8 a good meeting with the B of H workers of Stamford at Miss Edmund's Ch.A. Mission Room: a difficult gathering: how to unite Ch. & Dissent! Stamford stagnation, & keen political rivalry. It went off *wonderfully well!*"

Then on Saturday he was off again to Eton, where he spent Sunday preaching to the boys (who he thought "really attentive") and talking to the provost. There was some "private chatting" in the evening about recent negative press coverage of the school ("filthy articles") in the "John Bull". He had some rest in the afternoon and read "Miss Soulsby's pleasant essays on 'Books & Reading'".

Ned was at home from school and he is mentioned as accompanying his father on a trip to Somersby "over the wolds" on 6 August. They were driven by Dr Mansel Sympson (a physician, not an academic doctor) in his "motor". Hicks did not keep a car, preferring trains, so he often mentioned in the diary when an early adopter of the car gave him a lift about the diocese. The Somersby trip was for Hicks to preach at a church that had been restored, but there was the additional interest of seeing a copy of a bust of Alfred Tennyson placed there. This seems to have drawn some bigwigs: "The President of Madg. [Magdalen College Oxford] – then everybody else!" Even Lord Tennyson came, the poet's son, who had inherited his father's newly conferred baronial title.

He seems to have struck Hicks as a pompous ass, but Hicks won him round in an unusually detailed account of the exercise of his diplomatic skills. He was most insistent that Hicks had mispronounced the word "knowledge" when he read a quotation from a Tennyson poem in his sermon. "My Father always pronounced it as '*know*-ledge'," he claimed, "& wished it always so to be pronounced in the reading of his poetry". Hicks was able to keep his end up. He had avoided doing that, he said, because "Bernard Shaw had so roasted the parson in 'Candida' for saying the word like that". He made Tennyson laugh and was rewarded with reminiscences of the family home in Harley Street of Arthur Hallam, his father's great friend. They discussed the portrait of Arthur Hallam at Eton, which Tennyson the poet did not think was authentic. This was insider stuff and sophisticated, quite different from the conversational skills Hicks needed for other diocesan occasions. The range a bishop needed was enormous.

The pattern of big and little duties went on. On the August bank holiday, then the first Monday of August, the Hickses gave a garden party for their old friends from Salford. More than sixty came by train, and Agnes gave everyone "a packet of chocolate" before they set off back at 6 p.m. A week later, taking an interest in Record Society work, Hicks went to luncheon with Canon Foster and saw his "workshops" where "3 clever women were busy cleaning, mounting, & binding old Registers & other precious documents. His discovery, & use of *chiffon* for mounting". Professional record agents could be hired to do the slow, patient work of transcribing and checking.

A QUESTION OF JURISDICTION

An interesting ecclesiological problem presented itself on 18 August. This is a reminder of the expectation that a bishop would have a comprehensive command of a good deal of technical and legal knowledge. He had his chancellor to turn to, but nothing like the number of diocesan staff a bishop will normally have now. When summoned to the Archdeacon's Visitation, the vicar, whose name was Galton, "came, but under protest". He said the archdeacon had no jurisdiction over him. "He affirmed that Edenham Ch: was before the Reformation the private Ch: of a Religious House." He argued that that meant that the present church was a private chapel of the Earl of Ancaster and its priest essentially his chaplain. "The Archdeacon wants me to enquire into the matter" writes the still very new bishop. His analysis, recorded in the diary entry and "pointed out" in response to the archdeacon, evidently without a formal enquiry, made three points. First, "many other parish churches" had once been the churches or chapels of monasteries suppressed at the dissolution of the monasteries, and passing into the hands of private owners in the sixteenth century. If Galton was right, many questions would arise about the ownership as well as the control of the buildings and plate of the church. In any case, Mr Galton had been licensed as vicar. That meant he had accepted the right of the bishop to license him to a cure of souls in the diocese in the ordinary way. That would have been the time to raise this question, not now.

A RAILWAY STRIKE

Meanwhile, there was a general strike to contend with, which included a "great Railway strike", made official on 18 August. Hicks found he could not go to Grantham by train for a confirmation as he had intended so he "ordered a motor-car". Ned and Christina were in Salford with Mary and her family, and could not get home, though they managed to get as far as Grantham, where their father collected them and brought them back with him. He was able to confirm all the candidates, except one who was defeated by the strike. The family was always close and however busy he was, Edward Hicks saw as much as he could of his children and grandchildren. In late September he went to Manchester to see Mary and her husband and have tea with the Knoxes.

"WOMEN AT WORK" AND THE TRAINING OF TEACHERS

October brought days involving two areas of importance, and we can begin to see a new pattern of emerging "big" concerns with areas of special significance for Hicks as he got into his stride with the small things which filled so many of his days as bishop. One (2 October) was the question of "Women's Work" in Grimsby, discussed in a conference with all the Grimsby clergy: "No women at work, except a Church A. sister. It was *left to me* to see what I could do!"

The other (10 October) was a meeting about the future of the training college for teachers. The Lincoln Teacher Training College, established in 1862 as the "Diocesan Training School for Mistresses", was one of a majority of such colleges established by the mid-nineteenth century which were run by or under the auspices of the Church of England.

In 1846 a pupil-teacher scheme was introduced which allowed girls to rise from the status of senior schoolgirl to that of teacher. The heroine of Charlotte Brontë's novel *Jane Eyre*, published in October 1847, progresses from pupil to teacher in much that way, though for formal government recognition, pupil-teachers had to spend five years "apprenticed" to the head teacher from the age of thirteen plus; they were paid, the boys – who received about £10 a year – more than the girls; then (until 1863) they had to sit the Queen's Scholarship Examination. That qualified the would-be teacher, often a boy or girl from a relatively humble background aspiring to "social mobility", for a place in a teacher training college, and a maintenance grant. Those who did not take the examination could teach as "uncertificated" teachers.

These arrangements had to be updated when the Elementary Education Act of 1870 made it necessary to recruit more teachers in a hurry. Teacher training colleges were allowed to send out students as qualified teachers after a year's training. The standard required to pass the certificate examination was lowered. Teachers already working in schools could be recommended for certificates even if they did not take any examination. Within ten years the number of teachers with certificates nearly trebled. By the end of the century, universities were setting up colleges for teacher training, with no more than two hundred students. The 1902 Education Act set up a more coherent system of supervision, with Local Education Authorities.

Secondary school teachers were likely to be expected to have a degree and to be of a similar social class to their pupils. But the standards expected in training colleges, especially for girls, had to be raised. The establishment of a new superior sort of training college for young women was one of the achievements of Miss Beale and Miss Buss. Miss Beale (1831–1906) became headmistress of Cheltenham Ladies' College and remained there all her life. In 1885 she founded a training college for women in Cheltenham, St Hilda's, and in 1893, St Hilda's Hall in Oxford, which became St Hilda's College. Miss Buss (1827–94) entered women's education through a venture founded by her mother as a private school. In the late 1840s she went to the newly available lectures at Queen's College in London. There she found the young Dorothea Beale and intellectual stimulation. F. D. Maurice and Charles Kingsley were among those offering teaching, and Miss Buss was able to get certificates in geography and French and German. Then in 1850 she was able to move her mother's school to bigger premises and relaunch it as the North London Collegiate School. It had expanded by 1865 to about two hundred and fifty girls. In 1870 she founded a new school, the Camden School for Girls. The Cambridge Training College (1885) was another foundation in which she had a decisive hand. Both Miss Beale and Miss Buss became keen suffragettes, too.

By Edward Hicks's time as bishop, quite a battle was going to be needed to raise standards at the Lincoln training college. A meeting was held to decide what to do when Canon Rowe, the principal, retired at the end of the following summer term. "At last", says Hicks, it was decided to advertise the post openly. The Reverend E. G. Wainwright might have done but "unfortunately he has no University honours". In his Charge, Hicks was to confine himself to addressing the clergy on education only within a limited compass. At Scunthorpe on 27 June he spoke on "Day and Sunday Schools". For the Sunday schools he wanted to see less well-meant amateurism and fewer instances of priests taking the schools themselves. He encouraged training for the

Sunday school teachers, especially now that children were getting professional education on weekdays. He thought priests should teach in the day schools in their parishes.

Also in October 1911, Hicks "saw Disney & his Churchwardens. I spoke of the dissolute state of Skegness in the season". Skegness was a pleasant place to go for a few days' rest, the Hickses found, but there had been good reason to make it the scene of a mission on the sands earlier that year.

THE CHRISTIAN SOCIAL UNION

November saw a local conference of the Christian Social Union. On 28 October 1911, Hicks did his duty of presiding for the CSU at its meeting where the Medical Officer of Health gave a paper on the "Lincoln Housing Problem" and Hicks spoke too.

On 26 November the diary records that Henry Scott Holland came to stay. On this visit, Scott Holland preached in the nave "all about the underdog, & how H.S. always takes his 'side' and assumes that the upperdog is in the wrong". Hicks comments that it was "an audacious, & awakening, sermon which gave dire offence to Alexandra Melville, who never (I think) came again to the Sunday evg services".

Then the CSU held its conference in the Chapter House: "On Labour Colonies. Very discursive, very dull & rather ineffective." Scott Holland was still there on 28 November, when there was a "splendid meeting in the Drill Hall" and Scott Holland "spoke admirably".

The Bishop quite frequently saw cases of clerical idleness and incompetence and various kinds of misbehaviour, sometimes general, sometimes particular. He was learning how difficult these cases were to deal with. On 15 November 1911, he notes that "the Revd John Rees of Helpringham is a dreadful rotter! What is to be done with him?"

At the beginning of December, Hicks was commenting that he had had "a very busy time ever since September, but unusually so during the last fortnight or three weeks". "I am surprised at my success in achieving it," he admits. He also owns to the effect of family stress, concerns about her aunt Selina, aged eighty-seven, and "dear Edmond's awful illness", which seems to have been keeping Agnes away among her own family. She wired on 11 December with the news that he had died at 4 a.m. that morning. She was evidently now reconciled with her family after the apparent estrangement at the time of her marriage. There is a touching note on 8 April 1915, on a visit to Bath, that Hicks and Agnes walked "up to Coombe Downe" where they visited the graves of her father and stepmother and her sister Christine and her brother Basil and his wife.

PLANNING HIS FIRST VISITATION

A bishop's duty to supervise his diocese required him to conduct "Visitations". That meant sending out Articles of Enquiry, which Hicks noted he had done, in the diary for 15 December. The Visitation and his Charge to the clergy of the diocese was "fixed for June 1912", and it was going to be one of the most important things in that year. In the Charge as he eventually published it, he says he tried "to simplify and shorten the questions, so as to save the clergy trouble, and yet promote efficiency":

> *I have so long been a parish priest myself, that I know how irritating it is for a busy incumbent ... to be called to fill up enquiries and returns.*

The next day he had to make sense of the system of lay readers as it existed in the diocese. He held a luncheon to find out more. The provision of lay readers had been revived in 1866, in a period when there were not enough clergy to meet the needs of the Church of Engand faithful, especially in the industrial cities, which had seen a huge growth in population. Lay readers tended to exercise a "bridge" ministry between the social classes. They were unlikely to have had a "gentleman's" education, but it was considered an advantage that they could speak to the working classes in their own language and on their own terms. They might be able to get access to meeting rooms unconnected with the local church buildings, and they could do the sort of thing Hicks was so keen on by way of reaching out among people who did not usually go to church.

Lay readers were not ordained and could not by tradition officiate at Holy Communion. The difficulty was to fix the scope of the activities permitted to them. They could preach, with some restrictions, and teach in Sunday schools and Bible classes. The question of allowing lay readers to preach in the church itself was addressed in the late nineteenth century by making a formal end to the liturgical sequence before the reader stood at a lectern to preach. He was not allowed to use the pulpit. Permitting him to preach lay with the vicar. Evensong was favoured for these experiments. In the Charge the following year, Hicks spoke about lay readers and the special requirements for their approval, on Wednesday 19 June, at Horncastle. Archdeacon Bond, Hicks reminded his listeners, had been enthusiastic about fostering proper training for the diocese's lay readers and ensuring that they were admitted by the bishop for service in the diocese (and only in that diocese).

The year ended with a visit from Mary and John and some visits by the Bishop to "a number of the older residents in Minster Yard, to wish them a happy New Year".

Chapter 11

Settling into Harness:
The Pre-war Years

We have been following Edward Hicks almost day by day at the level of his own tentative discovery of what the job of being a bishop entailed, while he made up his mind how to tackle it and what sort of manner to adopt. Now he began to be more confident and to see that he could make a difference where there were big problems close to his own heart. The bigger picture was going to be tackled in his Charge.

This was going to take a lot of energy and his health was still worrying. On 15 January 1912, he was not well, "oddly giddy, with violent biliousness" but he pressed on with engagements including speaking at a temperance meeting. He felt "very poorly" afterwards and confessed to being *very tired*. And he would have to be careful not to allow campaigning and public support to get in the way of the routine care of his diocese. On 31 January he conducted a "Quiet Day" for the Lincoln clergy. On 1 February he went to London for a meeting of bishops, which he found "very dull" for two days.

TRADE UNIONS FOR WOMEN

Trade unions were now being formed among working women. A letter to *The Spectator*, published on 27 January 1912, set out some of the objectives of the National Union of Women Workers:

> *all who are concerned with the welfare of women … realize that it is of the utmost importance that women … shall be induced to join good approved societies. With this object in view the N.U.W.W. is forming a committee – (a) To collect information about the existing provision for women in friendly societies and trade unions, and (b) The terms upon which men's societies propose to admit women under the Act.*

Agnes and Christina may have strengthened Hicks's resolve to do what he could for this movement. Like other late Victorian supporters of social reform, he favoured the work of trade unions.

His own intellectual interests always remained lively. He often notes something he had been reading, and on 2 March 1912, he bought a set of Goethe's *Werke* from E. A. W. Peacock, one of his priests. But the chief event of March was the next stage in the long story of getting a new head for the teachers' training college, with its ultimate result of causing years of trouble. On 30 March, the training college committee met again. The Board of Education wanted a woman principal. It was agreed to get Rowe to stay on till Christmas "that we may have time to make arrangements accordingly".

CHRISTINA'S MARRIAGE AND BEDE'S LONG VISIT

By far the most important family event of 1912 was Christina's marriage to Edmund Knox, one of the sons of the Bishop of Manchester. Christina had not made dramatic or pioneering use of the freedom of choice her parents had given her. The two Knott daughters with an Oxford education, whom we met earlier, had both married, becoming Mrs Westacott and Mrs Scriven. Christina remained unmarried for some years after she graduated. As we have seen, she seems to have lived at home and helped her father and he quite often mentions that she has accompanied him on a visit in the diocese. She was already in her mid-twenties when she married Edmund Knox. Their children were to be Rawle, baptized by his grandfather in August 1913, and Penelope, born in December 1916.

The diary briefly notes in April that there had been "correspondence" with the young man and the next day "dear C. F. [was] in much anxiety". By July 1912 the banns were being read, and in August Christina spent part of her holiday with her own family and part with the Knoxes. When, soon after the marriage, her husband went to war, she was able to continue her work about the diocese while he was away fighting in France.

We hear very little of Agnes's feelings in the diaries (possibly because she had the opportunity to edit them before they were released for others to read). In them, she is often "AMH", sometimes "Agnes". She was brought up in an earlier generation, with its more restricting expectations, and there is no evidence that she was anything but happy being a vicar's and then a bishop's wife, and supporting her husband's causes, often by accompanying him, while enjoying her children and her interests.

Hicks's diary mentions a visit from Bede on 29 April 1912. This was a special event for the family because he worked so far away and could rarely come home. Matthew Bede, known to the family as Bede, was the eldest of the surviving sons. He was apparently not drawn to the church and ordination; he had a career in Burma working for a shipping line.

He had left his ship at Marseilles two days earlier and travelled north to Lincoln, to arrive well but tired and with "a boil on his elbow". He was still at home in June, when Hicks mentions a jolly party where "Bede entertained us" with dancing and "recitations". He dined with his father on 8 October before Hicks set off to preside over a large successful meeting on the White Slave Traffic Bill, so he seems to have had a long stretch at home before going back East.

Bede is largely absent from the wartime diaries. Perhaps he was too far away fighting in Mesopotamia for news to arrive very often. But he and his parents remained close. Hicks was concerned that Bede should be able to return to his former work and position when the war was over, and he noted on 22 May 1917 a lucky encounter with Sir Frank Forbes Adam (1846–1926), banker and man of influence in British India. "He was really nice," commented Hicks, and gave assurances that "if all is well & they have room", Bede could expect to be taken back after the war.

Hicks pressed this matter further on 13 June, using his contacts, when Charles Roberts took him to interview Lord Islington at the India Office. Roberts had been undersecretary for India and Lord Islington was his successor:

*I told him about Bede, his character, attainments, career –
how he would like a civil post, of administration, somewhere
in the Mesopotamian Region – if it comes under British
administration (as is likely). He offered to place Bede's name in
the hands of Sir Percy Sykes, who seems to be at present the civil
administrator of those parts.*

Bede is listed as receiving a CBE in a supplement to *The London Gazette* for 1946 as a British subject resident in Persia, so it seems his father's intercession was successful. His mother wrote at the end of his father's life in terms which suggest that she looked on him as the head of the family now, and expected to be able to rely on his support and help with the aftermath of the death of his father.

PEACE CAMPAIGNING AND VOTES FOR WOMEN

The Second Reading of the Parliamentary Franchise (Women) Bill was debated on 28 March 1912. Sir Alfred Mond rose to second the Bill by linking the question of women's suffrage to the wider debate about the consequences to society of allowing them to be educated like men:

> *The opposition to Woman Suffrage is based on two lines. The first is the effect which granting the Suffrage would have upon women, and the second is the effect it would have upon the State. I may say that most of the arguments on the first head, namely, the effect on women of granting them the Parliamentary vote, which forms a considerable part as anti-Suffragist speeches, is but a revival of the argument against the intellectual development of women as a sex which we have heard at every stage of that development. If you look back and read the speeches about the larger education of women, their admission to the universities, and the learned professions, you will meet with arguments about the hearth and home, and with arguments about the neglect of the husband, such as are put forward today, and those opposing the Parliamentary Franchise for women are doing so, largely in the idea that they can possibly stop the natural development of women, which has proceeded, is proceeding, and will continue to proceed whether you give them the vote or not.*

He took the opportunity to stress that women were now doing men's work and the scale on which they were doing it:

> *The fact that we have in this country over 5,000,000 of women engaged in earning their own living, over 2,000,000 engaged in industrial pursuits, surely is sufficient argument to those who still talk of setting up woman as a sort of china doll on a sacred*

*hearth to be worshipped from afar, a caricature of a creature
that in any time of human life has never existed and will never
exist. The woman is to take no interest in her country or in the
fate of her country, and in the economic conditions of the people
among whom she lives, but she is to be confined to the home and
to the wash-tub, to the cooking and the baby's cradle.*

In this climate of heightened activism, Edward Hicks agreed to
be president of the Church League for Women's Suffrage. Maude
Royden, prominent activist in many women's causes, commented,
"I doubt if there was another bishop on the bench who would have
done so". The League was not extreme. It planned to work through
prayer and education rather than holding demonstrations. Maude
Royden had a reputation as an excellent speaker. Mrs Giles and
her husband hosted a meeting of the Church League for Women's
Suffrage in their garden in mid-July 1912, when "Miss Royden
spoke *beautifully.*"

Hicks approved of the movement to win votes for women,
partly because of his evident fundamental and lifelong personal
belief in the equality of the sexes, but he also, pragmatically,
thought women might lend their voices to the temperance
movement and encourage restraint in drinking if they got the
franchise. Maude Royden said as much:

*I think Dr. Hicks hoped for an accession of strength to other causes
that he loved – the Temperance Cause above all, no doubt – from
the coming of women into politics. He realized, almost more than
any man I know, the bitterness of waste which we Suffragists felt
so keenly in agitating to be allowed to work not actually doing it.*

He was not the only sympathizer to think so. The view that women
were more likely to vote for temperance was expressed in a CSU
leaflet (No. 41).

On 14 May 1912, Hicks preached a sermon "on peace" at St Martin-in-the-Fields.

THE CHARGE TO THE CLERGY, 1912

In June came the Visitation of the diocese Hicks had been planning since the previous year. It was bound to distract him from routine business. On 14 June, John Wakeford, who had been vicar of St Margaret's, Anfield, Liverpool was installed as Precentor, canon in charge of the cathedral's music and worship, but the Bishop was busy speaking at Gainsborough on "Church and State", and got there only for the tea party afterwards. Hundreds had come from Liverpool to be present, he notes.

The Visitation and Charge was a process with a long history. It had begun before the Reformation as a method of ensuring that the religious "business" of a diocese was kept in order. A series of questions would be asked in each parish, covering such practical matters as the state of the church buildings, the names and number of clergy serving there, the baptismal roll, and church attendance. Many of these questions had to do with property or legal matters, and in the Middle Ages a notary would often do this work. Canon law in the Church of England required an archdeacon or the bishop to visit every three years, and once the Visitation had established what might be needed or desirable, a Charge to the Clergy could be drafted.

Edward Hicks characteristically took on the work himself. The process presumably took most of his available energies for stocktaking, because on 24 June 1912, the second anniversary of his consecration as bishop – three days before the Visitation ended on the 27th – he wrote only "God forgive my many neglects & overrule my follies & mistakes, & purify my character."

In his Charge, Edward Hicks took a large view and a long view of the state of the nation and the contribution his clergy might make to improving it. He asked them to consider: "What changes are to be made in the social order, now that Feudal England is gone for ever, and we find ourselves become a great and growing Industrial Democracy?"

Many radical thinkers of the late nineteenth century held that the industrialization of English society had led to oppression of the factory workers and the degradation of the working classes. They campaigned for something to be done about it, and Hicks had found himself among them, though not the noisiest and most outspoken and not a leader of such campaigns, but a steady, concerned, committed presence nonetheless.

"How are we to prevent the domination of the plutocrat, and the corrupting influence of the millionaire?" and "How to rechristianize the economic and social order?" Here Hicks was encouraging his clergy to think about some of the questions we still hear today (in different language) about the risks to ordinary people of allowing the rich and powerful, and especially the commercial interest and business lobbyists, to influence government policy.

That day's Charge address on 14 June had been the most newsworthy of them all. This was a topic which was going to draw reporters from the press, and he may well have felt it to be important to put that before the installation of the archdeacon. He had noted in his diary for the day before, 13 June, that "Reporters came at 6 to take down my Charge on Disestablishment etc!" The disestablishment of the church in Wales was afoot and causing much discussion nationally. "I have Welsh blood in my veins," confessed Hicks. He thought the Welsh Church should be disestablished and freed from the jurisdiction of Parliament and English law. In his Charge he revealed a dislike of the establishment of the Church of England, as something "of far greater advantage to the State than to the Church".

As we have seen, he called his Charge *Building in Troublous Times*. It was published (by Longmans) in 1912. This was not in itself noteworthy. Bishops' Charges were quite commonly published in a similar way, and it ensured that anyone who had not heard all his addresses on the different topics, as he delivered them one by one round the diocese, could fill in the gaps. First, gathering the statistics from his Articles of Enquiry, Hicks counted heads. More than ten thousand a year were being baptized but less than half that number were confirmed. The preparation of young people to make them ready for confirmation was, he felt, important. It needed modernizing. "I was myself prepared in the 'fifties by a really good head-master" – at Magdalen College School – "one of the High Church Oxford men; but his instructions were of a very dry kind, though the character of the man deeply influenced me."

The population of the county was steadily growing, chiefly in the "centres of industry", and there was therefore the further question whether the churches and Sunday schools and "parochial organizations" had "kept pace" with the growing need. New parishes were being formed and new churches built, but would they be enough? Hicks had appointed a commission to "consider the present anomalous boundaries of the parishes".

He gave much thought to the character and the role of the clergy. On the Thursday of the first week of his Charge in June 1912, he spoke at Louth, about "the character of the clergy". There had been periods of great laxity in the past, he explained, and he outlined them. He spoke encouragingly of recent improvements, though his diary bespeaks a number of worries. On Monday 17 June, at Spalding, he spoke about the duties of the clergy in terms which reflect not only his own lifelong experience but what he had been learning in the past two years. He said he thought the Eucharist was "a more intelligible and far more moving service than Mattins" and that with a few words by way of an address it could be the best form of service for a Sunday. But variety was good. He encouraged his priests to be "good and habitual visitors … Few clerical duties are so fruitful if properly done, both to parson and to people, as diligent visiting". In a large diocese, a sick priest might find it difficult to secure a *locum tenens* (a temporary deputy), so Hicks proposes to try to provide "a staff of priests ready for such emergencies". He wanted to see the clergy as "custodians" of their churches, "some of the loveliest and most interesting churches in the land". He approved of work "for the intellectual and social advancement of our people", using parish hall, reading room, library, club, whatever the parish had available: "I have known of lectures being arranged for winter evenings." Music was good too.

At Grimsby on 25 June, a Tuesday, he turned to "Temperance and Purity", the moral welfare of his flock, and devoted much of his address to the drink problem, though he included gambling. The Charge given at Brigg on 26 June was on "Home and Foreign Missions". Here again Hicks took a grand view, suggesting that "foreign" missions were now less remote, in a shrinking world where travel was making overseas cultures better known and more familiar. That meant there was no real gulf between mission abroad and mission at home. Energetic prayer for missions at home as well as far away was Hicks's recommendation. "Home Missions" should include "the training and sending out of men capable of fighting in the front of Christ's army" against the "evils of drink, of lust, of gambling".

WORKING WITH ARCHDEACONS

George Jeudwine (1849–1933), a friend of Hicks from Oxford, who had been secretary of the Diocesan Conference, had himself briefly been Archdeacon of Stow in succession to the admirable John Bond, who got a special mention in the Charge:

Was there ever a simpler life than his, richer in good works, or in humility and tenderness of heart? ... No one will ever know how much the better organisation of the Diocese, in all sorts of ways, owes to his mild wisdom.

Then in 1913 Jeudwine became Archdeacon of Lincoln. Jeudwine's successor as Archdeacon of Stow was the John Wakeford whose installation as Precentor Hicks had to miss on 14 June 1912, and who held the office until 1921. Wakeford was a high churchman who had caused eruptions in Liverpool by changing arrangements for services. He was to cause more trouble, culminating after Hicks's time, in his trial for alleged adultery. Hicks wrote in the diary in July 1913 about the arrangements for the two forthcoming archidiaconal installations.

An archdeacon was a powerful figure and it is easy to see how an archdeacon could become "arrogant". In the archdeaconry he had his own jurisdiction and was not acting as the bishop's delegate. He had to ensure compliance by his parishes with the law of the land and the law of the church, and personally inspect the churches and churchyards. (This is a task Hicks seems to have taken on himself, but informally and in order to get to know his diocese.) He had to hold Visitations each year. He had a right to a say in any plans for making pastoral changes in the diocese. He should protect any object of historical or archaeological or artistic value if he believed it to be at risk.

The Hickses took a holiday in August, beginning on the 6th at Caistor, with Christina. But she left on the 20th to join the Knoxes' holiday party in Worcestershire.

THE FORMIDABLE MISS TODHUNTER

After pressure had been brought to bear to appoint a woman as head of the Lincoln training college, Miss Winifred Todhunter

(1877–1961) was appointed to tackle the task. On 12 September 1912, Hicks reports that the "Lady Principal has come ... Highly approved of her", he says, not yet aware how much difficulty she was going to cause him. She had been educated at Cheltenham Ladies' College and the London Day Training College and gained a University of London degree in 1904. She lectured at the training college in Stockwell until she was appointed to replace Canon Rowe as the first female principal of the college at Lincoln. It is hard to tell from the diaries whether the trouble that followed was her fault or whether the existing staff simply resisted change, but she was going to cause Edward Hicks a good many difficulties and require the exercise of his utmost diplomacy.

TEMPERANCE CAMPAIGNING

A meeting of a National Convention, to demand the temperance laws which it had been promised would be enacted in the session of 1913, was held at Central Hall, Westminster on 13 November 1912. More than four hundred towns and counties and districts sent representatives. Leif Jones MP said that, on the basis of their resolution, he was "entitled to speak for constituents numbering not less than" 5 million people. Hicks was there and spoke. He noted in his diary:

> *Leif Jones in chair: but an interview with PM swept out of possibility by the row in the House. NB This is an attempt of the Classes to reassert the insolent contempt of democracy which was exhibited in the rejection ... of the Licensing Bill of 1908. It can only end in one way; by the defeat of the Classes. But it may cost a severe, & perhaps a long & strong, struggle.*

"I have much hope ..."

On 7 December 1912, well before the war began and took clergy out of the diocese, a conference of lay readers was held at the Old Palace in Lincoln. We already know that Hicks was a strong supporter of their work in the diocese. He was optimistic: "Much real discussion, & great good resolved to be attempted. I have much hope". He became increasingly aware that in parts of the diocese with scattered populations the clergy needed lay readers to help them. "[Mason] took me in his motor to see the outlying hamlets belonging to the Parish – Dyke, Cawthorpe, Twenty. It is clear that *one good Curate at least & half a dozen lay readers are needed for such a Parish.*"

On 18 December, Hicks briefly noted that it was his sixty-ninth birthday, a day on which he "motored to Horncastle to give the prizes" at the grammar school. "*Coeducation*". A clergy retreat was in process. He says they read Marson's *Life* of St Hugh at the meals: "It is clever, & readable; but has two faults. He relies too much upon secondary authorities outside the Vita Magna, & he is too 'slangy' & jocular".

There was a hint of things to come on 22 December when the choral Matins at the cathedral had "men from Barracks" there. He said they tried to behave but that "*none* knelt". They were completely unfamiliar with the liturgy or the hymns and could not really join in. Here was a body of ordinary young men who lived outside the reach of the church as a rule.

Chapter 12

The Last Year of Peace and the Run-up to War

Good relations with the city dignitaries were still being carefully fostered. Hicks began 1913 by entertaining the mayor and corporation to dinner on 2 January. The dean, who had said some unfortunate things, "very cleverly avoided dangerous points, & very largely restored himself to the good opinion of the Corporation. This dinner does no end of good. All the Chapter present – save the Archdeacon of Stow."

On 6 January Hicks was at the theological college at Kelham, where, he said, "everything is very plain: gritty: noisy: not very comfortable". Kelham was a house and theological college of the Society of the Sacred Mission, an Anglican mission order founded in 1893, which started work in South Africa less than ten years later. One of its central ideas was to welcome men who were not notable socially or intellectually or even spiritually, but men with a vocation, who could become workhorses in the mission field. It also allowed its members to choose the degree of their commitment.

The building – which was to be taken over for military purposes when war began – was an extreme example of Victorian Gothic design, by Gilbert Scott. He seems to have been so pleased with it that he reused some of the design elements on the façade of the Midland Hotel at St Pancras station in London soon afterwards. The Manners-Sutton family, who had owned Kelham, had sold it to the Society of the Sacred Mission in 1903 because they were short of money. Hicks seems to have found the trip worthwhile. He says he met "a large number of Principals & Vice-P's of Theological Colleges – all three kinds: Missionary, Graduate, non graduate colleges".

On 13 January the Hickses set off for one of their winter holidays, this time to Grasmere in the Lake District, in the snow. But they were soon back, and on 23 January Hicks went to London and made time to drop into the House of Commons. There he saw Leif Jones MP, an old ally in temperance matters who was just as eager to support the cause of votes for women. He "discussed with him the Franchise Bill, & W. Suffrage".

While he was there he noticed "the Women's Deputation leaving their interview with Lloyd George & other Ministers". Outside were:

> many women "picketing" the House of C. Scores of Ladies with sandwich boards, with mottoes.

The tone of the campaign was still perceived to be "ladylike" and diplomatic, at least as it was presented on those sandwich boards. Hicks gives an example of the wording:

> Labour men, we confide in your courtesy, & we thank you etc.

One of Hicks's favourite topics, the link between excessive alcohol consumption and social deprivation, was the subject of a meeting of the Christian Social Union on 25 January 1913, when he gave the address himself on "Drink, unemployment & Low Wages". Regular raising of the concern always seemed to him worthwhile.

THE BISHOP'S CHAPLAIN LEAVES

Like all the Anglican bishops, Edward Hicks had a personal chaplain, part of whose job it was to work with the bishop's secretary, planning the business of the day. The chaplain also travelled with the bishop, said Matins with him each morning, or Evensong, so it was bound to become a close relationship. The routine duties of a bishop's chaplain were demanding and it was not normally a post in which a young clergyman stayed for very long. At first Hicks's chaplain was the Reverend W. Rowland Rhys. But after a couple of years, he had had enough.

Hicks was fond of him and records on 6 February 1913 that he was "anxious" about him. He "is very gloomy, & is in doubt what to do". He was to leave on 22 February "of his own desire" and claiming that his health would simply no longer "stand the keen NE winds of Lincolnshire". Efforts to find him a living had failed. He would not accept one in the diocese and he had refused one from Southwark. Winchester had sought his services as a diocesan "missioner" but he said it did not "suit him". On 20 February there is a bleak note, "*Dear WR Rhys left me.*"

ENGAGING WITH METHODISM IN THE DIOCESE

On 15 February 1913, Hicks opened the "Wesleyan Missionary Exhibition" and on 22 February had lunch with "a Mr. Walker" who edited the Missionary Magazine and was involved in the exhibition. Lincolnshire was John Wesley's home territory; he was born twenty miles from the city of Lincoln. Methodism remained strong in the diocese and the new bishop was still developing his approach to Nonconformists in general and particularly the Methodists. His method of preaching outside churches in the "field", which he had adopted since the Fenny Compton days, was much what John Wesley and his followers had adopted in the eighteenth century, but it had to be tempered to Church of England needs.

The Reverend C. E. Bolam, vicar of St Mary Magdalene, came to see his bishop on 25 February 1913 because the dean was angry with him. Hicks says he wrote the dean "a letter of conciliation". It was not the first time he had had this sort of visit from Bolam. In November 1912, Bolam had come to tea and "to groan" about the relations of St Mary Magdalene's to the cathedral. It was a difficult situation. The original fabric of this ancient church, dating from Saxon times and probably the first parish church of Lincoln, had been buried beneath the medieval cathedral. At the end of the thirteenth century the parishioners were given a new site close by to build a church but they retained the entitlement to hold their own services in the cathedral in the chapel dedicated to St Mary Magdalene, "processing in" as of right. This leftover historical curiosity was exactly the sort of thing to prompt disputes. Bolam remained vicar from 1907 until 1926, when he seems to have lost his sight. The situation became something of a bee in Bolam's bonnet, but despite his persistent troublemaking on this matter, Hicks and he seem to have been fond of one another.

THE CHANCELLOR AND THE RISK OF SIMONY

At the end of 1912 the last entry in the diary for 31 December is a worried note about the resignation of Beesby from his living. The worry was about the possibility that there might be going to be an unlawful buying and selling of a living ("simony", so-called after Simon Magus's attempt to buy a place among the apostles in Acts 8:9–24). "Worrall the Vicar is selling the Living, & we happen to know that all is quite Simoniacal." Jourdain, the registrar, was to draft a letter. On 8 January 1913 is a note: "With Jourdain, to arrange another letter to Mr. Worrall about

Beesby. He wants to resign, & then sell to the Father of the man who is to be presented. It comes within the Act." The Act Hicks presumably meant to refer to was the Benefices Act 1898. That sets out a number of restrictions on selling the right of patronage to a benefice but he seems to have feared that this proposed device might fall within the law.

This was not the only instance where Hicks was concerned about potential simony in the diocese. On 26 February 1913 he was considering whether to do as the dean and Mr Bell of Bourne were asking, and bring an action against Thomas Cowpe Lawson in the Consistory Court. Lawson seems to have been a sound clergyman, low church, but liked by his parishioners, except some of the high church ones, of whom Mr Bell seems to have been a determined representative.

We have seen throughout this story how the aftermath of Tractarianism had been the division of the Church of England into well-marked "parties", high and low church, leaving moderates such as Edward Hicks in difficulties because he was exposed to accusations from each side that he favoured the other. It began to be difficult for ordained adherents of the Tractarian movement to get livings to serve in parishes, so some of them took to ministering in the slums of industrial towns and those of London. Trusts were set up to purchase advowsons (the right of presenting to a living), with the intention of ensuring that the "right" clergy, belonging to the approved category, were presented to them. One of these in Lincolnshire, Donington, had been purchased by a trust, for the purpose of ensuring that the priest who was given it would be an evangelical.

The Church Association also established a trust to buy advowsons; this was the body that had got Edward King prosecuted for ritualism while he was bishop. Both factions had been trying to buy the right to present to Bourne. Hicks comments that "It seems to be probable that the Ch. Assocn purchased the living of Bourne when it was vacant, that is, after the death of the previous incumbent" whose name was Manefied. To buy the presentation to a vacant living in order to give it to a preferred candidate would be simony; that would invalidate the presentation, and

> *If so, & if we can prove it, the Living is vacant, & Lawson is not Vicar & never has been. They want me to bring an action against L. in the Consistory Court. I must consult Jourdain, & my Chancellor.*

Hicks was not allowed to concentrate on this problem uninterruptedly for long. One of the concerns he had spoken about in the Charge was demanding his attention. On the same day, 26 February, he had already had an on-site meeting about the future of Bracebridge Church, where a growing population was going to make it necessary to rethink parish boundaries, perhaps build new churches, with all the consequential problem of the best way to "arrange" incumbents "between each other so as to undertake the visiting, teaching, confirming etc etc of the growing population". "At that corner," he said, having looked along the lane, "there should be a Church of some sort, & a *good man planted* at once."

On 22 April he and Jourdain interviewed Lawson.

> *I feel convinced that he is innocent of any malpractice, & knew nothing of any simony – if there was any. He is anxious to incur no danger to his good name … If he is ever in any danger of being ejected, he would wish to resign in time.*

In fact things looked black for him. Talbot, the chancellor, having been shown the evidence that "transactions, apparently simoniacal, had preceded the appointment of Lawson to Bourne", had advised that the case should be laid before the Crown. That might lead to the appointment of Lawson being declared void. The patron of the living in 1910 had been Hugh Lely, who was known to be willing to sell it, which at that time was lawful.

The case was heard by the then Lord Chancellor, Lord Haldane, and a compromise negotiated. Mr Lawson was to be given the living of Castle Bytham, which would be vacated for the purposes by its incumbent Mr Smith, who would be presented to Bourne by the Crown. This exchange of livings was successfully made in 1913. The diaries indicate that Lawson stayed in his new position without further controversy and the position about the advowson was eventually tidied up.

VICARS' WIVES: SOME EXPECTATIONS

The diary for 31 December 1913 has a telling note on the help-meet role of a vicar's wife. Hicks understood what might be expected in the Church of England, but perhaps not from the wives of dissenting ministers:

> *A letter from MacKennal saying he must leave. I feel sure that his wife is at the bottom of it. She has been brought up in dissent, & does not understand the status & opportunities of a clergyman's wife. & esp. a Curate's.*

One of Edward Hicks's earliest problem-clergy, noted on 24 November 1910, had been North-Cox, who "having broken down, resigns". So he had to be replaced. But the living's "Income [was] only £303 gross, & pretty certain to be nearly halved in 1918 when the corn rents are revalued". On 3 March 1913, it began to appear that it had not been merely the inadequate income which had caused the breakdown. Mrs North-Cox was, it seemed, a startlingly bad example of how not to behave as a vicar's wife.

> *Mr Wilson gave me some grave particulars of Mrs. North Cox. She drove him nearly mad: she has about £400 per ann of her*

own: is extravagant: & very vehement in anger: always in
debt: does not drink, so he feels sure: is very indiscreet in her
associates ... brings up her growing daughters very unwisely.

Agnes was, of course, a model clergy wife and always had been. But she could be critical. At Easter, which fell on 20 April in 1913, one of Hicks's own sermons brought him reproof from his wife. He had preached a University Sermon in Cambridge "on the perils of wealth". She thought it "would do harm ... I hope not: but feel anxious". On this visit to Cambridge they were shown over Newnham College by Miss Alice Gardner. "She is a little creature, very plain, & with no idea even of making the best of herself." He particularly disliked her dirty hands and her determination to show him everything so exhaustively that they had to insist on getting out into the sunshine.

TEMPERANCE WORK AT NATIONAL LEVEL

On 24 April 1913, Edward Hicks was in London for a meeting of Convocation. "At 3 went across to the House of C. & had a chat with Will Crooks. Then got hold of Leif Jones and G.B. Wilson, & we discussed UKA work etc etc." Will Crooks MP was a reliable UKA ally, though sometime his Parliamentary duties had to come first. On 11 November 1912, Hicks had been in Birmingham, where he was at a "Capital & crowded meeting (Annual) of Bm Auxiliary of UKA. Will Crooks was to have spoken: but he has been wired for from London to avert the *defeat* (*sic*) of the Govt.!"

THE ANNUAL STOCKTAKING: 1913

Hicks was silent in the diary on the 24 June anniversary of his consecration for 1913 except to note that he had caught an afternoon train for a visit to Burgh College. But on 18 December 1913, his seventieth birthday, he wrote a stocktaking note on the needs of the diocese which echoes the main lines he had set out in his Charge the year before:

> *We want more discipline, more zeal, more hope, more definite ideals. The Discipline I am trying to supply, with my Archdeacons. More zeal & hope I am trying to infuse by example & word. Definite ideals are difficult to conceive or inculcate in the present confusion in the Church.*

"The apparent lack of systematic visiting in the country parishes is a serious matter, & will need looking into" Hicks noted in a diary entry for 16 October 1913, at the end of the Diocesan Conference. The task of visiting the diocese in detail continued to take a good deal of his time and energy. Lincoln was still an enormous diocese and it was thinly populated in his time as bishop. Yet he saw it as a priority to visit as much of it as he could. Sometimes he was the first bishop in living memory to visit a particular parish. Entry after entry in his diary has him catching a train to make a visit to a parish, but he does not seem to have made a systematic plan. He found that there were plentiful opportunities or reasons to be present in a parish without making the priest feel he was being "inspected".

Hicks went about the diocese to meet his priests in order to build trust and form good relations with them. Yet he wrote comments in the diary which would often have undermined such good relations irrevocably if their subjects had read them. The diaries were at their most frank and growing franker when it came to descriptions of these individual strengths and weaknesses of the clergy.

PERSONAL FRIENDSHIPS AND PURPOSEFUL "NETWORKING"

The personal friendship between Hicks and Scott Holland seems to have been strengthened by their common ground of interest in the CSU. Hicks paid a visit to Oxford on 29 July 1913, where he had a "long chat" with Scott Holland at Christ Church, where he was then a canon of the cathedral, which went with the Regius Professorship of Divinity. We can only guess what they talked about. The next day the electors to a professorship in Latin was to take place, and they must at least have touched on that. But it would be surprising if they did not discuss their common interests in the area of the CSU activities. Hicks certainly read Scott Holland's work. He says so in a diary entry for 27 December 1913. "I have been reading lately some essays on 'Property' by L.T. Hobhouse, Rashdall, Scott Holland & others, with preface, by [Charles] Gore: excellent, but revolutionary."

MORE HOSPITALS AND NURSES

Hospital visiting had a "patronage" as well as a pastoral aspect for a bishop. When Edward Hicks paid a visit to Oxford on 29 July 1913, he took the opportunity to stop at Northampton on the way, because the Mastership of St Mary's Hospital had fallen vacant with the death of its previous holder, and the choice of the next one lay in the bishop's gift. He took it very seriously, visited the hospital and talked to the matron ("who was at St George's with my sister!") and the doctor, "& spoke with all the patients (52) both men & women … I learned a good deal," he notes.

His sister's nursing career perhaps made the Bishop more than commonly conscious of the importance of adequate training for nurses, whether gentlewomen or not. Mablethorpe Convalescent Hospital, "seen over" on 11 August 1913, caused Hicks some concern because "the Matron was not a trained nurse

(!) & curiously ill-mannered. I have no confidence in her ability, though I think her a good sort".

Some regulation of nursing training with a requirement of state registration had been called for during the 1890s, but there was disagreement among nursing leaders as to the requirements which should be imposed. The Midwives Registration Act of 1902 proved relatively easy to get through, but a House of Commons Select Committee on nurse registration faced an uphill struggle against the divisions of opinion in the profession. It reported in 1904, with strong recommendations, but no Bill followed. Some private members' bills failed to get Parliamentary support over the next few years. Although a College of Nursing (in the form of a professional association of nurses) was successfully set up in 1916 to improve education and establish professional principles, Nurses Registration Acts for the separate parts of the UK did not begin to go through until 1919. For England and Wales, the Act established the General Nursing Council. All this was going to affect the provision of nursing care in the demanding circumstances of the war, when suddenly a great many nurses were needed in a hurry.

August 1913 brought renewed concern for the Bishop over one of his clergy – and encouragement from another. The previous year, on a visit to Cleethorpes, he had decided the vicar, Dalby, was not "at all the man for Cleethorpes: he is narrowing & lacks vivacity that is needed for a multitudinous place like this nor does he seem to have vision, or hope". Hicks almost despaired: "taciturn, glum, & disappointed. I hardly know what to make of him, or to do with him!"

On the other hand, Edward Hicks always responded favourably to a promising clergyman. On a visit to Old Clee and Cleethorpes in August 1913, he made a note to "*promote*" Webb, the curate. Preaching on the sands later about the Prodigal Son, he was confronted by an indignant Mr de Lacy Read who wanted to know how the Bishop "could have the impertinence to come there, & tell people how to conduct themselves", when he "had a number of Romanising clergy" in the diocese and "had not the courage to put a stop to their doings". In this exciting area he could see that soon a new church "would be wanted" but he "found Canon Dalby by no means excited about it". "Dalby is getting old, grumpy, & less active. *Quomodo summoveri poterit* (How can he be removed?)" he asked himself. On a later visit, Dalby met his bishop "gruffly" in the rain and gave him cold meat for supper. He "told me plainly that he never heard me or saw me without feeling more of a tory than ever before".

A WOMEN'S DIOCESAN COUNCIL

In Lincoln moves were made in the autumn of 1913 to launch a "Women's Diocesan Council". This was clearly supported by Edward Hicks's wife and Christina, because they hosted it, though it cautiously confined itself to "women's matters" and did not venture into wider concerns. On 31 October 1913, there was "a meeting in our drawing room, many ladies present, to form a Diocesan Committee of Women". They planned to "form a Council, & so gather a Dio. Assocn of women which shall meet at a Dio. Conference of Women to discuss as Churchwomen matters which concern Churchwomen. It went well". Its first meeting was to take place the following April, attended by Hicks and his wife. He recorded "a large attendance" of over one hundred and sixty women.

THE GROWING PROBLEMS OF PROVIDING TRAINING FOR THE MINISTRY

Lincoln's own residential theological college, known as the Hostel, now entered another of its problem periods for the Bishop. The warden seemed satisfactory. John Clement Du Buisson, author of studies of Mark's Gospel, had won praise from the bishop for his preaching the previous year. Nevertheless, there were evidently discussions afoot about the quality and level of the training the Hostel could offer, particularly for students who arrived without a university degree. On 6 February 1913, Hicks had a visit from the warden of Stephenson Hostel, Sheffield, "who talked about the possibility for Hostel men getting a Univ. degree with him at Sheffield". No doubt he had the interests of his own institution and its future viability at heart as well as those of Lincoln ordinands.

The chancellor of the diocese had responsibilities for the ordination training college in Lincoln so the choice of the right man was important for that purpose as well as for judicial reasons. On 27 August 1913, John Octavius Johnston of Cuddesdon (1852 –1923) accepted the post of chancellor. This was quite a catch. He had been principal of St Stephen's House in Oxford and therefore had extensive experience of ordination training. After a period as a don in Oxford he became Examining Chaplain to a series of Bishops of Oxford, including Hicks's friend and ally Charles Gore. In 1895 he had become principal of Cuddesdon. He was, therefore, despite his extensive relevant experience, a potentially controversial appointment because of his known high church views, but he did know a good deal about training ordinands.

The chancellor's appointment settled, Hicks set off "at once after bkfast" to meet "the Warden & Holden (Vice P) in the garden". He "walked & talked with them". The running of the Hostel had been going along "most easily & peaceably" but he thought that in the interests of avoiding future territorial disputes, now "a new Memorandum should be drafted" by himself as bishop, "setting forth briefly but clearly the duties of either in respect of the Hostel". This should be "assented to" by the new chancellor and the warden.

The chancellor was indeed keenly interested in improving ordination training in the diocese. In May 1914, Hicks was to write that he was "full of ideas, & practical reforms" for improving ordination training arrangements in the diocese. The Sheffield overture was responded to. He and Du Buisson had "been over to the Stevenson Hostel in Sheffield". The plan was to "send Literates there, to qualify in Arts, & *not instruct* them in elementary 'Arts' at *our Hostel*". On 10 June 1914, the Bishop went to an "old boys" meeting of former ordinands from the Hostel. Then he was present at the "Hostel cricket match & tea. A number of old Hostel men to dine & sleep. Interesting talk with Varahon Hugh de Wells & Grosseteste etc". (Hugh de Wells had been Grosseteste's immediate predecessor, and he had done a good deal to reorganize the diocese administratively.)

THE DIOCESAN CONFERENCE

In 1913 the diary mentions the Diocesan Conference on 15 and 16 October. There was "good debate (on the Finance Committee's Report) … which did much good, dissipating mists & admitting light". More "brisk debate" followed on Parochial Church Councils. On the second day, Hicks jotted down observations on familiar and new speakers, with a sense that "I am living in a *new* age of the Diocese – with new men, & new needs. The old men spoke little; they are falling off" (he mentions Heneage and Thomas Cheney Garfit who "spoke prominently but tho' well meaning not brilliant"). "Torr *very* clever & good. Welby Everard a new man. Dr. Macdonald's paper very clear & well-phrased: Marris calm, brief, meditative & eloquent: like a young prophet." Edward Welby-Everard (1870–1951), of a family of baronets, had appeared in the diary at a "crowded Conference" on "the Wages & Housing of Labourers" in July 1912. The promising Reverend N. C. Marris was vicar of Morton. Hicks had preached in his parish on a "long & tiresome" rainy day in late July 1912 "to a fine gathering of the Aveland Sunday School Association". His early approval of Marris seems to have been justified. Hicks presided and the conference passed "a good Resolution" which Hicks himself had drafted.

Not to be discounted were leading laymen, local figures who had a place on certain committees and did not hesitate to press their views on Chapter and cathedral affairs. Thomas Cheney Garfit of Kenwick Hall, Deputy Lieutenant and JP, is first recorded as speaking at the Diocesan Conference on 15 October 1913. The Bishop was to become thoroughly irritated by the man in the end. Less than a year later, Cheney Garfit was being "rather difficult" at the Executive Committee of the Diocesan Conference on 19 June 1914, and it was to grow worse.

CLASS CONSCIOUSNESS

Before Hicks encountered him at Corpus Christi College, John Ruskin had been awakened to the need to question some of the assumptions of contemporary society. Outstanding among these was the notion that it was a necessary and uncontentious fact of the way things were that there should be a class of the privileged and a class of servants and labourers who worked for them. (He also saw that "commercialism", what in modern terminology would be called "market forces", had its downside.) Hicks had enjoyed a fair degree of "social mobility", rising from a lower-middle class background to an upper-class status. He had entered energetically into the late Victorian and early twentieth century debates about the disadvantages suffered by the working classes and how to help.

Hicks approached people in the friendliest way, rarely confrontationally, always with humane kindliness towards human frailties, though his comments in his diaries could be sharp. He talked down to no one and regarded no one as inferior, yet he often lets slip a class-conscious comment in a diary entry. To the modern reader some of his assumptions strike a jarring note. He often makes class distinctions. In the society of the time he could do nothing else. But did he think some of the laity "better" than others, and why was he so often concerned to find that one of his priests was not a "gentleman"?

The diaries are scattered with hints of a class-consciousness he shared with most of the people of England in his time, and which he applied without distinction to both laity and clergy. On a trip to Grimsby to preach to the Grimsby Guilds Union, Hicks made some cutting comments about Mrs Piggott-Smith, his hostess for the night. She was "a farmer's daughter & rather inferior middle class. Children nice… but with a vile accent" – 10 November 1913. Allsop of Grimoldby he reckoned "a nonentity but a gentleman" and absurdly fond of his "overfed" dog. His energetic wife "on her bike", "runs the parish" he noted in his diary for 21 September 1914.

TROUBLE AT THE TRAINING COLLEGE

Miss Todhunter was now making herself felt as the first woman principal of the training college. On 16 March 1914, the Bishop took the "chair at the Training College Committee, to try & smooth down many crumples. Fairly successful so far. Interviewed Miss Todhunter aftds". Two days later he was back, trying to reconcile differences. He used the methods of a modern mediator. On 18 March 1914

> *I to Tr. College, to try to compose a serious strife between Miss Todhunter & her staff (save one or two). I spent half an hour with Miss T. Then 1 Hr. with the Staff: then Miss Butterworth & then Miss T. Then Miss Turner & Miss Elwell,*

as representing the staff. Finally I brought these two to Miss T.
& made explanations, & they shook hands: I prayed with them,
& then gave them my blessing & came away v. hungry & tired
at 8.30.

Diocesan business

The country was close now to being at war. But the implications were not yet uppermost in the mind of our bishop in his annual stocktake. Edward Hicks treated this exercise of review partly as an occasion for spiritual self-examination:

Fourth Anniversary of my Consecration. God grant me grace,
& health & strength, for the coming year. I want to conquer
three besetting sins. I want also to be more guarded in speech:
this is difficult, for I am impulsive.

On the practical side, he judged that:

The Diocese is really beginning to be moved, & my plan
of weekend visitations is beginning to tell. I seem to have
accomplished little or nothing: but many things have (I hope)
been rather strengthened, & I am well satisfied with my
appointments – in particular those at the Cathedral.

Being a Bishop in Wartime

Chapter 13

War Breaks Out

Responding to the Outbreak of War

Edward Hicks did not find the war easy on his conscience. When he became president of the Church of England's Peace League in 1910 he had been wholehearted about its aim of "combating the war-spirit as contrary to the spirit of Christianity". He did not resign when war began, but he found he had to adjust his views of war and modify his public statements about it as the country entered the First World War.

The outbreak of war also changed things for the CEPL. It had to rethink its objectives and its position. With war an inevitability, it even began to be suggested that the League had done harm by giving the Germans the idea Britain would be easy to conquer and would offer no real resistance. The League almost apologetically published *A Little Manual of Prayers for Use in the Time of the Present War*. It had to find an approach which would win support. In April 1915 Hicks was to preach on behalf of the Church of England Peace "Society", as he absentmindedly wrote in London at Bow Church on "War & Manliness":

> *I tried to prove that our English sports on the one hand, & our mechanical labour on the other formed a "moral equivalent" for*

> *war, as training us in manly courage etc. There seems to have*
> *been a report of it in the "Morning Post" next day & [?] in the*
> *"Times".*

Some went on accusing the League's members of being unpatriotic. Was Hicks a patriot? What did he think patriotism meant? He was to find that out during the next few years. Before the war he had been, if not an out-and-out pacificist, very sceptical of the justification for the grandiose imperialism of a British Empire near the height of its dominant position in world affairs. Twice in his lifetime it had acted on the assumption that it was entitled to defend its interests by military intervention in South Africa. He had always been willing to speak out on policy questions and to take a lead on subjects on which he felt strongly. But his previous public position on British warfare had been taken in very different circumstances, before the country was faced with a real danger of imminent invasion.

A European war with Germany had been looming throughout the first years of Hicks's episcopate. Metternich, the German Chancellor, apparently even tried to interfere internally in British politics and force resignations of ministers making speeches Germany did not like. The British government had to consider which countries to treat as allies if the worst happened. It was realized that land war, if it began, would be between Germany and France. Germany would invade France. France must therefore be regarded as Britain's ally and supported as necessary.

Much of the recorded discussion in government in the run-up to war turned on strategy and the costs of preparing for war. A bishop near the east coast could not safely think all this was remote. His diocese was uncomfortably close to the sea across which, not far at all, lay the potential enemy. The general fear that the country faced invasion soon became very particular locally in wartime Lincolnshire.

At first the British government still saw the navy as the main British defence weapon, and it was suggested that an army could always be called into being if needed. There were discussions about how many Dreadnoughts would be needed (four, five, six to eight?). Winston Churchill was for a mere four (he wanted naval economy). Lord Fisher thought up to eight would be right. But it was gradually being realized that German sea power was expanding. In 1911 the Germans sent a gunboat to Agadir. Meanwhile, Lord Haldane was pressing for consideration of the costs of land forces on the basis of his specialist knowledge of Germany.

The Bishop of Lincoln was not the only one to wonder aloud whether war could have been avoided. Even before it started, Churchill wrote in a letter to his wife, Clementine, on 28 July 1914, "We all drift on in a kind of cataleptic trance". He meant the European governments which seemed to be moving to the tipping point like automatons. Yet, in the same letter, he said of Britain and her preparedness, "We are awake to the tips of our fingers". He wrote to her again a few days later: "There is still hope though the clouds are blacker and blacker … the apprehension of war hurts … interests more or as much as war itself." The financial system was paralyzed, he said. "You cannot sell stocks and shares." The interests and honour of Britain hung in the balance.

Edward Hicks was to find it difficult to keep to a clear position which could be stated consistently down the years. On 1 August 1914, he was writing, "Much excitement about the outbreak of European War: God keep England outside of it!" When war loomed ever more closely, he addressed a meeting of the Peace League on the beach at Cleethorpes. As he says in his episcopal diary for 2 August: "I spoke of the outbreak of war, & pleaded for *British neutrality* & was applauded."

But he was slowly brought to accept that neutrality would not be possible. Mistakes had been made by politicians and the consequences had to be faced. War was declared on 4 August. He did not mention it in his diary that day, but on 5 August he described his feelings:

> *This is a momentous day in the history of Europe & the world. I am still against this war ... Sir Ed. Grey & co. have either knowingly or unintentionally steered the nation into the most horrible war of European History.*

On 16 August he "preached on the War – but a Peace sermon".

Hicks came to think it was his duty as a bishop to give a public lead once war began. Too much was at stake for him not to make the best of it. His peacemaking energies gradually went into trying to argue that things must be different after this war, when disagreements between nations must be resolved by arbitration and small and vulnerable states protected from aggression by bigger and more powerful ones.

However, moderation and reluctance to fight was not going to be an easy position for a public figure to adopt. Particularly not when the finger pointing out of Kitchener's poster "Your country needs you!" was telling the nation's families that the military life was a noble calling, and one to which every man should respond as a duty in time of war. Conscientious objectors were going to be mocked as cowards, and girls would hand out white feathers to young men who did not join up. At the beginning of the war, "peacemakers" like Hicks, too old to fight but taking a very public and unfashionable position about the war, were still being accused of exposing England to German aggression by giving Germany the impression that they would not fight back if attacked.

Hicks could not assume that his clergy would all agree with him in any case. Not all the clergy of the diocese were men of peace. The Dean of Lincoln was surprisingly militant. On 3

August 1914, the Bishop "called on the Dean who is eager for war & for fighting Germany". By 29 August, the dean – though he had been a vice-president of the Church of England Peace League – was in "a highly warlike mood. He goes on drill & is beating up recruits etc." But if this urge to recruitment included the clergy, it was going to create a problem over pastoral provision for the diocese, going far beyond the gaps left by those who offered to serve as army chaplains.

War hits the diocese

The war made an impact on the diocese within days. On 1 August, even before war was declared, "Davis of Auborn called, & wanted advice about cancelling the Miss[iona]ry Exhib[itio]n because of the war (!): 'Drill Hall might be needed etc etc'." During August 1914, and for the summer and autumn of that year, the Bishop was repeatedly encountering diocesan problems created or heightened by the war. But he also had family issues on his mind – the arrival of two of his grandchildren, Mary's offspring, John and Fauriel. They were to stay with Hicks and his wife from August 1914 until the beginning of April 1915, when Christina took them home to their parents at Fallowfield. The strain of this extended period of childcare by busy grandparents no longer young was eased by the fact that the children had their nurse, Lillian, with them. A letter from Hicks to Mary during this period is quoted at some length by Fowler. He reassures her that the children are "well and happy, and wonderfully good in ways and manners. We think they grow fast, and they are a great joy and comfort to us all, especially to your Mother and to me". Mary was to have two more children, Agnes and Christina. Little Agnes is mentioned in the diary in October 1915, sitting at table with the family and "behaving quite nicely". Baby Christina was christened in June 1918.

Mobilization in August 1914 was speedy and highly visible. Hicks had been much impressed by the enormous size of Immingham docks when he visited them in October 1910. Now, on 6 August 1914, he recorded that the "Immingham oiltanks [were being] carefully guarded by thousands of troops ... At Lincoln crowds to see the 1st Lincolnshires off to France: their Barracks want to 'borrow'! mattresses for the extra soldiers who are there". He was already committed to "open" a garden party for the Society for the Propagation of the Gospel that day at Barrow upon Humber. He went, and he spoke on "the war & our duty & behaviour in this dreadful time".

This instant preparation for war was not confined to Lincoln. It was going on everywhere, especially near the British coasts facing the European mainland. Mobilization was equally noticeable in Sussex, another coastal county particularly dangerously positioned for invasion from continental Europe. Virginia Woolf wrote in a letter on 12 August 1914: "We left Asheham a week ago, and it was practically under martial law. There were soldiers marching up and down the [railway] line, and men digging trenches", and it was said that buildings were to be taken over for use as a hospital. "All the people expected an invasion."

People were not only inconvenienced by the war. They were frightened, and with reason. In Lincolnshire, priests and people alike were worried, and it does not seem from the diaries that those with local pastoral responsibilities were always much good at encouraging and reassuring their flocks. The Bishop did his best to provide an overarching air of confidence and comfort. On 18 February 1915, Hicks went to see Mr Usher, who had a collection of miniatures and old silver, was "in real fear of Zeppelins & Bombs", "and was going to put his best stuff in the Bank at once". His family needed his reassurance too. After a visit to his daughter Christina and her baby Rawle, who were in London on 20 October 1914, Hicks notes that she was "really anxious about the threatened German zeppelins and bombs". He seems to have felt something of a thrill. "Wonderful searchlights soaring up into the heaven, over the Thames, like horns of fire. London ... at night *very dark*" and, in the late afternoon, "vast crowds apparently returning to their homes as fast as they could".

Zeppelins – or the threat of Zeppelins – scared people whenever there was a warning of a "raid" over England. These Zeppelins everyone was so afraid of were rigid-framed airships, patented in the 1890s in Germany and the US. They got their lift from hydrogen or helium and their drive from internal combustion engines. By 1910 they were carrying passengers on a commercial basis for a German airline. These were not bombing raids of the Second World War type. Zeppelins were airships, slow and not easy to steer with accuracy, and that exposed parts of the country to accidental damage when the raiding craft drifted where they were not meant to go and dropped their bombs. The Zeppelins were apparently mainly used at first for reconnaissance flights by the German army and navy authorities. They could make it difficult for the British ships to get close to Germany or lay mines as they wished.

BUSINESS AS USUAL OR AN ALL-OUT WAR EFFORT?

Despite the war, the bishops held their regular meetings with the Archbishop of Canterbury at Lambeth Palace. In late October 1914 Edward Hicks was in London for the "debates at Lambeth" which were "all about the War". He says he felt, as he so often did at these meetings, "an outsider". He was able to be wryly witty about this – "I fear I am thought a bore, or a bear, or a bounder". A year later at the Bishops' Meeting at Lambeth, 26 October 1915, the discussion was still about the war and how the church was to calibrate its response. "We were mostly occupied with the War & its problems, & finally with the 'Spiritual Call of the War'."

In the end, Edward Hicks concentrated on the diocese and its people's needs and tried to maintain an air of normality in the churches as far as he could. But it was necessary again and again to consider whether adjustments needed to be made in the national interest. At home in Lincolnshire, on 11 September 1914, the Church of England Temperance Society held its local committee meeting and decided to try to go on with the CETS Festival at Gainsborough on 11 and 12 October. The committee, with its new secretary, the Reverend J. E. Meurig Davies, decided to try to arrange its next annual meeting for 1915 at Spalding. Once war began, the Church Army's mission locally also developed a new focus. On 15 October Hicks mentions the new arrangements which had had to be arrived at for the "Ch A Vans", "one to work at Lincoln with the troops, & the other on the coast, among the troops there".

The ordinary business of being a bishop with its tests and trivialities went on much as usual. Other families could be much less open-minded than his about women's expectations, as Edward Hicks discovered in a dispute over a wedding ceremony. On 2 September, the diary recorded the marriage of Ruth Giles and Julius West. Ruth's mother and sisters were "vehement feminists". They "desired to omit 'Obey'" from the marriage vows. The Bishop was faced with a problem:

> *The father would not come to the wedding if "obey" were omitted. They consulted me, & I was puzzled. But in the end it was agreed that I should read the marriage service "over them" at 8, omitting "obey", & "giving away", & other small things …, the Father remaining in our Vestry.*

There would then be a Eucharist at which Mr Giles read the epistle. This was accepted – "I feel satisfied that I did right, & saved the family from real difficulty".

Another ongoing issue was that of Miss Todhunter, at the college. Tull, the chaplain, also found her a challenge. On 3 October 1914, "Tull came to talk over affairs at the Tr. College. He says that Miss Todhunter keeps everything restless, & unsettled & is continually changing her arrangements". Hicks seems to have been inclined to think the fault or shortcoming lay with Tull. When, on 13 December 1914, he preached at the training college, he noted that "Tull is hardly clever or cultivated enough for Chaplain and Miss T does not like him, nor like to defer to him in matters which are really in his discretion".

There was the usual round of parish visits, followed by more shrewd diary notes about the incumbents and the general state of the parish in question. But now there were also notes about the impact of the war and its demands. On 21 September 1914, Hicks made "a round of visits" in a car, beginning after breakfast. At South Cockerington "old, white-haired, devout" Mr Handyside had a wife who was "not his social equal" but a "good, industrious woman". He was "deaf, as well as poor: very simple & gentle". When the Bishop arrived, "he was ringing the bell for War intercession", special prayers for wartime.

At North Cockerington, Hicks found an elderly clergyman and (he suspected) "bon-vivant" now very ill, and "two small, unrepaired, unrestored untidy churches … *In my patronage!!!*" Hicks wrote indignantly, with three exclamation marks and the underlining he always used when he wanted to emphasize something especially. At Theddlethorpe, St Helen's, he found only a "v. nervous charwoman in charge". The vicar was in London, ill in bed. Hicks wrote a worried note to himself. "NB What of the Ch. & Parish: who is in charge?" At Theddlethorpe, All Saints, the vicar was out, "worried because the Day school is commandeered by the Territorials". Skidbrooke vicarage produced the vicar and his sister. "He *knows nothing* of Parochial duty, & seems to be without desire to learn," wrote Hicks, in exasperation.

Wartime or not, a bishop had to decide what to do if he discovered really shocking behaviour in the diocese, whether lay or clerical. On 28 September, Hicks notes "NB Ludford had a bad name among villages hereabouts till recently". It was a village which received the failures of other places. It was called "'Long, lazy, dirty, drunken, lousy Ludford'. Apparently it is respectable now, but still very Wesleyan, but immoral". On 30 October he "Saw Archd. Wakeford about the V. of Biscathorpe, who drinks & does nothing: also Allnutt, who seems quite mad, & is reckless of truth".

The often amusing or charming eccentricities of the clergy of the Church of England were all very well. The question was still what sort of training the next generation ought to have and how high a level of education, including theological education, was necessary or desirable. The Hostel, which was supposed to be meeting that need, was under pressure from the outbreak of war.

At a meeting of the Hostel trustees in early 1914 there had been no shadow of the changes the war was to bring, just a decision to replace lost trustees with four new ones. But by September it quickly became apparent that the number of students was dwindling "because of the War". At a meeting on the 18th, it was recognized that "a number of students" from the Hostel had already "gone into the Army" and some who had been going to come were now unable to do so "for lack of funds or other causes incidental to the War".

It was decided to carry on until Christmas, making small economies where possible, then to take stock and make a decision about the future. "The Warden & the Ch, both were convinced that, after the War, there would at once be a vigorous demand for entrance into such colleges." To that end the chancellor – still full of ideas – "expressed a strong desire that the Hostel … should be advertised as a *graduates'* college … this step would put the college on a better footing". The theory was advanced that that would make the non-graduates keener to come "as by exceptional favour shown to brilliant & promising men".

For both financial and academic reasons, amalgamation seemed worth considering. Burgh College at Burgh le Marsh near Skegness had been a missionary training college from 1878 but was now a general theological college. The college at Burgh had had a crisis, which Canon H. H. Foster, the principal of the college, had to deal with. As Foster explained, it had arisen because the college's property was vested in only two private trustees. When the second one died he was found to have left everything to "a certain lady".

Foster hired a detective to find her but he had no luck. In the end she was found by chance through an advertisement for a Wesleyan Harvest Thanksgiving in Foster's own village, and she agreed to execute a deed vesting the property in the Diocesan Trust. On 20 November 1914, Hicks was conferring with the chancellor about the advantages of a temporary arrangement, in the hope that the war would be over by the summer. "Shall Burgh be invited to amalgamate with us for a while? Could we go on alone till Trinity?" Burgh pressed on and made a new appointment. On 19 November 1915, Hicks met

Beddow, who is to be the new Tutor at Burgh College. He has been educated at Kelham, whither he came from a Natl School. He has passed the London Intermediate, & is preparing to proceed further. He is pleasant-looking, has a nice voice & accent, & is altogether a thoughtful & promising man.

It was not only Theddlethorpe, All Saints, which had buildings being taken over to meet wartime needs. The Hostel was soon to face a demand. Petwood, the social-climbing Mrs Weigall's house, was to become a military hospital for convalescents too, and we shall see a takeover even of the Old Palace in the end. Among the pre-planned army hospitals in Lincolnshire was the 4th Northern General Hospital in Lincoln itself. This was one of the "Territorial Force" hospitals designated before the war. It was set up in preparation in the Grammar School in Wragby Road, and while it waited for the arrival of the wounded from the Front, it attended to "invalids" from the great camp of reservists and recruits at Belton Park. By 15 September it already had some wounded men from the Front. Hicks visited everyone there (he hoped it was everyone) on 19 September.

With the war, the "OP" (Old Palace) became a responsibility in new ways. On 11 September 1914, the "inspector of the Eccl Insurance (at my request) came to look over the Palace", apparently with a view to fire prevention in wartime. Suggestions were made about extra taps and a "bucket-pump". He "admired our garden hose".

WELCOMING REFUGEES

Belgian refugees soon began to cross to England. Early in the war, the Hicks family took in a party who stayed with them in the Old Palace for some months, and were treated in the end as family friends. In a letter to his daughter Mary on 23 October, Edward Hicks writes that six had arrived the previous night. "The Dean's car brought them up," he tells her.

> *They fled from Antwerp to Ostend: then at Ostend they had to hurry away in a steamer for fear of the Germans, leaving all their goods behind in "les malles" [left luggage] in the station. So, beyond a little bag, they had nothing save what they stood up in.*

Hicks did not apparently at first see beyond the immediate human need of this little group, their practical requirements and the interest of their different culture and assumptions. To Mary he wrote that their lack of appropriate fresh clothing "made them (they thought) look contemptible" and "was a real sorrow to them". Money they did have with them, and after a night's sleep they went shopping to buy "linen, collars, tapes, etc." They spoke no English and were "very weary – with sorrow, fear and long journeying". But working in the cathedral library was "Miss Jones, a recent fellow of Somerville", "a perfect French scholar" who "has lived long in France", so any language barrier was speedily overcome. They were found to be all one household, though not all one family, headed by a retired major from the Belgian army; a woman whose husband was fighting at the Front with a boy of five and her father; a housekeeper aged sixty-six, and a middle-aged maid. These six stayed with the Bishop's family until May 1915.

It does not seem to have occurred to Hicks at first when his own group arrived that where six had come others would follow. He writes about his own refugees with personal interest and no wider reflections. Yet a quarter of a million Belgian refugees settled in Britain for the duration of the war. Trade unions were nervous at first in case they took jobs away from their members. But generally there was popular sympathy and support, and much of the work of looking after the refugees and finding them food and shelter fell to private endeavour and local committees under the supervision of the national War Refugees Committee. The pressure on resources and goodwill mounted. A War Charities Act was passed in 1916 to provide for some overarching regulation, and the number of charities registered under it totalled 9,153 when a Question in the House was answered on 7 August 1918.

WAR AND FAMILY LIFE

Edward Hicks's own family was drawn into the war from the beginning, and far beyond providing accommodation for displaced Belgians and soothing Christina's fears for the safety of her baby. Hicks was well beyond the age when he could expect to be called to fight himself. But Bede, Edwin, and Edward (Ned) were of an age to fight.

When war began Bede enlisted. Although Hicks writes with some anxiety about his younger two sons when they were deciding whether to enlist, he says nothing in his diary about the making of Bede's choice. Bede had been working abroad. Once he had been commissioned as an officer, he sailed for Mesopotamia with a Volunteer Mobile Battery to command a "gang of scoundrels". He was gazetted (his name published in the official list) as a temporary captain and then as a major, and stayed in that theatre of war until he came home at the news of his father's imminent death.

Should the others join the army? By early September the decision had to be taken. Men were joining up "faster than they can train them". There was a family conclave. The family talked it over carefully.

"He wishes only to do his duty: he hates war and fighting," commented Ned's father to his diary. Ned was now twenty-two. On Tuesday 8 September Ned enlisted in "Kitchener's Army", through the "Office in Lincoln for Public School and University Men". A bishop's son and a university graduate would naturally be an officer if he joined up, so he set off for Oxford on 18 September "to put down his name for a commission".

Edwin, the middle brother, had been working in a shipping firm in Burma. He tried to enlist in Manchester on Friday 4 September, but he was rejected because he was short-sighted. "He will probably enter the Territorials," commented his father. Here Edwin was successful. The diaries note that he was gazetted in *The Times* on 13 November. However, the status of the Territorials was not secure. As Chief of Staff, Kitchener (1850–1916) had been a leading military commander in the Second Boer War (1900–02).

When the war broke out in 1914, he was made Secretary of State for War and set about recruiting an army of volunteers big enough to enable Britain to fight a long war. He did not think much of the Territorials, the volunteer reservists, whom he compared with the incompetents of the Franco-Prussian War forty years earlier. He wanted to build up a professional army to complement Britain's naval prowess.

Another family marriage was in the offing and this too was going to be affected by the war. In Manchester, Hicks and his wife had become friendly with the Boyds, who lived in Altrincham in Cheshire. There were evidently shared views on the bringing up of children, including daughters. Hicks wrote of James Boyd in a note of commemoration:

> *He was the gentlest of husbands and fathers, delighting not in the exercise of his own will, but in seeing others grow up and develop strong and tender characters like his own.*

The friendship lasted after the move to Lincoln and the families stayed in touch.

The Boyds' daughters, Alison and her sister Ida, were members of a group of friends which included the young Hickses. Hicks notes affectionately in his diary for 3 December 1914 that Alison and Ida had had a happy evening at his home with his sons Edwin and Ned and other young men, "All of them quite delightful young folk." Alison had recently been appearing in the diaries, in a car with Mrs Hicks on diocesan business and helping secretarially.

Then came the engagement. On 12 February 1915, Mrs Boyd wrote from Altrincham to Mrs Hicks "to say how much they approved the engagement between our Edwin & their Alison", which had been known for a couple of days.

In Salford the family had got to know Ruth Chamberlain, who had been running the local Girls' Club from 1895. She spent

Christmases with the family in Lincoln, including the Christmas of 1914. Despite their longstanding and lasting friendship, she remains Miss C, not Ruth in the diary. On 29 December 1914, Hicks records "some motor drives with AMH and Miss Chamberlain: so yesterday to Skegness, & today along the North Road ... the ladies enjoyed the ride".

TEMPERANCE CAMPAIGNING BECOMES NATIONAL

Wherever he went, Edward Hicks noticed the drinking habits among all the classes, and any clear adverse consequence for local people. At Spalding on 1 December 1913, he had made a note of "awful stories of drink, dirt & neglect in Vic. & Church" at St John's. He had had lunch with Mr and Mrs Gleed. "He was a *Wine & Spirit Merchant*." He was not alone in his concerns. The whole issue of excess consumption of alcohol was becoming a high-profile matter nationally.

He had also agreed to support the Lincolnshire Labourers' Temperance League in 1914. On 23 July 1914, it held a rally. The group seemed "in danger of collapse & disappearance". Hicks decided to do what he could to help. "I have got them to take [Proudfoot] as their Hon. Organising Secretary & they have made me their President. We hope to recover, vivify & extend it." He badly wanted to make support for temperance campaigning a cause his clergy could adopt:

> O that the Clergy wd help in this movement. It would be right, & wise, & nothing more expedient for the Church could be imagined ... to do right, with a disinterested desire of helping what is good.

In the House of Commons Debate on the King's Speech, 13 February 1914, Leif Jones MP spoke on temperance, stressing the concern of responsible bodies and professions, including the churches:

> *The demand for a further reform of our licensing law comes not alone from temperance organisations; it comes in ever-growing volume from the Churches, from benches of magistrates, from the medical profession, and from social reform workers of every kind throughout the country.*

He mentioned a meeting in Queen's Hall:

> *A few days ago I had the honour of presiding at a great meeting in Queen's Hall held upon this subject. It was a crowded and representative meeting. I will venture to read to the House the names of the speakers of that meeting. They were: The Bishop of London, representing the Church of England, and Dr. Clifford, who spoke for the Free Churches; we also had a Roman Catholic priest speaking, while we had a lady representing 160,000 women who are members of the British Women's Temperance Associations. We had my hon. Friend the Member for Barnard Castle (Mr. Henderson), speaking for the Members with whom he is associated and we had Sir Victor Horsley, representing the medical profession; and I think I am justified in asking the Government what other question there is in their programme which would command such widespread and, let me say, respectable support as this question?*

It was suggested that a solution might lie in allowing local communities to decide their preferences. On 30 May 1916, Hicks went

> *at 7 with GPC Wilson to Middle Temple Hall, where we had a fine meeting of the Royal Courts of Justice Temp. Assocn. Lord Parmoor (of all men!) in the Chair: myself & Leif Jones*

the speakers … I spoke blandly but simply for T.A. & for Local Veto, & carried the meeting with me. Jones excellent on the national Waste of the liquor traffic.

Chapter 14

Not Over by Christmas

The war was not "over by Christmas" and the Hicks family had to think seriously about how they were going to manage, with tax increasing but their income not. They were not rich. Many bishops at that time came from comparatively wealthy families, but they did not. Edward Hicks sometimes worried aloud about money in his diary. It mentions the state of his bank account several times, which seems to have been quite an anxiety to him. On 6 January 1915, he noted that his quarterly stipend had arrived, but because of "War taxes" was only £984 seven shillings and sixpence, not the usual £1,059 seven shillings and sixpence. "It will be a difficult year", he concluded. On 8 January he and Agnes were off for a fortnight's holiday in Malvern, so they felt they could still afford a holiday. By October 1915, Edward Hicks and his wife had to have "a chat about reducing our Establishment quite considerably & living in a part of the O.P. *very* quietly, so as to save expense".

This may have been decided on for another reason than shortage of money. Hicks and his fellow bishops became conscious that they must set an example. While ordinary people were suffering the deprivations and discomforts of wartime, it would be inappropriate, they thought, for them to be seen to go on living lives of comparative luxury in palaces, attended by numerous servants. There were discussions in the meetings at Lambeth about economizing and shrinking episcopal establishments. The Bishop of Wakefield was apparently managing with three rooms and two maids for just his modest household, consisting of himself, and the Bishop of Bristol had "abolished late dinner". Hicks mentions his own family's similar economies several times. Normal etiquette was dispensed with at Lincoln, even in the Old Palace. "The judge dines with us at 8: no wig or robes, *belli causa* [because of the war]."

There was some conscientious formal reflection on the war in the Bishop's household. "After dinner I read much of Loisy's 'The War & religion' to AMH & Miss Day".

WOMEN AS "GUARDIANS OF THE NATION'S MORALS" SEEK TO JOIN THE WAR EFFORT

On 17 March 1915, Hicks records an

> *interview with Miss Williams (Miss Savill could not come)
> to ask me about the possibility of our organizing a concerted &
> simultaneous mission to women of all ages in the Churches &
> Chapels of Lincoln City this Spring or Summer. I to appeal to
> the Clergy. It is in view of the War & its call, its temptations,
> its opportunities.*

The transition from seeing women as custodians of modesty and of the home lives of the nation, to accepting them as fellow-workers and wage earners, was forced on the country by the exigencies of war, but it was not universally welcomed. And many saw it as a merely temporary necessity. Edward Hicks, of course, did not; he was strongly in favour of anything that improved the lot or advanced the cause of women.

Some individual pioneering females such as these two made the most of the opportunity to engage actively in war work.

Sometimes it was work of their own invention. In the same month, Hicks reports in the diary that Miss Steedman, "a Grey Lady, & grand-daughter of Bp. Wordsworth, ... has lately been engaged in the 'Mission to Munition Workers' at Woolwich: a very interesting & open-minded person".

But was this at a cost to a type of "femininity" valued by society? When *Commonwealth* (to which Edward Hicks had contributed) had been launched as a CSU journal on 1 June 1880, there had been high hopes that women would write contributions for it. Yet even this socially aware publication displayed a mixture of assumptions about women and their interests. The journal seems to have held firmly to the belief that women have a moral (or potentially an immoral) influence on their children before birth through their "mentality" (and thus behind every great man stands his mother). It spoke of "the womanly reverence for moral ideals" and promised that in the new publication:

> *complete moral enfoldment of the people will be continuously maintained. Very little heed will be given to the minor considerations of elegance or refinement of style in the writing which may be admitted ... Women of high organic caste will write here, and will present their views of the disabilities of women, and of the Maternal Functions of women.*

Performance was patchy, as it turned out.

Peacemaking among the clergy and another anniversary of Hicks's consecration

The clergy could behave with folly and indiscretion. On 1 February Hicks was trying to deal with the "senseless indiscretion of Jacoby: innocent, but a fool". The vicar had been having young girls to see him alone in his study in his lodgings late at night. There were hard pastoral decisions to be taken as a consequence of sexual misdemeanours; for example, on 25 May 1915, Hicks decided not to ordain a man who had indulged in "some indelicate talk to some students at St Chad's" and gone over to Doncaster and met a pretty girl whom he did not know in the street, took her to a Picture-House, gave her tea "and when they parted at the station he kissed her".

The running sore of relations between the dean and the vicar of St Mary Magdalene seems to have remained unhealed. Hicks appears to have had a sneaking affection for Bolam the unruly priest. On 18 February 1915, "Bolam came to be cheered up. He was". Perhaps the affection was mutual. On 6 July 1916, Hicks found Bolam on the same early train to London. "At Grantham he bought and *gave me* Dr Cox's new Guide to Lincolnshire." Hicks was evidently touched. "It has some misprints, but is full of nice things: I wonder if they are all true!" (The St Mary Magdalene affair was to drag on and on. On 3 January 1919, Bolam was there again to see the Bishop, insisting that the church "was not needed, & should not be reopened: but what is to come of it?" asks Hicks.)

Wakeford, the archdeacon, was beginning to look like a problem. On 26 February 1915, Hicks wrote: "At 2 to Deanery, where the D. complained seriously of the arrogance of the Archdeacon of Stow, etc. The other four will demand a Visitation & call for new Statutes! (Can I not myself curb the man?)" Wakeford could be severe in his Visitations. On 13 July 1915, Hicks wrote a note about "poor Cooper" of West Rasen. Nevile of Wickenby had alerted the Bishop that the archdeacon had "crushed" him "at his Visitation for not filling up the Enquiry papers aright". Apparently he had filled in the churchwarden's form himself (though at the churchwarden's "dictation"). "I hope this quarrel will blow over," comments Hicks.

Widowhood in wartime happened to both "women" and "ladies". But each "class" had different options when a husband was killed. On 8 June 1915, Hicks made a visit with his daughter Christina to a war widow who "has busied herself restoring" a house. He realized that occupying herself in this way "had distracted her from her grief". For the ordinary woman the grief was likely to be compounded by urgent practical questions of money and what they were to live on.

In June 1915, with the war well under way, Hicks took stock of his achievements at the end of another year since his consecration, but again concentrating on the spiritual and diocesan rather than the national or the state of the war:

> *I am sure that I am securing the goodwill of the diocese, &*
> *especially of the Clergy. My simple plan of visiting quietly &*
> *informally every Parsonage & Church in the Diocese is telling*
> *more & more. Each Sunday I have been preaching 2, 3 or 4*
> *times. I can feel my feet stronger as time goes on. For all this I*
> *thank God & take courage. More & more however I perceive*
> *my great unworthiness, & my sins: as also my grave deficiency*
> *in manner, dignity & address. But such as I am, I will go on,*
> *relying upon God's mercy & goodness, & trying to live as in*
> *His presence.*

Rhys, the former bishop's chaplain, seems to have recovered from his depression and kept contact with his former bishop. Fowler quotes a letter of 25 June 1915, in reply to one from Rhys, evidently asking how things were going as Hicks began the sixth year of his episcopate. He told Rhys that everything seemed to be going well in his own work. He has a "sense of increasing confidence and friendship between the Bishop and his Priests", as a consequence of his "plan" "of visiting informally every parsonage and church in the Diocese".

However, stressed Hicks in this letter, "the War is dreadful, in every kind of way". He mentions his sons Edwin and Ned, then being trained, and to "be sent out before long" to fight, and the forthcoming loss – when he too went to the battlefield – of Christina's husband, Edmund. The war "upsets everything: of course, it is the negation of order". Here we can glimpse the close knowledge of one another's feelings and thoughts which could be expected to develop as bishop and chaplain worked together. The shorthand note about the "negation of order" would have conjured up for Rhys Hicks's familiar love of orderliness.

Not that all the family news was sad in 1915. On 15 May Edwin and Alison were married, "a pretty but very quiet wedding, without music". After an equally quiet family luncheon, the couple drove off to Derbyshire for their honeymoon. The speed of the wedding after the engagement was announced may have been because in wartime the young husband was soon going to have to go and fight.

Alison and Edwin had a little time together first. On 9 July 1915, Hicks describes a visit when "Edwin had come in from his route-march" and Hicks saw him and Alison at their home. He met them together again at the Old Palace on 18 October 1915. There were more family visits, until Alison had to go to her father, who was seriously ill at the beginning of 1916.

Once Edwin and Ned had both decided to join up, the strain for the family did not end. On 6 and 7 July 1915, Hicks saw Ned "off for Devonport, to sail for Egypt". Henry Newsum, son of Clement Newsum, whom the Hickses had got to know while he was Mayor of Lincoln in 1911, was also going. Hicks wrote "his parents there of course; it was a stirring but simple farewell. The Major nearly wept as he made a long speech to Ned". By 4 August Henry Newsum was back, wounded in the thigh, and reporting that he had seen Ned in the battle on 21 July, and thought he was safe. Ned's parents were still waiting for a letter, his father notes. The human cost of the war came home to the family very quickly.

On 15 July 1915, the Bishop visited the vicar of Swayfield and his wife. In the rectory garden she sat sewing "under an extemporized summer house ... Rather a lively elderly woman," he commented. They had four daughters "all at work". One of them was "a Secondary Teacher of distinction at Bromley, Kent – who is an ardent Suffragist (as they all seem to be) & therefore much approves of me! Some pleasant sallies therefore".

This charming picture of a clergy family with advanced views on the role of women encapsulates the Bishop's dilemma. Hicks had well-developed opinions on the innate intellectual equality of men and women. His family seem to have strengthened his convictions about that. But campaigning for social, educational and political equality in contemporary society as a bishop was quite another thing. In defending the rights of women there was a risk that he would get himself into trouble even if he tried to avoid politics and the risk of adverse publicity. Yet the needs to be met were connected. It was thought to be a fair question whether the lower classes and women had enough education to understand what they were voting about if they were allowed to vote. The only way to answer that was to improve women's educational opportunities. And activism among women themselves – such as the suffragettes engaged in – was controversial. In this idyllic scene in a rectory garden, Hicks apparently met with approval for his opinions on all this.

Church Unity

In a diary note of 6 July 1915, Hicks mentions that there had been a discussion at a meeting of Convocation he had attended in London: "Leading Wesleyan ministers" had asked for a meeting "at their Central Hall [in Westminster] about possible reunion with the Church":

> *I spoke warmly welcoming the project, pointing out its vast*
> *possibilities, & adding that I was cradled in Methodism, &*
> *was unworthily made Bp of the Diocese from which Methodism*
> *had its origin.*

The archbishop put him on the proposed committee at once:

> *"Would I be one" said the Archbp. I consented. It may come to*
> *nothing: & may be only one of the Bp. of L's bubbles: but it may*
> *lead to something very momentous.*

There seems no doubt that Edward Hicks's time at Oxford, and the people he talked to there, had put him on the path to a more middle-of-the-road Anglicanism, and a fair tolerance of "ritual", and such ornaments as the candles on the altar which had proved so controversial at Fenny Compton. But before this national initiative took off, he had been well disposed to friendship with the Methodists in the diocese, though he was well aware that Methodism had its own divisions.

Ned becomes a Roman Catholic

These are all examples of the routine work of the diocese, modified now the country was at war. But one thing loomed very large. A major concern of 1915 was Ned's decision to become a Roman Catholic. It was not that Hicks had any dislike of Roman Catholics as individuals. In February 1915 he had found himself meeting a group of refugees who were waiting for him on a visit to Thornton le Fen in order to show him their respects and "kiss the Bishop's hand". They appear, though they were Roman Catholics, to have regarded him as fully a bishop and they knelt around him for a blessing, which he gave. This ecumenical moment, which evidently gave Edward Hicks pleasure, came before events which upset him very much.

Hicks seems to have shared the continuing rooted official Anglican objection to Roman Catholicism. As bishop he had at least to pay that objection lip-service, in any case. Subscription to the Thirty-Nine Articles – required of all Anglican priests on admission to their "titles" or "livings" – included accepting that the Bishop of Rome had no jurisdiction in the realm of England (Article 37). Roman Catholic "reunion" was not yet being attempted in the Anglican Communion, and would not be seriously considered until after the Second Vatican Council, still half a century ahead. So it was quite a shock to the family when Hicks's own son Edward (Ned) became a Roman Catholic. He minded very much, but he did not reject the young man.

The first moves towards this decision are hinted at in a diary entry for 2 November 1915. Ned had written to his sister Christina "full of his religious difficulties, & the Roman question: from which it appears that Ronnie Knox has decided *soon* to go over to Rome". Ronald (or Ronnie), it will be remembered, was the brother of Christina's husband, Edmund, and a family friend as well as Ned's confidant during his time as a student at Oxford before he graduated in 1914. Knox had become a Fellow of Trinity College, Oxford in 1910. He was ordained as an Anglican priest in 1912, and became chaplain at Trinity.

Ronnie came to the view that the law of the Church of England "was not absolute, but represented a kind of contract between you and your parish". If the incumbent and his parishioners came to agreement about, for example, some point of ritual or observance, no bishop could have authority to intervene and require something different. This difficulty about episcopal authority was something he felt in connection with Anglican not Roman Catholic ecclesiology. He gave a paper to the Corpus Christi College Church Society. "Church circles in Corpus sat rather aghast; even my friend Mr. Hicks (who afterwards preceded me into the

[Roman Catholic] Church seemed uncertain how to take it." Yet Ronald became a Roman Catholic in 1917 and was ordained as a Roman Catholic priest in 1918. Ned went part of the way.

Edward Hicks's diaries have nothing to say about any conversations with the elder Knoxes over Ned's dilemma and Ronnie's influence. Ronnie did not have a great deal to say about his father in his spiritual autobiography, until he mentions his confirmation in 1903, by his father, who was then Suffragan Bishop of Coventry, moving to Manchester later in the year. His father was strongly evangelical but had been very interested in the story of the high church Oxford Movement. There must certainly have been sophisticated and informed theological discussion in a household where the father as local bishop was balancing his own prejudices. Yet perhaps the elder Knox failed his son as a confidant in this inward struggle.

Ronnie's chief ecclesiastical confidant as a boy was not his father but, surprisingly, "the then matron in college [Eton], to whom I am indebted for much salutary instruction and correction, as well as sympathy". She was his "safety-valve".

Among the kindnesses I had from her was an introduction which became interesting later ... She had been for some time a nurse under the Universities' Mission to central Africa, a mission which owes its whole origin to Tractarian inspiration.

She introduced him to the Bishop of Zanzibar, Frank Weston, who was to take a lead in a controversy which would shake both church and British public.

Between the ages of sixteen and eighteen, Knox read a good deal about the Oxford Movement and even more poetry and the classics. "I read something of Bishop Gore: he had been kind to me in Birmingham, where he was my father's diocesan, and the murmurings of old-fashioned people who thought him over-liberal had not reached me." He was doing his reading at Eton, where he says he had "few like-minded people to exchange opinions with".

At home, says Ronnie, "my views were known, and doubtless regretted, but never led to the smallest discontinuance of kindness on one side nor (I hope) of respect on the other – certainly not of affection on either". He was not at first

> *attending services in Manchester of a kind my father disapproved of. Nor did I feel my position equivocal as the son of an Evangelical champion, for these were the days of Mr. Birrell's Education Bill, when my father would appear on platforms side by side with Lord Halifax.*

His father was restrained in his response. He allowed himself only to comment, "I need not say what your return [to the Church of England] would be to me though I am conscious that my hopes of it must reckon with difficulties almost insurmountable."

But meanwhile, as Ronnie Knox notes, Ned had moved on ahead of him.

> *I suppose about the end of the summer term [1915], Mr. E. R. Hicks, whom I had long known as a friend and recently become connected with by family inter-marriage, had written from Gallipoli to tell me that he was contemplating submission to Rome; he has had trouble before, and I think that the piety of the Irish troops to which he found himself attached produced a strong impression. My advice to him was … that I was in no position to advise. I think it was about the end of the summer holidays that he wrote to me from Egypt announcing his reception into the Church.*

So perhaps his father was wrong in thinking he had been quite so much the follower when he was influenced in his decision by Knox.

The uncertainty Ned was feeling in 1915 is put down by Hicks in a diary entry for 7 November to the fact that he had "been very poorly in body". On 19 November a letter from Ned arrived written from the train on the way to Alexandria and saying he was going to be received into the Roman Catholic Church before he was sent into action. "Alas!" writes Hicks. He makes no other comment in this entry but he had more to say a few weeks later on 17 December, after Ned had been received:

> by the R. C. Bishop of Jerusalem, in the "Greek Catholic" Church of Alexandria. O me miserum. *[Woe is me.]* He will repent of it some day. He has been much under the influence of Ronald Knox, & shares the rigorist views of the Bp. of Zanzibar & the rest. I cannot see how I could have avoided this: I dare say he looks upon me as a very lazy, & indifferent sort of Churchman & Xtian.

In October 1915 and again in December (then with the "heavy" news of Ned's defection to the Roman Catholic Church), Hicks could only write to Bede and to Ned himself, both fighting overseas. Ned was home in September 1916 and his father "had a long talk" with him.

THE DIOCESAN CONFERENCE

Diocesan business had to continue. Hicks's remarks in 1915, when the Diocesan Conference was held on 17 to 18 November, are very brief. It was well attended and went off well, but we do not learn much more.

The dean evidently found Cheney Garfit as irritating as his bishop did. On 19 November 1915 the diary says: "At 12.15 Maintenance Committee. Well attended. The dean retired very soon, *huffed* at some rude utterances of Cheney Garfitt about the

'New Rule of the Chapter' etc." But Fry must have been less of a habitual peacemaker than Edward Hicks, given his long-running dispute and apparent bad relations with the Bolam who once came to Hicks "to be cheered up".

THE BISHOP AND THE SOLDIERS

Edward Hicks may have been against war in principle, but he liked people. It would not have been in his nature to refuse to speak to those who chose to fight or to manufacture bombs and weapons. As soon as the country was at war, the diary records him confirming soldiers, and visiting soldiers in training camps and wounded soldiers in hospital. Those whose consciences prompted them to become soldiers he treated kindly. He shunned no one. It was one thing to disapprove of war in general and to try to live as a man of peace. It was another to do the duties of a bishop in a country at war when the consequences were not going on in a country thousands of miles away and at home almost everyone was affected.

His change of attitude went further than that. He got to know and respect – even admire – the soldiers when he saw them preparing to fight. As early as 15 September 1914 he had found himself watching the men learning to be soldiers at camp, especially a "cycle corps" drilling ("very pretty"). He even made a visit to see draught horses destined for the Front at a depot with a horse hospital, and talked to the men looking after them.

He discovered that soldiers found they needed religion, even if they had not thought they did before they joined up. On 3 January 1915, he preached at a Soldier's Service – "Essex Terr[itoria]ls, & *very* nice men ... At 3 I dedicated the new Chapel-hut at the Camp on Wragby Road ... Col. Ivatt read the Lesson beautifully. I wish I knew these military men better. They are admirable".

The number of special confirmations held for soldiers may be an indication of an awakened awareness of the importance of religion among ordinary people who felt their lives endangered. The rise in wartime confirmations could also suggest that there may have been some recent slippage in the normal routines of confirmation in the Church of England. On 27 June 1915, Hicks "preached to a *Church-ful* of soldiers: a fine sight. Then at 2.10 motored with Col. Arthur Taylor to the Camp, for a Confirmation at 2.30". Here he "confirmed some 40 territorials in the open air in a lovely corner of the Park, near the Lake, under the trees. Then tea outside the Mess tent with the Chaplains".

On 5 October 1915, we read that Meurig Davies "wants to go as a Chaplain to the forces: he wd do for Welshmen only!" exclaims Hicks with gentle humour. Hicks knew Davies well because he had become the new secretary of the Church of England Temperance Society on 12 October 1914.

Hicks had first got to know Paul Ashby, another man drawn to army chaplaincy, while doing the rounds of the diocese to meet his clergy. He was Rural Dean of Ness, and had travelled with Hicks from Stamford to Uffingham on 5 July 1913, at the end of a day when Hicks had made an immense tour:

> *Seen each man & family at home: visited each Ch. With its parson: prayed & talked with them: got a notion of them: & (above all) they had got a notion of me.*

Hicks ran into Paul Ashby again two years later, on a train on 18 October 1915. He "told me many facts about the Front, & his experiences as a Chaplain". Ashby was to serve as a chaplain in Egypt next. Hicks was evidently struck by the insights he was able to give into the realities of what the serving soldiers were facing. Ashby also helped him to realize how difficult it was going to be for soldiers to adjust when those who survived returned to their homes. An experienced chaplain's sensitivities could be useful. Ashby spoke "very admirably" at the Diocesan Conference, as noted on 28 September 1916, "warning us not to make things in Church different from what the soldiers had been accustomed to: they would otherwise be disappointed when they came home".

For some of the clergy, the passionate patriotism which tempted the clergy into army chaplaincy seems to have proved permanently damaging. On 5 November 1915, Hicks notes that McIntyre "wants a Chaplaincy ... Poor fellows: the *War fever*!". McIntyre reappears in the diary on 19 March 1919, in one of the telling glimpses of the stresses of clergy life the diaries offer, when Hicks took him as chaplain on a expedition. He

> *smelt strongly of Whiskey. I had a serious word with him afterwards, & he confessed to having had some. I also spoke seriously to his wife: but she has been ordered a little claret by her doctor! I anticipate a downfall here.*

On 19 December 1915, Hicks noted that from the point of view of a diocese at home, "the shortage of clergy in this war-time is serious". On 13 February 1916, writing about the parish of North Willingham, he says resignedly, "Pedder & his wife are good, & gentlefolks, but quite lunatick (*sic*): however, they may serve for war-time!" That did not necessarily make it straightforward to reinstate returning clergy at the end of the war.

THE WOUNDED IN LOCAL HOSPITALS

Hicks had a new and more personal experience of wartime hospital visiting from 1915. On 27 October 1915, he visited Henry Newsum, the mayor's son, who had been shot in the thigh in August 1915 in a battle in which Ned Hicks had also fought. "He seems to be slowly recovering, but the wound discharges a good deal, yet less than it did. His father was there: we travelled home together."

When Edward Hicks made hospital visits like this to the casualties of war who found themselves being nursed in his diocese, what did he see? He did not commit such impressions to his diary in painful detail, but others who wrote about them give us a clear picture of the scale of what was being asked of the nurses. Vera Brittain describes some horrors in her own nursing experience. She knew that some parents would be visiting their son, a boy of twenty, for the first time. He had lost an eye. His head had been trepanned. He had fourteen other wounds. "He is the most battered little object you ever saw. I dread watching them see him for the first time."

On 25 November 1917, Hicks reports in his diary on a visit to Mablethorpe, where the "Chaplain of the N. Staffs" took him to luncheon at the Mess, "Then walked with him & called at the Convalescent Hospital – full of soldiers".

WHAT ARE WE GOING TO DO ABOUT THE HOSTEL?

The problem of billeting the greatly increased number of nurses needed for the extra hospitals caused much disruption in the diocese as buildings were requisitioned and their normal functions denied them. Commandeered buildings, whether for hospital use or for accommodation, were not always suitable, at home as overseas, and the displaced normal activities which had been using the buildings could suffer.

On 26 February 1915, they were still planning to go on till Trinity running the Hostel in Lincoln as a college for ordinands, with "finances & prospects" to discuss. However, the Hostel was soon to be subject to a wartime takeover of the buildings (for rent) by the War Office. The trustees met to discuss this "proposal" on 12 June 1915. They were discussing it again in January 1916.

Trustees of the Hostel met apud me [at my home], to attend to

> *the proposal of the War Office to take the Hostel about middle*
> *of April as a home for the 200 (?) new Nurses needed for the*
> *doubled huts on the Wragby road!'*

The loss of the use of the Hostel building was to have a long-term adverse effect on ordination training in the diocese.

MEETING THE WOUNDED AT THE STATION? MORE WARTIME WORK FOR WOMEN AND JOBS FOR THE GIRLS

Hicks's diary for 26 September 1915 notes that Miss Caroline Herford (1860–1945) is "busy now meeting the wounded at the station. Last night, & tonight *very* busy: wounded coming in fast from the great *Forward Movement* in France, Belgium & (Gallipoli?)".

Miss Herford was another of the fearsome organizing women the Bishop mentions with careful respect. He had known her through his daughter Christina. Caroline Herford had been educated in Manchester schools and at Brunswick Street College for women, which was the precursor to Owens College as a route to higher education for women. She had a period at Newnham College, Cambridge in the mid-1850s.

She became one of the instigators of the project to create a "higher" girls' high school for Withington. The first meeting to discuss this possibility was held in her drawing room at Lady Barn House School where she was then headmistress, in October 1889. When the school was launched, she taught biology there. This was the school Christina Hicks had attended before she went to Somerville. Miss Herford spent the war as a university lecturer in Manchester from 1910 to 1918 and working as a commandant for the Red Cross. Her pupils found her awe-inspiring. She was clearly an authoritative figure to be met by if you were a returning wounded soldier.

As in Lincolnshire so in France and Flanders, women had to be found who were capable of meeting the wounded as they arrived and ensuring that they were sent onward appropriately.

2 September 1914: ... Arranged I send 2 nurses for day and night duty to the Railway Station – selected one for both day and night duty who could speak French. Admitted the patients including 3 officers who had been at Red Cross Hospital. By evening Hospital full.

7 September 1914: ... saw Surgeon General who discussed the question of putting Sisters on the trains for duty. Considered that Sisters on the Stations at suitable places would be the better arrangement for the moment. Nurse Nunn took some officers down in Hospital train to St. Nazaire.

It was also essential to find women to put in charge in the hospitals who were capable of managing them adequately:

7 September 1914: ... Went to No. 9 opened in the Race Course, Miss Osborne appearing to manage only fairly well.

OTHER WAR WORK FOR WOMEN

Not all women who put in work in aid of the war effort made such an impact. Hicks notes with gentle irony on 26 November 1915, "Miss Walker & Miss Dallas at work at [Pressing-hay] for the army: war work for (educated) ladies!" He was forward-thinking about the position of women in contemporary society, but his sense of humour stopped him tub-thumping on this point in the way he did about the dangers of alcohol.

Perforce, women in the lower social classes were doing the jobs of absent fathers and husbands: chimney sweeping, bill-posting, hearse driving, grave-digging. Mrs Pankhurst led a women's march through London, demanding a right for women to work in wartime with all the men away. Could this be expected to continue once the war ended? Would the men not want their jobs back and the women back at home cooking and cleaning for them? The trade unions were hostile, for fear that would bring wages down and affect the position of male workers post-war. Politicians and press were patronizing – especially Lord Northcliffe – and saw this as a temporary emergency measure. The position of those reluctantly conceding the inevitable was that women were delaying marriage for the nation's sake, "helping the great cause of freedom", but they would naturally expect to leave work and marry as soon as possible.

The realities of the extent to which industrial work by women in wartime, especially in making munitions, had changed the working practices of the nation became apparent. At the end of the war, the Church of England Committee on Social Problems published a report on *Christianity and Industrial Problems* in which it pressed for more equal wages. Women had recently been doing men's work, but they were paid much less, and it was assumed that they were not going to be the breadwinners. "A legal minimum wage is indispensable to women," said the report:

There ought … to be a change in the attitude of society towards the industrial employment of women commensurate with the importance of the part which they have played in the war. During the last three years large numbers of women have undertaken work hitherto reserved for men, and new standards with regard both to wages and to other conditions of employment have begun to grow up.

However, the committee was not in favour of married women working; it thought men's wages should be raised so they could support their families.

THE END OF ANOTHER YEAR OF WAR

One respect in which the war must have felt more "real" during 1915 was the intensification of Zeppelin raids. The fear that Zeppelins would be used for bombing did not prove to be altogether well-founded at first, but from 1915, the Kaiser ordered bombing raids, excluding historic and public buildings but soon allowing London to be included.

There were twenty raids that year, some blown off course. Lincolnshire and East Anglia were especially vulnerable because of their position. A raid is described in the diary for 8 September 1915, when the buzzer sounded and "the town was as dark as pitch & silent as the cemetery". The response of the community was "a triumph of cooperation", wrote the Bishop approvingly. The Bishop's flock were, however, perhaps less sensitive to their duty to "reflect" on the war. On 31 December 1915 Hicks wrote "to Boston to preach tonight in the Parish Church – a War Repentance and Intercession Service. Church dark: Lantern: only a fair attendance".

But the ordinariness and good order Hicks always tried to maintain was still in evidence. Hicks's relations with his chancellor seem to have remained very amicable. At the end of the year, the Hickses offered him a bed in the Old Palace while the drains at his own accommodation were being attended to. A diary note in early December 1915 records that "the Chancellor is sleeping & living chez nous: *drains*". In 1915 Ruth Chamberlain stayed with the Hickses again at Christmas, though otherwise they had only the "close family" party.

Chapter 15

Army Chaplains and Conscientious Objectors

In the background of these large-scale events and needs, the business of the diocese had to be kept up with. The now-familiar pattern of affectionate amusement runs through many colourful little episodes. On 7 January 1916, Hicks was consulted about "superintending the supply of hay for the army!" The diary makes it obvious that Hicks always put diocesan needs first, though that often overlapped with the concerns of wartime. On 31 January 1916, the night of a raid involving nine Zeppelins which were scattered across the Midlands by the weather conditions, the warning buzzer went before dinner so the palace put out its lights and everyone went down (into the cellars, presumably) to hide. They got hungry and had something to eat by the light of a single candle. They waited. "By degrees the servants crept off to bed." The Bishop and his wife went on waiting until after midnight they heard the trains begin to move again. They too went to bed, to be woken at 2:30 a.m. by the buzzer announcing that the raid was over. This was to be another year of frightening attacks. At the end of March 1916 there was a five-Zeppelin raid on "the Eastern Counties" which did "much damage, esp. at Cleethorpes!" Hicks noted another big raid in the diary on 23 September 1916.

ARMY CHAPLAINS

For much of the war, clergy could choose freely whether to join up (to do war work or to fight) or not. Some clergy went further than their colleagues who had chosen to serve as army chaplains. They felt it their duty to join up, and leave their parish work for other kinds of war work. As soon as the call came to join the armed forces and before it became an obligation under the Military Service Act of 1916, Hicks was faced with the problem of how to respond to clergy who, although they were free to refuse, found they wanted – in some cases – to become soldiers. On 16 December 1915 he records in his diary that he "Addressed the Junior Clergy concerning 'Clergy as Combatants'".

As the war began to kill and wound so many of the male youth of Britain, the call to arms moved from voluntary to compulsory. The Military Service Act of 1916 imposed conscription on single men between eighteen and forty-one, but it exempted the clergy from call-up, including ordinands near ordination. The First Schedule to the Act listed exceptions, including "men in holy orders or regular ministers of any religious denomination". The position of men in training for the ministry was not wholly clear though. On 4 February 1916, Hicks says he had heard about "an extraordinary Army Order, dated Jan. 28. *Exempting Roman Catholic priests & Ordinands* from enlistment. I wired to the Archbp. Of C. for further information". Many of his own diocese's ordinands were busy enlisting.

The 11 February 1916 prompted a diary note that the Committee of Burgh College had held its annual meeting:

> *Seven of the men have been enlisted today – which thins the College ... Five or six Burgh students to tea: they had been examined by the doctor, & some rejected & others enlisted. They*

are all to sleep at O.P. tonight: the military authorities seem quite careless of their health & comfort – as usual.

The problem of exemption of ordinands exercised a meeting of Convocation on 15 February. There was a discussion of "exemption of Theol. Students nearing Ordination etc."

Those already ordained were certainly exempted by this Act, but not all of them wanted to be.

W.W. Leeke, who enlisted in spite of my wishes, is now in difficulties. He attested before the Act, & is now accordingly called up: but the Act exempts the Clergy: how then does he now stand?

Exempted clergy remaining in England who did not choose to fight might still not be available to serve parishes. Their bishops could "release" them for other sorts of contribution to the war effort. On 25 July 1916, Hicks mentions a

young London parson, whom the Bp of London has released, that he may work under the authority of the Dept of Munitions in visiting employers on behalf of the boys who are crowding to the m. works, & see that some good supervisor is placed in each of the Works: his duty being simply that of a Scoutmaster, or Captain of Boys' Brigade, in brothering or fathering the lads, & looking after their moral & social welfare. I was much interested in what he said of his work & experiences.

Nationally, the bishops as a group tried to get a picture of the work of the army chaplains. Before the war there had been commissioned regular serving Army chaplains, mainly providing pastoral care for soldiers in garrisons stationed in England. Local clergy had provided extra support as appropriate.

The rigid structures of the Victorian class system supported the whole system, for clergy, like officers, were "gentlemen", mainly drawn from the professional, middle, and upper classes; the "men" were from socially lower planes, less well educated, and as the call-up process showed, often less good specimens physically than their social betters because they had not been so well fed when they were children.

Only the Church of England, the Presbyterians, and the Roman Catholics had official chaplaincies among those commissioned (eighty-nine, eleven, and seventeen respectively in 1914). In addition there were thirty-seven "acting" chaplains (not commissioned), drawn from other denominations. (The Nonconformists were sometimes an exception to the rule that ministers of religion did not come from the lower social classes.)

Now army chaplains were serving in France among soldiers going into battle, and discovering that the high ideals with which they had joined up had become mud and misery and pointless sacrifice. They were going to be dealing with deaths and supporting the injured and the frightened. There were rumours that they were not doing it very well. There had been no special training, nothing to prepare them.

At a meeting of bishops at Lambeth, on 25 May 1916, the Archbishop of Canterbury gave his impressions of a visit to France at which he had "chiefly visited the Chief Chaplains, & enquired into their work & prospects" – "His impressions were highly favourable". That, it was admitted, was a change. Things had not been going so well shortly before. He had been given to understand that the chaplains were now "valued, encouraged & asked for", unlike a year ago. Another entry in the diaries a few months later gives quite another view. On 4 October 1916, Hicks wrote:

Mitchell ... told me of his experiences at the Front in France: he sees no signs of spiritual revival among the troops; but they are quite responsive to religious appeal, but dreadfully ignorant of religion. The nation needs simple & plain teaching.

Most of Hicks's direct experience of the chaplaincy work of his clergy was local. To the army and the navy was added an "air force", which came formally into existence as the Royal Air Force on 1 April 1918, from which year the first chaplain-in-chief was appointed. Hicks had some contact with both naval and air force chaplaincy needs. He could be very frank indeed, especially after a year or two of dealing with chaplaincy problems. On 8 February 1919 he was to write of E. L. Clarke

> *late Navy Chaplain for 20 years, an old Hostel man, & very much alive – now Chaplain of the R.A.F. [came] to discuss the Chaplaincy of the Aerodrome at Hemswell. Burrow of course incapable, greedy & litigious: Eastwood, whom I recommended last September has not played up: alas! He is to poke up Eastwood ... & try & square Burrow so as to get the use of his Church for services: it is close to the camp.*

It all caused senior churchmen a lot of worry. In London, on 31 January 1918, says Hicks, "I found the Archbp still dealing with problems about the War & Chaplains."

He made a number of visits between 1916 and 1918 from which he was able to see some of the difficulties arising in the chaplaincy work in the hospitals where wounded soldiers were being taken.

A letter to *The Times* from "Edward: Lincoln"

It was not only the complications of war service for the clergy which caused a bishop difficulties. Equally problematic, pastorally speaking, were those laymen who did not want to fight, especially those who had a rooted objection to taking life, even in wartime in the service of their country. So in 1916, the year's big political issue for Hicks was the controversy about the conscientious objectors. He was moved to rare public protest in a letter to *The Times* signed in the formal convention as Bishop of Lincoln and noting in his diary that he was writing it:

> *As I read of the handling of conscientious objectors by some local tribunals, I am visited by some painful fears … The will or capacity to take an enemy's life is not the only element in good citizenship … Is the nation, in its military zeal, slipping into the old vices of intolerance and persecution? Conscience is a sacred thing. Is private judgment to be swept wholly aside in time of war? … it is perilous to trample on conscience [4 April 1916].*

The passing of the Military Service Act, on 27 January 1916, with the adjustments in a supplementary Act of Parliament on 25 May 1916, set out the ground rules for deciding exemptions. Apart from the clergy, a man might be exempted if he was being trained for – or was engaged in – work of national importance; if he would suffer serious hardship if called up; on grounds of ill-health; or "on the ground of conscientious objection to the undertaking of combatant service". So in principle, conscientious objectors were also exempted for being called up for military service under the Military Service Act of 1916.

The conduct of Quakers was in some respects surprising. The traditionally pacifist Quakers, although they could claim exemption, eventually joined up in such numbers that it has been suggested that perhaps a third of them were in active service. The Quaker John Graham reflected on the situation which had been brought about by conscription in the Antipodes just before the First World War and the "partial departure under very difficult circumstances from the absoluteness of the testimony against all war … " He saw it as acceptable to serve in ambulance units and in a medical capacity and to support refugees – "Though we cannot fire, we did not keep out of the firing line". The handful of Friends in Australia and New Zealand are, he knows

> *called upon to bear repeated imprisonments for the maintenance of their testimony against compulsory military drill. There has been widespread resistance of which the little body of Friends forms the steel spear point … If conscription were tried in England, no one in the Society has any hesitation whatever in promising the Government a similar experience on a larger scale*

he warns. The question as he saw it was whether in "modern times" war had somehow become worse on an unprecedented scale. Graham had no truck with the argument that whereas an offensive war is bad, a defensive war may be justified. All sides commonly claim merely to be defending themselves, he observed.

THE TRIBUNALS

Certificates of exemption from the requirement to fight could be granted by local tribunals. The certificates could be absolute, conditional or temporary. There were appeal tribunals, and a central tribunal was provided to consider further appeals if the first appeals failed. Conscientious objectors could have a hard time before these tribunals. Tribunals tested their sincerity, but not necessarily consistently and the outcome could be a matter of luck.

Edward Hicks knew how chancy and how difficult it might prove for a man to satisfy a tribunal that refusing to fight really was a matter of conscience for him. As a bishop he wrote letters on behalf of "Con. Objectors". Influence could certainly make a difference. A letter from Edward Hicks to his old friend and ally, the politician Charles Roberts, now presiding in a tribunal, could be expected to have some effect. On 17 July 1916, Hicks mentions in his diary "Mr Sharpe & Mr Effield, 2 ILP & NC Fellowship men", on whose behalf he had written to Charles Roberts. Other conscientious objectors might not be so lucky as to have influential supporters with the right contacts.

Some leading intellectuals took a harder line. In July 1917, Hastings Rashdall wrote to C. C. J. Webb (1865–1954) (a medievalist, another of the loose grouping of late Victorian "social philosopher" scholars with which Hicks was still periodically involved). Rashdall wrote to comment on the paper on "The Conscience" which Webb had sent him:

> *The only criticism I would make is that you hardly seem to admit sufficiently that it may sometimes be the duty of one individual to do something which nevertheless it may be the right and the duty of other individuals to shoot him for doing.*

He thought it could hardly ever be justified to refuse to fight when the nation needed soldiers:

> *There are certain possible circumstances in which (though I should personally be disposed to think them very rare) a man would really be justified in refusing to serve, but, if his fellow-citizens take the view that he ought to be compelled to serve, it is right for them to compel him to serve if they can.*

MEN OF CONSCIENCE AND REPEATED IMPRISONMENTS

The battle to stay out of the fighting did not end with getting exemption. Conscientious objectors soon began to find themselves subjected to some brutal treatment, imprisoned not once but repeatedly for continuing to "object". Edward Hicks signed two memorials to the Prime Minister and supported Lord Parmoor to the extent of heading a list of signatories to a protest in support of his attempt to call a halt to it. On 24 May 1917, the Bishop noted in his diary "At 4 I (with the Archbp) to H. of Lords, where he was to support Lord Parmoor in asking a question about the treatment of Conscientious Objectors".

Lord Parmoor did ask his question. He asked whether exemption should be conditional or absolute. He said conscientious objectors should not find themselves imprisoned more than once for what was, in effect, the same offence. They were being court-martialled, sent to prison, serving their sentences, then when they came out they were court-martialled again and sent back to prison, each time with twenty-eight days of solitary confinement to serve at the beginning. It was not surprising that some of these men had suffered breakdowns and worse – "lunacy has been caused by punishment of this kind".

Whether it would be safe to let such men out is, of course, an important question for a nation in wartime:

There are five or six hundred of these men, I believe, and it has been thought that when they come out of prison they might take advantage of their freedom to spread opinions inconsistent with national interests at the present moment. This is an objection which one has to consider.

But, suggested Lord Parmoor, there was a remedy under the Defence of the Realm Act to protect against that. The Archbishop of Canterbury spoke, strongly condemning the conscientious objectors:

I do not suppose I need say that I have … no sympathy with the convictions that these men hold … they seem to be absolutely intolerable and inconsistent with the ordinary working of a civilised community.

Earl Russell noted that some of these individuals made things more difficult for themselves by refusing to do any kind of war work, even as non-combatants:

> *the most obstinate of these men take such a very high view of their own conscience and its dictates that they will not accept any alternative service.*

It was not intended – or initially expected – that conscientious objectors should be allowed to take their objections to such an extreme that they refused even to do war work which did not involve fighting or the use of weapons. But some did and this further controversy was the result. Hicks did not speak in this debate. He could have done, and he was clearly concerned enough to attend. But he did not use the voice he might have had if he had been willing to become an active speechmaker in the House of Lords.

For those who were prepared to do war work but not actually to fight, the options were less painful. Virginia Woolf wrote to her sister Vanessa on 28 June 1916, to comment that Duncan Grant's efforts to get exemption had ended with his being allowed to do farm work instead of fighting: "It's very odd about Duncan, isn't it?" She went on to report some gossip about the way conscientious objectors were being treated:

> *We dined with the Heseltines the other night and there we met one of Asquith's secretaries, who said in confidence, that all C.O.s in future who are imprisoned are to be interned as alien enemies.*

The story was mentioned again in another letter – "The latest rumour is that all C.O.s are to be interned as Alien enemies".

Asquith spoke in the House of Commons, in response to such concerns. The question in the Notice Paper to which he prepared a reply was:

> *if, in view of the number of cases of alleged brutal treatment by Army non-commissioned and commissioned officers of conscientious objectors, supported by the evidence of the victims and witnesses, and the repeated refusal of the War Office to have an independent inquiry made into the allegations, he will grant such an inquiry into a few selected cases which can be supplied to him?*

The popular imagination had been captured by one particularly disturbing and now famous case, but others were raising various questions about the way the system was working. A question had been asked of the Undersecretary of State for War about a conscientious objector named Arthur Slater. Is he, it said

> *detained in the military prison at St. Alban's; if so, what is the sentence he is serving; by what Court he has been sentenced; what is his present state of health; when will he be allowed a visit; and why is he not given the benefit of the Army Order of 25th May last?*

MPs rose in turn. Another question was asked as to

> *whether four conscientious objectors, named Hayward, Bishop, Reccord, and Fromow, have been for more than six weeks at Shoreham Camp, and have during that time refused to obey orders; why have they not been court-martialled; why were they removed on 23rd June to Seaford Camp; whether it is intended to send them to France; and, if so, whether they will be allowed the usual five-days' leave before going abroad?*

The Undersecretary of State for War was asked

> *whether he is aware that many conscientious objectors who have been refused exemption by the tribunals have had*

> *testimony borne to their genuine convictions and courage by*
> *commandants, governors, commissioned and non-commissioned*
> *officers, and men; and whether, in the case of men who are more*
> *than once court-martialled or tried as conscientious objectors, he*
> *will order that such testimony shall be taken and considered by*
> *the Court?*

The undersecretary asked them to wait to hear the Prime Minister.

Asquith made a statement as promised the next day, after he had been reminded that "Monday's Order Paper" contained "twenty-five questions on the subject of conscientious objectors". Rowntree said their treatment now amounted to "persecution for religious conviction". Asquith's statement set out

> *The procedure to be adopted by the War Office in the cases of*
> *soldiers, under Army Order X, of 25th May, 1916, sentenced to*
> *imprisonment for refusing to obey orders.*

This situation arose in the case of conscientious objectors who had been refused exemption and found themselves in the army and then simply refused to obey orders. They were being treated like any soldier and brought before a court martial. From now on, promised Asquith, these would be referred to the War Office and if they had been before a tribunal, "the records will be consulted" – "Those who have knowledge of the man's antecedents, such as ministers of religion, may be consulted":

> *The men who are held to be genuine conscientious objectors*
> *will be released from the civil prison on their undertaking to*
> *perform work of national importance under civil control. They*
> *will … cease to be subject to military discipline or the Army*
> *Act so long as they continue to carry out satisfactorily the duties*
> *imposed upon them.*

Honest objections must be respected but cheats should get their deserts, he concluded.

Chapter 16

National Mission

By 1916 the overarching political position had changed. The Liberals and the Conservatives were now in a coalition government, and the growing rivalry among the Liberals between Asquith and Lloyd George resulted in 1916 in the triumph of Lloyd George, who became Prime Minister.

How politically moderate did Edward Hicks remain in these changing times? This was almost as important a question from the point of view of his reputation as the need for visible moderation in his "churchmanship". There are clues about his real preferences in his earlier outward political behaviour. At the election of 1900, he had supported the local Liberal candidates in Manchester. A letter of Samuel Proudfoot to *The Modern Churchman*, written after the publication of Fowler's biography, hints that he may have been less attached to the middle ground than he tried to seem. "He distrusted Conservative politicians … He was almost a fanatical Radical"… his "perfect control" … "frequently gave the impression that he was more 'moderate' than [he was], but only to the superficial observer". His earlier life and loyalties suggest that his natural leanings would put him somewhere between the modern Labour and Liberal Democrat parties as a voter.

Probably Edward Hicks always saw the whole question of politics through the prism of the attitudes and priorities he thought were truly Christian. His own interests lay in trying to make things better for people practically and locally, so the question for him was likely to have been whether any one party could do that better than any other. He was not the only bishop to take this line, in which "Christian socialism" is not quite the same thing as modern political Socialism, though it is its close cousin. In 1905 the Christian Social Union (CSU) had published a pamphlet by Charles Gore, Bishop of Birmingham, on Latimer, a sixteenth-century Protestant hero of the Church of England, which he entitled *Bishop Latimer as a Christian Socialist*. "Latimer was", he wrote, "the prince of Christian socialists, the forerunner of the Maurices and Kingsleys and Westcotts of later day".

Not only established industries and the tasks of their workers but the whole social framework of the nation was changing under the pressures of war. Edward Hicks had lingered on the fringes of the active campaigning for social reform which had its leading lights in the late nineteenth century. He was not commonly listed among the notable names, as a high-profile national figure, a Ruskin or a Webb. Now he had to rethink his beliefs and his priorities.

Hicks's overt party politics had never been sharply defined. All his adult life his political opinions had tended to the socialist or liberal. "Nice people: though tories!" neatly sums up his attitude to the Conservatives. Was he going to lean more towards the Labour Party or the Liberals? As a supporter of the Christian Social Union, did Hicks become a "socialist" in a party political sense? At heart he probably remained a liberal, but with a small "l". As we have seen, when he became bishop, he made friends of certain Liberal politicians, especially C. H. Roberts, who served as Liberal MP for Lincoln throughout his episcopate.

Writing in the *Manchester Guardian* on 8 December 1904, in an article on the Christian Social Union, he had compared the priorities of the leaders of an emerging socialism. He compared the approach of the Scotsman Keir Hardie (1856–1915) with that of Will Crooks, an ally we meet in these pages, but whose socialism was, he feared, of a more militant trade unionist brand. Hicks wanted *Guardian* readers to understand the difference between a caring attempt to improve people's lives, and a radicalism which might disrupt the social order.

THE NATIONAL MISSION

The bishops had now began to discuss the holding of the National Mission, partly to encourage a population which was oppressed by war and personal loss. They discussed it at a meeting in January 1916, and it was planned for that autumn.

The National Mission was further discussed and planned for in the diocese. Hicks became enthusiastic:

> *The extraordinary feature of it is that its aims and scope exactly correspond with what I have been always insisting upon as the duty & call of the Church, viz, to appeal not only to individuals for their conversion to God, but to appeal to the Collective Church to take collective action in Xt's name in order to remedy the national evils & social sins of England. God help us in this great endeavour.*

By 17 May he was organizing the mission in his diocese, a "crowded Meeting of Clergy and Laity from all parts of the Diocese, & some ladies" of the Women's Diocesan Association. He "charged them concerning the general Mission". They only wanted to know "*What to do?*" He "constituted them a Diocesan Evangelistic Council" and sent them off to form district groups and get to work. More arrangements about committees and groups followed, and more crowded meetings at which Hicks felt he had fostered enthusiasm and "good was done". He was consciously trying to be "daringly idealistic", feeling "the exceptional nature of our days". He went so far as "intentionally" to seek to show "the duty of the Church collectively to Social Reforms, besides driving home as well as I could the more obvious duties".

On 2 July 1916, again in connection with the National Mission, Hicks "gave an Address on the War etc. & its call; & the Natl Mission" in the marketplace at Spalding. The approach of the proponents of the National Mission in the diocese was generally broadly inclusive. In June 1916 Hicks wrote in the diary of Miss Elliott and her "demonstration of a Reformed Sunday School ... *Crowded!* But everybody seemed to enjoy it".

Before the mission took place, however, Hicks received bad news about his youngest son. On 10 July Hicks wrote:

AMH showed me a telegram to say that Ned was wounded on Th. 6th by a piece of shrapnel which entered his rt leg in front, a little above the knee. We heard later that it had been got out, & he is doing well but of course in bed.

The next day they had to play host to Randall Davidson, the Archbishop of Canterbury, his wife, and his chaplain, so they could not give themselves up to worrying. Davidson was coming to preach in connection with the National Mission. The dean "in his car very kindly met" their distinguished guests, and the next morning at 12:15 p.m. was the Missionary Festival Service. The nave was crowded. The archbishop preached well, Hicks thought, taking as his text the beginning of Mark's Gospel, with its account of the way John the Baptist preached the coming of Christ – "a fine sermon, setting the Missionary problem in its larger light, with much force of logic & feeling".

Then there was a lunch which was well attended. There was "no *butter* but much real sense & kindliness". The archbishop "seemed very happy & quite at home", but his party left straight away and Hicks returned to the cathedral in the evening to hear a quite different sermon, on the mission in wartime, by the Bishop of North and Central Europe:

> *A wonderful sermon on the War, its call, its uplift of so many soldiers: the certainty of social change after the War; the need of the Natl Mission, & the certainty that international world problems, & the problem of Missions would be forced upon us more than ever.*

Randall Davidson had problems on his own mind, especially the case of Sir Roger Casement, who had been sentenced to death for high treason in connection with the Easter Rising over Home Rule in Ireland in 1916. The archbishop was under pressure to campaign to save him, but in a letter of 14 July he expressed his reluctance. He had formerly had a high regard for Casement for his work in the Congo and central Africa. But now he feared he had been "mentally affected" if the evidence made public was right.

CONVALESCENTS

Hospitals or places for recovering soldiers to convalesce were being opened at Woodhall, Horbling, Boulham, Spilsby, Bourne, and Mablethorpe. At Spilsbury, on 19 July 1916, a day packed with duties, Edward Hicks found time to make a visit first to the drill hall, "converted into a *beautiful* hospital, with wounded soldiers". At Woodhall, what had been intended to be the new Gentlemen's Home – of which the Bishop had laid the foundation stone a year earlier – was "*just* able to be used, & is filling with convalescent soldiers" he noted on 16 March 1915. There was a "little Conv[alescent] Red + Hospital" at Horbling, which the Bishop visited on 2 March 1916. On 12 March, Hicks visited the Convalescent Hospital at the Hall at Boultham. A "little

Hospital" at Bourne also seems to have been for convalescents. Hicks says he spoke to them when he made a visit on 20 October 1917. His sense of what was needed must have been heightened when Hicks's own son Ned and his son-in-law needed hospital care as wounded soldiers from 1917. Edward Knox, Christina's husband, was moved to the Royal Northern where he recovered.

During wartime, with its special and sometimes very personal demands for hospital visiting, Edward Hicks did not lose sight of the needs of ordinary patients. The Lawn Hospital, which was over a century old, had begun as a lunatic asylum. On a late August Sunday in 1916, after preaching at the cathedral, Hicks "called (by request) upon a Mr. Barnes at the Lawn Hospital". Mr Barnes had worked for the Post Office. Hicks noted: "I should judge that ambition & vanity were his besetments, & that overwork broke down his brain." He was "very mad, & told me he owned the Lawn, & most of Lincoln: was married to Princess Mary, & was Almighty God". Hicks "spoke kindly with him", and then talked to Dr Russell about him. He was told that there was "v. little hope".

By now it was September, with the date of the actual mission approaching. The Wesleyans sent their good wishes. When Hicks spoke on the National Mission at Haxey in mid-September, he was given a bed by the Sheppards that night.

> But [Mr Sheppard] was perpetually harping on his good family, & his wife's noble relations, & the dormant peerage, &c. &c. I forbore to say anything that might offend; for I wished to make him & his wife as happy as I could.

On 21 September 1916, the Hull District Synod of the Wesleyan Methodist Church & the Lincoln District sent letters of goodwill and support for the National Mission. This was evidently seen as a Christian, not a denominational, mission. Hicks preached in the cathedral on 4 November to launch the week of mission. The week seems to have had mixed success and his own open-air preaching at the Engineering Works on 6 November did not go well, he felt – "I was like St. Paul at Athens". The 17 November saw a "sparsely attended" and distinctly bad-tempered meeting of the Consultative Committee of the mission.

Changes of opinion could take Christians out of the mainstream Church of England without their realizing it. On 6 February 1916, he wrote a long diary entry on the strange developments at St James church, Deeping St James, where he had celebrated the Eucharist that day. (More can be read about this affair and Frederick Tryon, its vicar, at the end of this book.) Dryly he says he rested in the afternoon and read an essay on "Missionary Methods".

Successful missionary activity could prompt a request such as Hicks received on 23 February 1916. The churchwardens of Bracebridge Heath Mission Church came to see him

> *wishing to have their lay-reader Ordained … They had no idea of raising the add[itiona]l funds requested for paying a Curate. I must see Stafford Smith: for I fear this "Mission" is getting independent & out of hand: these men had not consulted their Vicar!*

In March 1916, Hicks described in his diary a meeting at Spalding with "all *the nonconformist ministers* in the town". The local vicar had called it and the Bishop "spoke on the general aspects of the problem of Reunion":

> *I noted that the older men – Mr Yates e.g. – were rooted in the old Puritanism, but the younger men were open-minded, & saw the force of Modernism etc. Mr. Spendelow – Baptist, & brought up a v. strict Calvinistic Baptist, – was very kindly.*

INDUSTRY AND THE WORKERS, BOTH MEN AND WOMEN

In the diocese, industry was now giving its energies to the war effort. When war began, the firm of Clayton and Shuttleworth turned its efforts to aircraft manufacture. In 1916 it made parts for an airship for the Admiralty to be called the "Submarine Scout". As the war prompted the urgent development of aircraft for warfare in the air, more contracts followed, from the War Office as well as the Admiralty. The War Office ordered the Sopwith Triplane, then changed its mind. Nevertheless, forty-nine of these machines were built for the Royal Naval Air Service, beginning in 1916. There followed a contract for the Sopwith Camel, of which more than five hundred were built between 1917 and 1919.

For ordinary women who had to work for a living, the choices were mostly limited to some form of domestic service, or employment in a factory or shop. The types of factory work available changed with the war, with the mass production of munitions, but there was not enough of it. Hicks wrote in the diary for 1 April 1916 about a tea party with local factory owners, Shuttleworths and Rustons, together with Miss Connell of the Labour Bureau. They met to discuss the local employment situation for women. The problem was apparently that the local women, daughters of factory workers, did not fancy domestic service, but there were not nearly enough jobs for them, even in the munitions factories:

> *We talked by arrangement of female [labour] in the munitions works, and the prospects of immigration. It appears that the girls & women of Lincoln dislike domestic service (children of foundrymen & mechanics) & cannot find enough industrial occupation. The munition works do not absorb a tithe of them.*

Yet, munitions work, even if there was not enough of it to go round, was going to be a key area of potential employment for the women of the diocese.

ROUTINE DIOCESAN BUSINESS AND SOME LONG-RUNNING PROBLEMS

In the end, Tull gave up the struggle to work with Miss Todhunter in the training college and resigned, as Hicks noted on 4 January 1916. On 20 January 1916, it was agreed to offer the chaplaincy to Jeudwine, to "exercise authority, & employ a deputy". Jeudwine had been an Archdeacon of Lincoln from 1913 and might be expected to be a force to be reckoned with in dealing with Miss Todhunter.

The committee saw all round the problem. After a 3 November 1916 committee meeting, Hicks commented that "Miss T. is regarded as an exceptionally good Principal". It was recognized that the staff (and the principal) were underpaid, and that heating and kitchen provision badly needed improvement. Hicks notes to himself that "a few years ago Church had most of the training colleges but now only 1/3. Need to ensure Church Colleges *first-rate*". Miss Todhunter is recorded as having at least one signal achievement to her credit in raising academic standards. In February 1886, the Committee of Management had approved the establishment of a library. This went no further at first than the setting aside of a cupboard in the Lecture Hall. In 1899 there were still only 485 books in the college library. Under Miss Todhunter the library got an annual grant of £25 and a reference library began to be built up. It soon had 1,500 books.

There seems to have been some bad blood between the subdean and the Precentor of Lincoln. On 25 February 1916:

At 6 the Subdean & the Precentor came, by appt, to see me & talk over the dispute that has arisen between them concerning

a W.C. which belongs to the Subdeanery, but intrudes into the
wall of the Precentory. After a quiet discussion for nearly and
hour, I got little light: but promised to go & see the place.

This bad feeling seems to have run on all year, despite the Bishop's best efforts at reconciliation. On 17 November 1916 "the Subdean was ready to 'put his knife' into the Precentor in connexion with the Positive Organ employed at the Convention".

Diocesan demands still took up much of his time. In April 1916, the vicar of Potterhanworth had been cutting down trees and building new cottages. "On the whole, he has done well by the village. I wish he were more of a parson & less of an estate agent." On 8 April 1916 "the Chancellor [Johnston] & the Warden [Du Buisson] to confer with me about the Hostel". It was decided that it should close in June. On 27 June 1916, there was more conferring with the same two about the Hostel, to try to ensure that after the war it would be possible to reopen it and ensure that its work carried on. They looked at the memorandum "on the Relations between the Chancellor & Warden" which Hicks had drafted in 1914 when Johnston came.

It has never been completely revised, or agreed upon, for the
simple reason that the new Chancellor & the Warden & the Bp.
were all such friends, & so well understood each other ... & we
had no desire to delimit our frontiers.

But "we thought it wise to revise & draft the memorandum as a guide for those who may have to revive the Hostel, & start things afresh" after the war when they got it back for ordinands.

On 10 May 1916, Hicks wrote with amusement:

The Chancellor was away in London for the day, claiming a
book that had been stolen (?) from the Cathedral Library. He
proved his point & brought the precious volume back at night.

*He came into us after our supper at 8, & entertained us all with
the story of his day.*

Hicks tried to follow up exceptionally worrying cases such as that
of Mr Simmons, but they were not at all easy to deal with. By 25
June 1915 a meeting had to be called "to discuss the state of this
parish, & the Revd. T. C. Simmons' administration of the place";
then a Commission of Enquiry was started. But Simmons was still
there, though being complained of as "mad", in October 1916.

There was an Executive Committee meeting about the
Diocesan Conference of 1916 on 25 August when the
troublesome Cheney Garfit was "rather heated & contentious"
but Hicks restored good relations. The afternoon discussion at
the conference in September was "discursive & tame" because the
topic was vague, but Paul Ashby spoke well about the end of the
war and the problems which he thought would arise when the
soldiers came home. It was decided not to hold a conference in
1917 and to let the Executive Committee deal with any business
which was essential.

TEMPERANCE IN WARTIME

The years 1910–18 were a high point in the activities of the
United Kingdom Association, but the UKA was losing hope and
momentum by the end of the war. The war changed expectations.
On 4 August 1914, the King had issued various orders and
prohibitions about alcohol which were thought to be appropriate
for wartime. During the war, the UKA concentrated on arguments
similarly deemed appropriate for wartime. Lloyd George had made
a speech at Bangor in February 1916, "Drink is doing us more
damage in the war than all the German submarines put together."

In June of that year, at a local temperance meeting, Hicks
records that Leif Jones "made a great & clever speech".

"Prohibition during the War, & six months after" was the theme. It was, commented Hicks, "odd how strongly the Church was represented in the affair". There was also some effort later on this day in Louth to reach local children before they could become habituated to alcohol. A meeting for children was held "to whom I gave a Band of H[ope] Address", employing, it seems, some stock stories and illustrations he had found appealed and made sense to children: "(lion & mouse – watch – Rly train)". Turning out to listen despite a Zeppelin raid, the temperance enthusiasts in Cleethorpes were not put off. In June 1916, Hicks heard Canon Dalby making a speech there, urging an end to drinking to the end of the war at least, and a year later he sat in a chair on the back of a lorry in a procession going to a public meeting of the Lincolnshire Total Abstinence Union at Cleethorpes. There was strong enough concern about the alcohol problem in the country to enable Leif Jones to present Asquith with a memorial with 2 million signatures later in the August of that year. Many pressed for complete prohibition of the sale of intoxicants in wartime.

THE ANNUAL STOCKTAKING

On 24 June 1916, Hicks's annual stocktake of his achievements for the year still looks at the same "domestic" priorities for his work in the diocese. Even the National Mission is assessed for its local impact there:

1. I feel my position stronger in the Diocese, & the National Mission is helping me with the Clergy & others.

2. If I have not conquered my obvious sins, I think I can see them more clearly: – viz. evil thoughts, vanity, irritability – & also, a lack of composure & due dignity...

3. I think I have made a little progress in prayer, but O so little ... The next 4 years will be full of great events & issues – social, religious & moral. I might be found useful by God.

By 25 August 1916, at an Executive Committee meeting, Cheney Garfit was "rather heated & contentious – not with me, but all the others!" Hicks used his best peacemaking technique. "I befriended him, & all ended well." At the conference itself, on 28 September, attendance was low "owing to the war" and Cheney Garfit was controlled by others, being "squashed by Ld Heneage & the Dean". Cheney Garfit did not hesitate to take up the Bishop's time, as when he took up twenty minutes complaining "I had not dealt fairly with the Evangelicals".

Hicks admitted his views sometimes offended his clergy. In September 1916, he had been asked to address a "breakfast" for deanery clergy on "The personal life of the Clergyman in relation to social movements ... This moved me to a frank declaration of my views & feelings," he wrote in his diary. "I fear I astonished them. But they needed it. I think the time for reticence is over: we must be frank & fearless, – though endlessly kind." This does not seem to have gone down very well with the local clergy, who were perhaps expecting something less challenging. "They *tolerated* me, as an oddity," he wrote. Yet there were inevitably new needs to be met in wartime. On 23 October 1916, there was a meeting over the CETS provision of catering for soldiers in CETS huts. Proudfoot spoke and Hicks rated his words "thoughtful".

Some of the clergy of the diocese who felt very strongly the tug to join in and "do their bit" could be very inventive. Cobb, the vicar of Waddington, was visited on 8 September 1916, and Hicks wrote admiringly in his diary:

Cobb took us to his workshop & showed us how he turned the little aluminium discs etc. for aeroplane joints. They have to be exact to 1/1000 of an in. & even beyond that! He has never had one sent back! Before ordination he had been learning the art of a nautical instrument maker.

Chapter 17

The Loss of a Son

From mid-December 1916 to 11 March 1917, Hicks was ill for three months, and had to make brief catch-up notes in his diary. This was shortly before he was made a member of the House of Lords on 14 March 1917. Bishops enter the Lords as members by seniority and he had now been Bishop of Lincoln long enough to earn the privilege. That day he was presented by the bishops of Llandaff and Norwich, "& stayed on for the debate on the new Cotton Duties & India". He then became quite a regular attender, with more days in London expected of him as a result. He "read prayers" as "duty Bishop" in the House of Lords on 19 March and 22 March. In between, on 21 March, he had tea with Leif Jones at the House of Commons and also "had a few words with Asquith. Read Prayers at 4.15".

He was in London again for Convocation at the beginning of May. He went to the House of Lords on 2 May "& heard the Archbp. protest against Reprisals. Thence I hastened away to dine with the Bp. of Croyden (also Bp. Of Willesden – Perrin): a good talk on Temperance politics, when I advised them not to leave the CETS". But even when it became more familiar, the House of Lords was not a forum in which he seems to have felt tempted to be a speaker, even though he says he voted.

In April 1917, Ned was in hospital in Lincoln "for a further operation on his knee". His father visited him there a week later and found him bored in bed.

Then Edwin died of meningitis in Amiens. Hicks heard the news on Wednesday 16 May 1917. He puts it between two other items in the diary for that day, after a detailed analysis of what happened at the chancellor's Bible class at 11 a.m. and before a note that he had confirmed "three men in khaki from the flying-camp at Carlton" at 5:30 p.m. In reality, the news had come with the morning post. "Letters came announcing that dear Edwin died on Sat. last in Amiens, of cerebro-spinal meningitis." His comment is awkward, formal. "It is very sad: but people most kind." Then he had gone to the Bible class and concentrated hard on the discussion.

In this tragedy, as in other painful family events, he is very restrained in what he says in his diaries, though Agnes, in editing them after his death and removing some family comments, may have taken out some of what he said. The next day was Ascension Day. It brought an "influx of letters of sympathy concerning dear Edwin's death, & one or two further details of his illness". He went to Evensong at the cathedral. "More letters, & a quiet evening: with books on Social Reconciliation at the end of the War." He expressed surprise – and was evidently touched – at the even "greater volume" of letters of condolence he received in the next few days: "We have more friends than we know of, & their sympathy is a real support, as far as it goes".

His way of coping was to carry on as normal. On 18 May "about 40 came to luncheon. We would not have it put off for our sorrow's sake". From Tuesday 22 May to Friday 25th he was in London, at a Bishops' Meeting at Lambeth Palace working hard on a report, listening to a debate on conscientious objectors in the House of Lords, dining with Miss Picton-Turbervill to discuss "Women in the Church". On 22 May, after a meeting at Lambeth Palace when the pastoral needs of girl munition workers were further discussed, he went on to the House of Commons in search of Leif Jones, but did not find him or Charles Roberts to talk to. But he "walked away with G. B. Wilson". The diary does not say, but he seems to have left Agnes with Christina in Lincoln to comfort one another, with Christina no doubt in heightened fear for her own soldier husband's future safety.

Edwin's young widow, Alison, reappears in the diaries from time to time, though she is not mentioned there in the days immediately following his death. The Hickses seem to have done their best to make her feel she was still a member of their family. She remained in London and Hicks records that he saw her again in July 1917 and in 1918. He found her busy, actively at work, and not short of opportunity. He notes in 1917 that she is at Devonshire House (still then an aristocratic house) "well-occupied there with nice people. & therefore happy".

THE CLERGY AND NATIONAL SERVICE AGAIN

On 11 March 1917, the Bishop had "had long converse with Arch[deacon] Jeudwine about the Clergy & Natl Service". As we have repeatedly seen, this was becoming a problem area both within the diocese and nationally. By May 1917, Hicks counted more than ninety of his clergy who had left their parishes to work in various war-related capacities (factories, farming, education). On 19 June 1917, Hicks

> met the Conference of Archdeacons & Rural Deans. In the debate on Natl Service I discovered some jealousy of the clergy who are working in munitions & other services, on the part of the men who are left behind: very odd & rather painful.

Among the tasks which had fallen to the clergy who remained in their parishes, rather than leaving them to work for the war effort themselves, had been that of providing for the spiritual care of parishioners who joined the forces. This had been a "war work" task from early in the fighting. Soldiers were asked for the names of their vicars on joining, and the parish clergy received a letter of enquiry about them. One standard letter of recommendation of this sort survives in the following wording:

> *XXXX has joined the Army. His address will be Private*
> *XXXX. Etc. He gave your name as that of his Clergyman.*
> *It will be a kindness of you write to the lad [Crossed out and*
> *"him" typed over] and also to the Reverend YYY, Chaplain*
> *at the Station, for whom I enclose stamped and addressed*
> *envelope. Any information favourable to him/the lad will be*
> *helpful towards his success; while you may be sure that any*
> *communication you make to the Chaplain will be regarded as*
> *confidential, to be used only in a way that will help the recruit.*
> *If you are from any cause unable yourself to [do this please*
> *identify someone] "interested in him" who will.*

For those who felt called to offer more than this kind of home-based reference service for the departing soldier to ensure that he had appropriate pastoral care in the army, the obvious way to "serve" was as a chaplain to the forces. The diaries are full of references to such chaplains.

Not all the chaplains to the services actually served overseas. It was possible to do this work while remaining in one's parish or diocese, or at least in England. Hicks had a good deal of contact with the work of those who were giving pastoral support to troops in training in the diocese or those who had returned injured and were being nursed in local hospitals. On 29 May 1917, he had some talk with Bolam, "about his Chaplain's work at Carlton – and Scampton's needs". Scampton was one of several "flying camps" in Lincolnshire, each with about seventy-five to a hundred men. Here men were trained for the new "arm" of the armed forces, which was to become the Royal Air Force. They had to double as the home defence too, because the trained pilots were needed for service abroad.

PREBENDARIES' RIGHT TO PREACH IN THE CATHEDRAL

On 25 April 1917, Hicks was informed by Canon Woolley "about the grievances of the Prebendaries in the matter of the 'right' to preach on Sundays etc at Holy Comn. I shall have the controversy brought before me shortly". Canon Woolley seems to have had had rather a bee in his bonnet on this matter. In the 1920s he was still pressing for reform. He submitted a memorandum to the subcommission on Lincoln in 1926 in which he suggested that the residentiary canons had taken control of the cathedral from the later nineteenth century and that the prebendaries had found themselves excluded.

The trouble from the prebendaries first brought to the Bishop for determination in 1916 was apparently prompted by Canon Townroe. Hicks had noted on 17 November 1916 that he and the subdean had been "rather critical & tiresome" at a meeting of the Consultative Committee of the mission. (But he was capable of making a helpful suggestion, as he apparently did when the cathedral had a royal visit on 9 April 1918, and he proposed "the suitableness of a word of prayer for the nation & armies etc.")

Hicks made his determination and his Visitor's Decision in full is given in the diary:

> *My Dear Canon Townroe, After careful and impartial inquiry I am convinced that the Dean and Canons Residentiary form the only body which has the governance of the Cathedral and*

its Services. If so, they were within their rights in making
some changes, and even trying some experiments, with a view
to render the Cathedral Services more helpful to the people at
large. That you were requested to preach at Mattins rather than
at the Celebration at 11.30 involved no misuse of their powers
nor the infringement of any rights enjoyed by the prebendaries
[Decision dated 29 May 1917].

"HOME REUNION"

Hicks's own relations with the Nonconformists in his diocese, especially the Methodists, seem to have been uniformly positive, though he certainly did not carry all his clergy with him. He worked partly by organizing shared Bible study and theological discussion, though this could lead to disagreement as well as to better mutual understanding and an enlarged sense of Christian community. Seeking ecumenical reunion was a step further, however.

The subject of reunion came up again in June 1917, when certain questions about mutual recognition of ministry became thorny, as commonly happens in ecumenical dialogue where this is frequently the sticking-point preventing union. Hicks describes a meeting of "our Bible Class: 4 or 5 Nonconf. Ministers being there, & an equal number of ourselves". They discussed 1 John 4:1–3 and then the essay by C. H. Turner in the *Cambridge Mediaeval History* "on the historical evolution of the Xtian Ministry". Turner was a friend of Charles Gore and revised his *The Church and the Ministry* in 1919, "improving" it, to Gore's strong approval. The discussion revealed that the members of the Bible class were divided on Christian unity. The youngest Wesleyan minister present was all for it. But his senior said division was a good thing, "suiting all tempers, & stimulating zeal" etc. The next day Hicks heard Cheales's Address on Home

Reunion. It "made dear old Canon A. E. Moore almost jump out of his seat: presently he arose & 'delivered his soul' against going to meet Nonconformists".

The annual note which Hicks liked to write on 24 June, the anniversary of his consecration, seems hasty this year. "I could have wished for more leisure for quiet meditation. If I had to moralize or take stock, I might write exactly what I wrote June 24, of last year."

On 2 July 1917, there is a note of plans for a "service on Aug. 4 in the Arboretum *for all citizens* to be conducted by Ch. & Free Church alike". This took place on the third anniversary of outbreak of the war. "I was anxious about this united Service, but need not have been."

GOVERNMENT MOVES TO TACKLE THE SOCIAL PROBLEMS ARISING

Against the background of the detailed daily life of the diocese, there were very big issues to be addressed. The life of the nation was feeling the effects of war. There are hints in the diary that as Bishop of Lincoln, Hicks could see among his own people the implications of the great wartime social changes for the class system in which he had grown up. And of course he was now closer to the seat of power, hearing debates in the House of Lords and not just reading about them in *The Times*. Lord Salisbury commented in the House of Lords debate of 7 November 1917 on the nature of the social change which was ending the old comfortable features of the class system:

> *My Lords, we belong, many of us, to the old squires of England, who lived among our people, looked after them, and were friends with them. There was no division of classes, no two nations, as between us and the people who worked for us, and who I believe have been and are still fond of us. But, undoubtedly, when you*

look outside the ranks of the squires, the landed interest – and look
at the industrial conditions of England, a different set of things
prevails. A certain harsh industrialism of which I have spoken
has been responsible for what we have seen, and certain feebleness
and insincerity in the Governments who have had to deal with
the working-class questions.

Wartime exigencies had prompted plans to get sergeants and corporals to apply for commissions (temporary ones for wartime only) and be "temporary gentlemen". But class differences were not so easily expunged.

On 15 October 1917, Edward Hicks had

Some quiet talk with Lady Julia about Chas Roberts & his
going to India. I find her indignant that CR should have been
willing to go out "in the retinue" of ES Montague – who had
"deserted" Asquith. He is not a Commissioner.

Montagu was Undersecretary of State for India from 1910 to 1914, and Charles Roberts followed him in the office from 1914 to 1915. Hicks may not have been in a general way an activist in party-political matters, but he had noticed that "the tide of partisan jealously runs high & deep between the followers of Asquith & Lloyd George". After his conversation with Lady Julia, he even allowed himself an indiscretion. "I reported this to CPS[cott] to whom it was an interesting revelation. CPS is now a close friend of LlG."

Commissions of Inquiry were an important fact-finding device of the moment in politics. On 17 November 1917, Lord Salisbury called in the House of Lords for debate on the reports of the Commissions of Inquiry set up in various parts of the country to look into industrial unrest locally. They were exploring the changing relationship or employer and employed and also, inescapably, the class system and its contemporary adjustments.

A speech explaining the purpose of the Commissions was given in the House of Lords by Viscount Milner on 7 November 1917.

> *The Commission to inquire into the subject of industrial unrest was appointed on the 12th of June. The Reports of the eight sub-Commissions were presented on the 17th of July, together with a very useful summary calling attention to the principal points in them ... Some of these recommendations were not so much suggestions of practical reforms, or definite action which the Government could take, as the enunciation of general principles, excellent principles, which I should be the last to question.*

"There was not merely politically but socially a repercussion" of events "upon the labour situation and the social situation".

Viscount Milner tried hard to show sensitivity to the feelings of the "working classes", but he takes the class distinction itself for granted:

> *It is so very difficult, in discussing this subject, to avoid a sort of attitude of intolerable patronage towards the working-classes which I should desire to avoid. On the other hand, there is also a temptation – if I may use such a word – to truckle to the working-classes, to say things which we know or think will be pleasant to them, for the purpose of earning their applause. I shall try and avoid both risks, and I assure your Lordships, and any others, that I for one approach this subject in a spirit of the deepest sympathy with the working-classes.*

What he read in the reports, he said, was mistrust. The workers did not believe that the government would restore the pre-war conditions for workers as was promised.

The underlying reason, he suggested, was the state of relations between employers and employed. He drew attention to Disraeli's novel *Sibyl,* in which is depicted "the chasm which divided the two classes at that time. He spoke of the two nations – not the same division as *The Times* made the other day, the division between the rich and employing class and the poor".

> *There is education. I am not suggesting – do not know whether I shall command the assent of educationists in what I am I going to say – I am not suggesting that education necessarily should be pushed forward now. It is not urgent, in the sense that it cannot wait a year or so; but there is a question which cannot wait at all, and that is housing. I urge the Government not to neglect the housing difficulty.*

The Archbishop of York spoke.

> *our workers … have been harassed and harried, in a way which it is difficult for us to understand, by confusion in the orders for recruiting and medical examination. They have resented the system of leaving certificates, by which it was open to the employer to dismiss the man and not open to the man to leave the employer. They have, above all, been annoyed and irritated by the constant confusion between Government Departments, and by the consequent delays in the settlement of many important and pressing questions.*

The archbishop asked what plans had been framed for demobilization of the soldiers when the war ended. What was the government doing to ensure that there were not going to be more problems for ordinary people when the soldiers came home needing food and jobs and housing? This needed attending to without delay, he urged.

Problems about another urgent matter were looming. Before the war, the trade unions had won various concessions, which had been set aside in the exigencies of wartime. What was to be done to ensure "the restoration of the trades union regulations"? "It bristles with difficulty":

> *On the one hand, it is difficult to know what these regulations precisely are. I fancy many of them have hardly ever been written down. It would be exceedingly difficult to get evidence as to what has been suspended and as to what is to be revived. Many of them would be plainly inconsistent with the necessity of increased production when the war is over. And yet the Government are under the most solemn pledge to restore them, and the only way out of the difficulty obviously is that any modification of those former regulations should take place by consent of the trade unions themselves.*

THE STRENGTH OF BRITAIN MOVEMENT, AND CALLS FOR PROHIBITION

The UKA was still making its appearance in the diaries during the last years of the war and beyond, though during the war, some felt it was "idle to expect that the Temperance cause can escape the setback which other social reforms have had to meet". In a Lady Day Letter in 1917, Hicks wrote "The Drink Question has reached a curious crisis in Parliament". There was a plan by the Cabinet to cut down the output of beer from 36 million to 10 million barrels. "Well, of course the vast wealth and influence of 'The Trade' make this Government quite alarmed at their difficulties." It was alleged that no one could get elected as a Tory MP unless the "Trade" approved. Hicks saw the "[Drink] Trade" as the enemy of working people, but that made him enemies. He was even accused of heresy for advocating teetotalism.

G. B. Wilson was the UKA secretary with whom Hicks seems to have worked most actively. An example of the familiarity of their working together is in the diary for 19 October 1915. Hicks had been in Manchester:

> *Went over to UKA Office, had a nice talk with GB Wilson.*
> *Then to Central Hall, where we had an old-fashioned Council*
> *Meeting. Leif Jones ... masterly speech.*

On 15 October 1917, Hicks was in London, where he attended the "Council of Forty" of the UKA. The next day the council met and there was a "fine speech by Leif Jones". Again and again the pattern of making the most of an opportunity to meet is noticeable. In late September 1918, on a visit to London for a reunion meeting with Methodists, including clergy and laymen, "GB Wilson came to talk things over with" Hicks on temperance questions. He came to dine in January 1919 "to discuss Prohibition in the US".

Total Prohibition in the United States was later to cause more problems than it solved but the temperance movement in England included supporters of the idea of a total ban during the war. A "Strength of Britain Movement" poster survives from 1916 headed "THE REAL WASTE that is helping the Germans & draining away Britain's Strength". Under a dramatic picture of a leaking tank, the poster goes on:

> *Since the War began, Alcohol has wasted*
>
> *1. enough food to last the whole nation 100 days...*
>
> *2. Over 4,000,000 tons of coal*
>
> *3. £4,000,000 of the people's money*
>
> *4. Man-power equivalent to the entire nation standing idle*
> *100 days.*

The call was "to stop this enormous waste on Alcohol till the War is WON".

But this call for "prohibition" was focused on the special needs of the nation in wartime, and it went further than the temperance movement had generally done.

In his diary for 20 March 1917, Hicks records going with G. B. Wilson to Queen's Hall for a meeting on prohibition "organised by the Strength of Britain Movement ... Booth of L'pool in chair: a fine meeting & fine speaking. *But* the Govt is against it! alas! Bp of Llandaff's Resolution in H of Lords. Lord Milner's speech!"

The Strength of Britain Movement prompted some correspondence in *The Spectator* in 1917. On 11 May 1917, *The Spectator* published a letter deploring the failure of the government "to act on the mandate of the great meeting in Queen's Hall in March" and announcing a "national demonstration" to be held at the Albert Hall on Saturday 19 May. *The Spectator* gave the movement space again in 1919:

At the International Conference on Alcoholism, representing twelve countries, held during the sittings of the Paris Peace Congress, I had the honour, with Dr. C. W. Saleeby, F.R.S.E., and Mrs. Wakefield Richardson, of representing the Strength of Britain Movement. I presented our record of work at the session (presided over by M. Emil Vanffervelde, Belgian Minister of Justice) relating to war-time measures for curbing the liquor traffic. This record refers to the Conference of business men and others, called by the editor of the Spectator in January, 1916, which led to the inception of the movement ...

The Committee feel that though absolute Prohibition was not attained, yet the diminution of the pre-war output of beer to one-third and of spirits to one-half, has so effectively increased the efficiency of the nation and assisted the proper conduct of the war that the effort was well worth all the time, energy, and money expended.

WOMEN: A MORAL DANGER TO THE TROOPS?

Women who found work as waitresses in the military camps were commonly regarded as posing a moral danger, a temptation to the soldier. The problem was sufficiently worrying to have been discussed by the bishops at Lambeth on 25 May 1917. Hicks records that Billborough, the Bishop of Dover, had told him "of the employment (quite new) of girls in Flying Camps, for certain kinds of manual work ... They will need some care!" he comments.

A further solution was to enrol or enlist the waitresses in an organization which could impose rules and expectations on them, a Legion of Women. Hicks went on 6 June 1917 to Harlaxton Flying Camp. "Here we saw the Chaplain (a new but very nice man (Partridge)). We learned how careful & strict the WO is in the discipline of the waitresses". The waitresses "dress in Khaki, are under the governance of a Lady Supt, have very strict rules, & are discharged at once, if unruly. They are part of the Army itself. I am well satisfied – if the system is well worked". Otherwise "the opportunities for mischief are obvious".

Hicks was not the only bishop to be concerned that women were being employed on munitions work in factories where they had to live away from home. On 22 May 1917, he was at a meeting of the bishops, including the suffragans, at Lambeth Palace. In the discussion there was "a good deal about looking after the girls whom the Ministry of Munitions has *herded* by thousands in huts away from their homes, untended & uncared for – save in body".

The women munitions workers in the diocese of Lincoln needed a welfare officer. So did the women who worked in the flying camps, providing catering. On 12 June 1917, the diary notes one of a series of meetings at which his wife presided as "Bishop's wife". There was a

Committee of Ladies with AMH [Agnes] in the Morning Room. We reviewed the situation … (a) munitioner women: (b) young women engaged in Flying Camps. It did not seem that we could do very much; but our ladies were to get into touch with their Superintendents.

Christina took a lead in some work in the diocese during the war designed to help mitigate these difficulties. The Somerville College record gives some details of this "war work", which included being honorary secretary of Lindsey Women's War Agricultural Committee as well as welfare officer, Ministry of Munitions, Lincoln. The war agricultural committees for individual counties were launched in the autumn of 1915 to try to improve wartime agricultural production. Women were encouraged into work on the land as a Land Army to replace the male agricultural workers missing at the Front. The Ministry of Munitions was created from 1915, when a shortage of shells was becoming a crisis.

Apparently the women working in the camps did not all present a moral danger because on 15 December 1917 Hicks held a "simple Confirmation" in the cathedral which included "several soldiers from Scampton & some nurses & 'Brown' women workers".

"VOTES FOR WOMEN" AGAIN

On 18 December 1917, Hicks went to the House of Lords, on the "second day of the Debate on the 2nd Reading of the Electoral Reform Bill, which includes votes for women". For this visit, on his seventy-fourth birthday, Hicks attended the debate in response to a special request. "I did not want to waste time or money by a cold journey in mid-winter. But the Church League for Women's Suffrage wanted me to be there as the vote was expected tonight," he explains. He did not regret it.

It was rather an interesting Debate. Ld Halsbury (as Ld
Chaplin later) cursed the Bill, but cursed still more their
wretched fate in finding themselves forced to support it, lest, by
opposing it, they might imperil the Govt whom they trusted
to carry through the War! The Lord Chancellor & others also
spoke: I was silent.

The speeches, of course, are on record in Hansard. What Lord
Halsbury actually said was, "I shall be voting for a Bill which I believe
to be a bad Bill and a mischievous Bill in its effects hereafter", but
better than bringing the government down. Viscount Chaplin was
willing to admit that his views on "woman suffrage" had changed.
On some points "my views, I frankly own, have been more or less
modified". But he still agreed with John Bright's point in a speech
in the Commons that if women were allowed the vote they would
have to be allowed to stand for election:

Are your Lordships prepared to see women in Parliament,
in the other House, or in this, taking their places upon these
benches and exercising all the rights and privileges that your
Lordships enjoy at present … I can only say that I am not.

It seems that Lord Halsbury was essentially saying that this huge
constitutional change was not something to be rushed through in
the exceptional circumstances of wartime:

I think that it is a very bad Bill because it is brought in at a
time when it does not admit of real consideration. To re-create
a whole Constitution is a thing that you ought not to do in
the middle of a great war. I suppose that no one would doubt
such a proposition. If you bring in a new Constitution at such
a time you are probably bringing into conflict every one of
the great questions that have pervaded the political life of the
last century, and you should not do that at a time when His

*Majesty's Ministers ought to be, and no doubt are, employed
every day and every hour in the consideration of those things
which must arise in war. It is wrong that at such a time you
should have all these political questions brought together and
decided without the consideration that they ought to have and
would have received had they been brought forward at a more
opportune time.*

The Marquess of Crewe reminded the House that many jobs were
now being done by women to meet wartime needs. That made
it harder to rule out their eligibility for the rewards of political
engagement. They got both the vote and the right to be MPs in the
end, but not until after the war.

WOMEN AS LAY READERS?

Another area of prolonged debate about the changing position
of women had one of its heightened moments in 1917. The
shortage of clergy during the First World War made it necessary
to relax the restrictions on the uses to be made of lay readers.
Could women be lay readers? Now for the first time women were
licensed as readers in nearly two dozen dioceses.

On 28 October 1915, Hicks had mentioned Sister Violet,
"an ex-deaconess, who was allowed to come & nurse her
cousin Miss Cole". The grateful invalid had made her wealthy
by a large bequest in her will and now she was taking a house
and "corresponding (by request of the Deaconesses Association)
with all the D[eacon]esses who are unattached to any Society,
or isolated all over the world". Deaconesses had been accepted
in the Church of England in the later nineteenth century, when
the movement arrived from Germany. They had been doing good
work in the second half of the nineteenth century, especially
in areas of urban poverty. They tended to live in more or less

informal sisterhoods, not taking strict vows like nuns. Nor were they ordained. They were not the same as deacons and they could not aspire to become priests or bishops.

What was the potential role of women in the life of the church beyond this provision to enable those who felt this calling (mostly gentlewomen) to work to help the urban poor? Hicks was not a radical about the ordination of women. Maude Royden of the Church League commented that though "he desired to see women on the same footing as laymen in the Church, with the same opportunities of service and the same rights", "he did not agree with those who, like myself, desired to see them on an equality throughout, even in the priestly office". When he found he could not go this far he resigned the presidency of this league.

Edward Hicks's resistance to the suggestion that women might be priests did not extend to women preachers. He commented that Maude Royden had preached "a fine sermon" at the City Temple on 18 March 1917. A remark of 26 April 1918 suggests he really had appreciated it because he referred to it as the basis for a sermon of his own that day at Robey's ironworks. Yet she had broken new ground in being accepted as a preacher there.

This was a controversy of the moment. In the diary for 24 May 1917, Hicks notes that he dined with:

> *Miss Picton-Turbervill who collaborated with Streeter in the little book "Women in the Church" & Miss Leaf who lives with her. (Miss PT told me that women were now being invited to read the lessons (as laymen) in Churches. Canon Charles & his wife also with us. A pleasant evening.*

Burnett Hillman Streeter (1874–1937) was an Oxford don and cleric.

Miss Picton-Turbervill (1872–1960) was allowed to preach at North Somercotes in Lincolnshire after the end of the war, a first for the Church of England. This was one of Hicks's problem parishes. The archdeacon, John Wakeford, and Samuel Proudfoot, always one of Hicks's close friends, disagreed over whether it should have been allowed. He had to deal with the controversy which arose over this episode. Edward Hicks was well aware of the contemporary discussion which was afoot, and willing enough to go as far as he felt he could in giving women an equal role with men in the church. But the time had not yet arrived when even a radical and rather "feminist" bishop could put his support behind the ordination of women.

CONSCIENTIOUS OBJECTION AGAIN: THE PROBLEM OF ILL-TREATMENT OF OBJECTORS

The topic of conscientious objection, which was important to Hicks because it affected his clergy and people, was discussed again in Parliament on 14 November 1917. The problem of subjecting conscientious objectors to successive terms of imprisonment was still causing concern. Lord Parmoor was leading resistance again. Once more, notable examples were put forward. Joshua Rowntree, a Quaker, son of an MP, with an Oxford degree, had "accepted the post of lecturer at a Settlement for men and women who desired to continue their education at continuation classes": "He is now serving his second sentence of two years hard labour in Armley Gaol, Leeds, where, according to the last report, he was in hospital." Here was another Quaker "wantonly withdrawn from about the most useful work that could be done, from a national standpoint, at the present time, and condemned to debility of mind and body". All sorts of punishments were described. Prisoners were being subjected to extreme cold; one had died of consumption; one had been chained up in extreme heat in Egypt. This, it was suggested, was torture.

One infamous case involving the alleged mistreatment of conscientious objectors had come to notice in Edward Hicks's diocese, at Cleethorpes.

This was the setting for the controversial Conscientious Objector case of the summer of 1917. The matter had been discussed in the House of Commons on 4 July when Mr Needham had asked the Undersecretary of State for War:

> *whether his attention has been called to extracts of a letter from James Brightmore, the Pit, Shane Camp, Cleethorpes; whether the punishment described has been awarded with his consent; and whether Brightmore is allowed to receive letters from his relatives?*

Charles Trevelyan had a question too. He:

> *asked the Undersecretary of State for War*
>
> *(1) whether he is aware that it is stated at Cleethorpes Camp that James Brightmore, who has recently been subjected to ill-treatment there as a conscientious objector, is being sent out at once to France; whether, as Brightmore has proved the genuineness of his objection by suffering two terms of imprisonment, he will see that the man is not taken out to France;*
>
> *(2) whether his attention has been called to the treatment of James Brightmore, D Company, 3rd Manchesters, at Cleethorpes Camp; whether he is aware that among other ill-treatment he was kept for a prolonged period in a pit 10 feet deep and 40 inches by 18 inches wide, and full of water at the bottom; whether the fact that he has served sentences of 112 days and six months' hard labour are sufficient proof of the genuineness of his conscientious objections; whether he will cause inquiry to be made into the case; and whether, if the*

allegations are not disproved, he will call those responsible for the proceedings to strict account?

The reply was that

This allegation has previously been brought to my notice, and in consequence on the 28th June I directed that a staff officer should proceed at once to Cleethorpes Camp to interview every conscientious objector there and to receive his complaints and to forward a full report. I received a telegram yesterday that a report was on its way, but it has not yet reached me. There is no truth in the suggestion that Brightmore is being sent to France.

The questioning became remorseless. Mr Whitehouse

asked the Undersecretary of State for War whether he can supply any information as to the case of James Brightmore, a conscientious objector, at Cleethorpes; whether he was placed in a hole in the ground about 12 ft. deep which contained water; and whether he was supplied with blankets and an oil sheet and told he would be kept there until he gave in or was sent to France?

The Undersecretary of State for War replied:

I have received a report on this case, but as regards Private Brightmore the matter yet remains somewhat obscure, and I am making further inquiry. But I am able to tell my hon. Friend that as the result of the visit of an officer of the staff of the General Officer Commanding the Humber Garrison, the complaints of all conscientious objectors at Cleethorpes have been investigated, and steps taken to ensure that they are treated in every way as other men of the unit. The case of Private Brightmore calls for further investigation, but of the

*four other conscientious objectors who were personally seen by
the staff officer, three had no complaints and one complained
that he did not receive his full rations.*

Mr Whitehouse had another question. He

*asked the Undersecretary of State for War whether he can now
give any information as to inquiries made concerning the
allegations of ill-treatment of a conscientious objector named
Jack Gray, No. 58541, 84th Training Reserve Battery, in the
camp at Hornsea; whether he was frog-marched, put into a
sack and repeatedly thrown into a pond, and pulled out by a
rope round his body; and whether under this treatment he has
given in?*

Once more the Undersecretary of State for War found himself
unable to answer fully:

*No reply has yet been received to my inquiries, but I will not
fail to write to my hon. Friend whenever I receive the reply.*

Mr Trevelyan was still not satisfied. He next

*asked the Undersecretary of State for War whether he has yet
had a Report on the case of five conscientious objectors, Garland,
Middleton, Price, Keighley, and Davis, in the 3rd Manchester
Regiment; whether they have been sent to France; and, if so,
whether he has had them returned to England in accordance
with the promise of the late Prime Minister?*

This time a reply was available following enquiries:

*On the 19th June a letter was dispatched to headquarters in
France saying that there was reason to believe that these men
had been sent overseas, having been summarily awarded*

detention without being given the option of trial by court-martial, and further requesting that in the event of their being brought to trial by court-martial they were to be sent back to this country to undergo their sentence. I have not yet learnt whether they have been returned to this country, but I will communicate that information to my hon. Friend as soon as it reaches me. Reports from the Command concerned show that these men were irregularly sent to France, and that they should have been remanded for trial by court-martial in this country.

This is a record which suggests that the treatment of conscientious objectors was neither fair nor consistent.

Further discomforts arose from another quarter. Men who had been called up and not tried to escape by claiming that they had conscientious objection could feel very strongly about any CO being "let off". On 24 July 1917, Hicks records that "Alex. Wilson … has joined the Friends & has today been to visit Henry Brightmore at Cleethorpes, a C.O." At a comment from the colonel, the Bishop put the other side. The colonel told him that "The men are almost in *mutiny* about this C.O. being let off: they will not be persuaded to go out on to the next draft etc." Hicks notes, "They little knew my views, & were astonished when I gently let them know".

Hicks's position was not uncontroversial among the bishops. In one of the debates in the House of Lords, the Archbishop of Canterbury stressed that no one had envisaged what had happened, that men would refuse even to do work instead of fighting. The Bishop of Oxford spoke on the "embittering effect which the treatment of conscientious objectors is having" on people.

At home in his diocese, he did his best to support individuals whose conscientious objection was telling against them. On

19 October 1917, he writes, "to Training Committee, where I succeeded in securing a grant for Pickering ... this student being a C.O. is in ill odour with many." Pickering had made an earlier appearance in the diaries, on 3 May 1913, when he and "Mr. Barham [both] of St. Paul's Brotherhood, Sheffield" wanted the Bishop's

> *sympathy & advice for their Hostel etc., & P. wants me to ordain him. They are the originators of a Lay settlement of earnest Churchmen for work (esp. Temperance & Purity) amongst lads & youths: Sheffield a very bad place.*

Hicks also did his best to offer comfort and approval pastorally. On 6 December 1917, the diary notes, Guy Hayler "told me the story of his 3 sons, one in the army & 2 C.O.s!" On 6 September 1918, the diary records, "I tried to visit a C.O. at the jail: Fenner Brockway, Editor of the 'Labour Leader'."

THE ROUTINE WORK OF THE DIOCESE

"Emergency theology" sometimes became a challenge as the war continued. Hicks's clergy came to him with difficult questions arising out of the fortunes of war. What was the right thing to do in a situation of life and death where a soul's eternal future might be at stake? In September 1917

> *Bunbury came to discuss something he had done as Hospital Chaplain. Was he right? The f. & m. [father and mother] of a young flying-officer had brought him to the bedside of their son aet. 18 who had had a "crash", & was unconscious & dying. He was unbaptized: for his F. had "wished him to decide for himself when he grew up". The Father was now sorry & wished he had done otherwise.*

Bunbury had baptized him and Hicks approved "thinking of the faith of the [fam] and infant Baptism, & the fundamental fact of the Love of God".

There were also examples of unusual practical pastoral devices invented by the clergy. On 13 December, the Bishop stayed the night at Gainsborough with the vicar, Mr Marris and his wife. "She is a wonderful woman: no servant but all in order, & herself always nice & pleasing in dress & manner." He wrote about Marris at some length. Marris was

> *full of the doings of his soldier son Oswald, & the d. He is doing a v. good work in looking after his "soldier-boys", whom he writes to every week. They number now 77. Sometimes sweethearts or wives will ask him to write "to our –" Once a sweetheart came to ask him to write a letter for her (!) which he did. He has become passionately devoted to the poor, & the manual workers, & their cause: quite a socialistic democrat.*

Hicks's optimism in that Charge of 1912 was still being justified. A "little Mission Church" depending on lay readers won his approval on 23 December 1917.

> *It was at New Boultham … The Triumvirate of Lay readers were there, & active. An excellent lady organist played the American O. The room about half-full – which a little disappointed me: but all was hearty & reverent. A good work is going on.*

Chapter 18

Looking to a Post-war World

The year 1918 began badly for Hicks. "*Aegrotabam* ... I was not well" he wrote in a note covering 1 to 4 January. He made himself get up and go into town in the end and he says he was grateful to his suffragan bishop for taking a confirmation for him. He commissioned a few lay readers on 5 January, including Mr Culverwell, a "nice young fellow who helps old Mr. Grayson", one of Hicks's vicars, who had been "invalided from shell-shock". The next day he learned that the dean, who had gone to preach before the King at Sandringham for Epiphany, had ruptured a blood vessel and was "dangerously ill". Fry was to recover and live until 1930, but this was no moment for a tired and ageing bishop to lose the support of one of his key diocesan figures.

The next day, 7 January, a letter of attack by "BEWILDERED LAYMAN" appeared in the *Lincolnshire Echo*:

> *Sir, May I without comment – which I'm afraid would be too caustic for publication – call attention to the Bishop of Lincoln's extraordinary attitude on the war.*
>
> *"For England to join in this hideous war would be treason to civilisation and disaster to our people. God save us from the*

war fever." (A message from the Bishop prominently published in the "Daily News and leader" of August 3, 1914).

"We felt in August, 1914, that we had no alternative open to us except everlasting disgrace. So with an awful sense of responsibility and even of fear we (as in duty bound) embarked upon it." (Lincoln Cathedral, January 6, 1918). Yours etc., BEWILDERED LAYMAN.

Hicks inserted the cutting into his diary but no responses, so perhaps Bewildered Layman did not succeed in beginning a campaign of disapproval.

Did Hicks betray his pacifist principles as Bewildered Layman accuses? It is not easy to be a bishop. If you speak out about public affairs, people will say that is not your role as a church leader. If you keep silent about national problems, people will say you are out of touch with ordinary people. Either way, your public pronouncements are remembered. Your critics may throw your first thoughts back in your face if you change your position in the face of events. "There is always a certain viperine element in the lower Tory Press & its publications, that seeks to attack me, & misrepresent me with Churchpeople," wrote a weary Hicks.

On the same day in January another issue that was bothering him was temperance, as his diary records. He and Agnes had been to Colwyn Bay for a few days' holiday, stopping off in Manchester on the way.

At Manchester I called at the UKA & had a nice chat with GB Wilson: he is sad & anxious about the Alliance, & has little faith in the grand schemes of dear Proudfoot for getting a larger membership. He complained of the dubious loyalty of Bingham & others, who were ready at any moment to baffle the President in any place because of their utter dislike of Lady Carlisle & her circle.

These are worries focused on the personalities and internal politics of the movement. But he also felt that the whole cause was at risk of failure:

But I gather from all that he said that the urgency of Drink Restriction is being felt increasingly & the feebleness of the Govt on the question is being realized by the people at large.

A few days in London followed from 15 to 17 January, where he did duty in the House of Lords, saying prayers and even voting, but *"against"* a Referendum on women's suffrage (against the Referendum, not the cause itself). Back in Lincoln, he was able to get a full account of the collapse of the dean. He had fainted getting out of bed, fallen and hurt himself, and then during the service he fell again and blood was seen coming from his mouth. The authorities at Sandringham sent for doctors and Mrs Fry, who was brought from home by car. But it had turned out not to be serious, only a result of the earlier fall which had broken a blood vessel in his "stomach".

Agnes was feeling the strain too. On 27 January Hicks wrote that she was

not well: complains of rheumatism & pains in the nape of her neck, & has a poor appetite. She feels the strain of catering for a large household at a time of great & increasing scarcity of all the means of life.

But he had to go back to London for the Bishops' Meeting and to act as one of the bishops who consecrated the Dean of Durham as Bishop of Hereford on 2 February. He also attended a meeting with the Methodists about reunion, where the familiar problems about what modern ecumenism would call "mutual recognition of ministry" got in the way.

Back in Lincoln that afternoon, he found "Chapman, father of a C.O. waiting for me: sad interview – alas!" Alison, the widow of his dead son, was there too, "looking well, but rather tired: she is brave & dutiful". (A year later, the following February, she was there again "'fagged out', & betrayed this morning a bronchitic cough & slight temperature. The weather was snowy & inclement. So she was kept in bed".)

Hicks took what comfort he could from his home life, although the diary often lacks the whimsy and gentle wit of earlier years. He says he was "much moved" to have Alison, Christina, and her husband there when he celebrated Holy Communion at 8 a.m. in the cathedral the next morning, 3 February. Then it was back to London for Convocation and back again to Lincoln, a commuting schedule which was now becoming punishing.

MISS TODHUNTER CAUSES TROUBLE AGAIN

Replacing the chaplain at the training college had not resolved things. On 9 February 1918, Chatterton, now chaplain, came to Hicks to complain "about his trying experiences as Chaplain: Miss Todhunter's ill-temper & 'Catholic' rigour". Miss Todhunter herself went on to buy and rename after herself a successful girls' school in Manhattan, and the college grew into what is now Bishop Grosseteste University.

THE LOSS OF A SUFFRAGAN BISHOP

MacCarthy, Hicks's suffragan who had helpfully taken a confirmation for him in January, had visited him on 20 October 1917 with some bad news. He had foolishly entrusted "a London friend" with, as Hicks confided to the diary, "all his savings, expecting a *very* high percentage, but *nothing* came of it!" The worry was seriously affecting his health. Now he wanted to retire from his bishopric at Christmas and from the rectory at Easter (with a pension).

It was urgent to find a replacement. Not for the first time, an existing "colonial" bishop came in handy in an emergency. In the Middle Ages it had come to be believed that the "orders" of deacon, priest, and bishop were indelible. Once the Holy Spirit had made a man a bishop, he would always be a bishop. He could retire from a particular bishopric but he remained a bishop.

MacCarthy's prospective replacement, Bishop John Edward Hine (1857–1934), from Stoke, came to discuss the appointment with Hicks on 13 February 1918. He had already been to stay with MacCarthy to learn what was involved in the post. He was medically qualified and had served as a missionary as well as a doctor in Africa, and seemed keen to be MacCarthy's replacement. However, Stoke was seven miles from Grantham, Hine had no car and there was no public transport. He would need to be paid travelling expenses. With this and the income from the Stoke living and an additional £100 (we are not told where from) he would be able to live and support his two sisters who lived with him.

At that first meeting, Hicks had found him pleasant enough though "rather taciturn". In June 1918 he instituted Hine as rector of Stoke and also made him a prebendary, giving him the Prebend of Langford Ecclesia.

> *He is a great traveller, with a wonderful memory: thinks in the concrete: not reflective; positive & happy in his beliefs, but has seen enough of the world to be tolerant & wish to round off angularities … The two Miss Hines are nice, gentle ladies: not young: the tall, big one is very delicate & can do little. The little one, the younger – is very quick & active in mind & body.*

On 2 March, attended by the two archdeacons and the chancellor and his chaplain, Hicks deposed one of his priests, William Miller Reid, from his orders. He described it as "a painful experience, which I hope never to repeat". Reid had been causing trouble at Immingham docks and had been the subject of a deputation of protest from "vigorous members of the Natl Union of Railwaymen" because of his "overbearing ways". But that would not have led to the rare and extreme sanction of deposing a priest, and the diary does not explain the reason for this quite exceptional act. John Wakeford was also causing difficulties by his "unwise behavior", which had prompted a local rebellion and his own loss of temper. Hicks repaired the fences by making a visit on 9 March where he let everyone have their say, and Wakeford "very kindly kept himself very quiet".

March, which Hicks described in the diary as the season of "my Spring Confirmations", meant "almost incessant travelling" and confirmations sometimes twice a day. Numbers were good, which gave him hope, "but it is a sad time, & one notes the large number of people in Church that are dressed in black". On Palm Sunday (March 24) he came close to complaining (in Latin) in his diary about noisy small children at Matins (*puerculis presentibus*).

On Wednesday of Easter week he had a visit from Mrs Hill, who confessed to being a "slave of drink" ("port wine"). She had given up alcohol for the past two months but she said she and her husband "had never been warned of the danger", though she now remembered an address the Bishop had once given at Woodhall Spa. Her husband was ill with liver disease and they were now destitute. She wanted to move into his diocese, but the Bishop of Ely and their vicar at Godmanchester said she must go into a home. "The disgrace & the cost!" she cried.

After Easter, Hicks and Agnes went "quietly" away for a few days in Skegness, and he mislaid his pectoral cross, causing much upheaval for Agnes who "raised the hue & cry". They were back for a royal visit to the Munition Works on 9 April. The dean showed the King round the cathedral, and Hicks took charge of the queen. At Hicks's spontaneous suggestion, the party knelt and he said "a few words of simple, extempore prayer ... for the nation & for the soldiers".

Then it was two days in London again and the news of the Manpower Bill which "*conscripts* the Clergy for Non-Combatant Service" for the first time, so desperate was the shortage of military manpower by now. Hicks held a meeting in Lincoln with the two archdeacons, to consider what steps to take. The proposal was quashed within days "probably through the influence of the Irish RC Bps".

Nevertheless, there was controversy in the newspapers. J. E. Chelmsford argued in a letter to *The Times* on 15 April that clergy were needed in their parishes more than ever now that wives were widowed and children left fatherless. In the same issue was recorded the Parliamentary debate on certificates of exemption, in which Leif Jones took part. Would it end with every man in the country being called up, it was asked, even if he had "only one leg or no leg at all?"

The 27 April 1918 was spent by Hicks in drafting a circular to the clergy about enlistment and National Service. Then on the 30th he was at a meeting of Convocation in London, where he notes, "Most of the day occupied in discussing the duty of Clergy & National Service & esp. enlisting in active service."

Some of his clergy were apparently still keen to join up for active service. On 7 September 1918, Hicks visited Browne, vicar of Keelby. "He is not at all a robust man: but his patriotism led him to *enlist* as Private." He had never been sent abroad, but was put to work in the canteen and had now had an operation. "He lies very weak, but may eventually get up, & home, *for a time only*", according to the doctor. Perhaps his experience had led to a rethinking of his simple ideals and he found he had a lot to think about. "He seems very shy of spiritual appeals, or dry: so I found."

Patriotic feelings could be strong and simple among the clergy. On 13 September 1918, Hicks records, "Walker of

Kettlethorpe came & told me of his difficulties … would like to get a Commission in the Army: aged 47 – to be a Lieut. in the Infantry. This I rejected." He seems to have diagnosed an underlying restlessness and suggested Walker should seek a change of living. Talk to your patroness, he urged him.

All this posed complicated problems of ethics. Should those in holy orders be willing to kill, even to save the nation from a dangerous invasion? Hicks does not discuss all this in his diaries. His focus is always on the individual and his welfare. He does not judge. He accepts that his clergy are engaged in painful and honest struggles. A bishop in wartime could find himself short of priests if his clergy joined the army, but he never seems to have urged that point of view on a clergyman determined to leave his parish and join up.

There was some friendly sparring with his personal chaplain, who refused to be paid and had been secretly repaying the £100 a year which Hicks had insisted on giving him, by any means he could, such as putting money into Hicks's account at the bank, or that of Agnes. Hicks's energy was returning a little, and with it pleasure in his work as a bishop. On 15 April he wrote in delighted capitals that he had taken part in the founding of the new high school for girls in Grimsby. His routine activities went steadily on in the diocese and in London.

LEAVING THE OLD PALACE

Meanwhile, the Hickses had been moving house. The 24 April 1918 was Lincoln's Day of Prayer for the war crisis. It was also the day when Hicks noted that the "considerably increased Income Tax as declared by Monday's budget" was going to make it impossible for them to go on occupying the Old Palace "as we do at present". They would not be able to afford it.

He seems to have acted quite rapidly after this to offer the

Old Palace for use as an "additional Hospital" for the Red Cross, because on 18 May representatives of the Red Cross came to have a look, to see if the Palace would be suitable. They thought it might, if they could afford to staff it with doctors and nurses. On 5 June, the diary records, the Red Cross had said "*they do want it at once*". There was an empty house in Vicar's Court, which had once been Canon Foster's, or the house once occupied by the physician Dr Mansel Sympson who sometimes drove the Bishop about the diocese. Into one of these the Hickses thought they could move in order to live more cheaply, if the Bishop kept his study in the Palace and use of the chapel.

Hicks's diary speaks rather proudly of Christina's energy and achievement in her war work, where she could do something to help and support ordinary working women whose potential employments had been radically changed by the war. Late in the war he wrote a diary note on an exhibition she had organized which he had gone to see with her (15 May 1918):

> *With Tina to town, to see the Women's Exhibition of War-works & workers at Boots': WAAAC; WRN; Land Army, & others: a remarkable crowd & show. Outdoor meeting at Cornhill. Miss Stack came later to stay (WAAC) for the night.*

Christina's war work exemplifies the tacit expectation that while ordinary women would be getting their hands dirty doing new sorts of jobs, gentlewomen ("ladies") would serve on committees to help them. They would be unlikely to be found in the munitions factories themselves.

ANOTHER VISITATION OF THE DIOCESE

Hicks was now preparing for a new Visitation of the diocese, after four years of war and a lot more experience of the diocese and its needs. However, he was ill during the period of this Visitation. On 8 June he wrote his diary entry for 28 May 1918, when he had begun his Visitation at 11:30 a.m. at Lincoln. "Delivered the first part of the Charge *extempore*". He planned to cover six topics, and to do it twice, an item at each place, as he worked his way from Lincoln to Grantham, Sleaford, Horncastle, Louth, Spilsby, Boston, Spalding, Grimsby, Brigg, Scunthorpe, and Gainsborough. The six topics were to be the war and the current Manpower Bill; the Prayer Book, attitudes to the Papacy and the Reformation; Christian Reunion; the Christian citizen; the position of women in the Church; and labour and the Church. But on Trinity Sunday afternoon he had a "violent bilious attack" which "the doctors pronounced" to be caused by an enlargement of the liver. He took as much rest as he could over the weekend between the Horncastle visit on the Friday and the Louth one on the following Tuesday, and managed to carry on. On Friday 7 June he sat down with Agnes to discuss whether they should or must leave the Old Palace and if so, where they should go to live. The following Saturday was to be the baptism of the Hickses' new grandaughter, Mary's child, who was to be called Christina Margaret. Edward Hicks was to have christened her himself, but his doctors "forbad the journey" to Manchester and Agnes went off alone to be there. Journeying soon went on, however, and Hicks returned to his travels and his duties.

MOVING DAY

Edward and Agnes chose Vicar's Court to move to and on 15 July there was "*much moving of our goods*" into it. After this hurry there was a delay, because the War Office mislaid the paperwork and the new hospital was "still waiting (impatiently)" for its certificate when Hicks went to visit the Old Palace on 7 September to have "a look" at it now it was ready to serve as a hospital. It was able to hold an Open Day preparatory to beginning work on 25 September. All this was perhaps to be wasted effort because the incompetence and delay with the paperwork and the decision-making was overtaken by the end of the war. By 1919 the talk was of returning buildings to their normal uses and how long it was going to take.

INDUSTRIAL RELATIONS BECOME UNSETTLED

As it dragged on, war was making the workers nervous about what was going to happen to pay and working conditions when it was over. There were signs of discontent in Lincoln as elsewhere. Working conditions had been improved by hard campaigning by trade unions before the war. There was fear that the loss of manpower and the changed arrangements the war made necessary would make it unlikely that what had been achieved would be restored when it ended. These were all live concerns in the diocese.

John Henry Whitley (1866–1935), Liberal MP for Halifax from 1900, had an industrial background. In 1917 he was appointed to the chairmanship of a committee which was to report on "The Relations of Employers and Employees". This was conceived to meet a wartime need, and to seek solutions to the growing concerns about industrial unrest. The *Whitley Report* proposed that there should be regular consultation meetings, though these failed to establish themselves in most industries.

Sidney and Beatrice Webb were at a high point of their influence as socialist intellectuals. They had taken a radical and challenging view of the changes to workers' conditions during the war, seeing them as part of a conspiracy against the working classes:

> *The Munitions Act and the Defence of the Realm Act, together with the suppression of a free press, has been followed by the*

Cabinet's decision in favour of compulsory military service.
This decision is the last of a series of cleverly-devised steps –
each step seeming at once harmless and inevitable, even to the
opponents of compulsion, but in fact, necessitating the next step
forward to a system of military and industrial conscription.
(Beatrice Webb, Diaries, 6 March 1911 – 8 December 1916,
p. 714, 2 January 1916, http://digital.library.lse.ac.uk/objects/
lse:six767gol)

When she wrote this, Beatrice Webb claimed that this amounted to the creation of a "servile state". Conscription would begin with unmarried men (without the vote) in industries not unionized, and then it would take married men and other industries too.

Christianity and Industrial Problems was published in 1918 as a Church of England contribution to this discussion. The first edition sold well but there had been some criticism of its analysis and proposals in 1918, and by 1927 there had been a General Strike. The text was reissued in 1927, unchanged, but with a context-setting preface by Edward S. Talbot, formerly Bishop of Winchester, in which he explained its intentions. He had chaired the "body of members of the Church of England which had prepared it". This body met frequently, and "thrice it sat for successive days". The report, he stressed, "sprang out of the War". (Hicks had commented of Talbot at a meeting in 1914 that he was "as usual" "on the fence".) The foreword to the original 1918 edition was written by the Archbishop of Canterbury. This report had been one of five commissioned by the church. Its theme was to be "Christian principles and their Social Application", especially in relation to industry.

The report pointed to the "unjustifiable position of subordination in which many wage-earners were placed by the organisation of modern industry". It favoured the idea that trade unions would be able to maintain a balance. It took the view that the fostering of the motivation of sheer greed was a bad thing. "Economic motives are good servants but bad masters, and the danger of a society which exalts them unduly is that it may evoke a spirit which it cannot control." It stressed the dangers of the coexistence of poverty and riches in times when there is more wealth but it is unfairly distributed. "Many have too little, while others have too much." It cited recent research on earnings. It framed the motto: "Co-operation for Public Service, not Competition for Private Gain, the True Principle of Industry."

This was the framework within which the Church of England was looking ahead towards taking a moral lead in social affairs at the end of the war. The refugees, who might have complicated things, began to remove themselves. The Hickses' group in the Old Palace seem to have found lodgings elsewhere early on.

THE WAR TO END ALL WARS?

Hicks's mentions of the Church of England Peace League in the diary in the later war years are few, but he still seems to have hoped that some kind of international peacekeeping organization would be established to prevent future wars. In November 1918, Miss Huntman, then its secretary, dined with the Bishop "& we discussed our plans for the Annual Meeting in January". When the meeting took place on 22 January 1919 it was looking to the future and approving the plans for the formation of the League of Nations at the conclusion of the war. There was a "fine speech" by the Bishop of Oxford, Charles Gore, and another by Canon J. H. B. Masterman (1867–1933), author of books on British politics and foreign policy. "All were very much pleased with the meeting", which adopted a Resolution:

> *That this meeting trust that the terms of Peace now being formulated in Paris, will be based in the principles of a League*

*of Nations, and that the League will embody & establish the
ideas which have been proposed to the world by such men as
President Wilson & Lord Grey of Fallodon.*

ECUMENICAL ADVANCES AND THE FUTURE OF MISSION?

Hicks was still willing to attempt reunion of the divided churches. On 31 January 1918, following the proposals of the previous July, about forty "Churchmen & Methodists" met at London House and discussed possibilities of reunion. The bishops of Oxford and Winchester were there but Hicks thought they were "likely to make *canonical* difficulties". Oxford did have proposals, but only if they did not involve such concessions. He thought that if the Church of England were disestablished and disendowed, "& Bps humbled themselves", then "the Methodists wd accept *reordination*". Hicks was impressed by Herbert Workman (1862–1951), the Methodist leader.

The missionary college at Burgh continued its work, though precariously. On 8 February 1918, Hicks noted in the diary that Burgh "cannot be run for a *profit*, without larger numbers".

MEETING NEEDS IN THE WOMEN'S SERVICES

Women in the armed services asked to be confirmed. Some WAACs who came for confirmation on 13 April 1918 "had their Directoress with them also. AMH & Miss Codrington gave them all tea, in the White Room". These were the women of the Women's Auxiliary Army Corps, another innovation of early 1917, intended to help meet the desperate need for more manpower. They were to serve at a lowly level, to do only administrative work, and they were not to hold commissions. On 21 June 1918, the Bishop "confirmed 4 W.R.F.s from Carlton". On 5 July 1918, "AMH & I drove over to Cranwell Church, where I confirmed 21 persons, of whom 3 were 'Wrens' & the rest men from the Camp."

There were enough of these servicewomen by the end of the war for it to be worth providing them with their own amenities within the diocese, as the Bishop records on 31 October 1918: "Opened Club Room for Service Women in Uniform at 3 pm … (NB It was full next evening, Sat., & on Sunday when I looked in at 8 pm.)"

"I SEE LITTLE THAT I CAN DO"

In June 1918, taking stock under the heading *Incipit nonus annus episcopatus me* ("Here begins the ninth year of my bishopric"), Edward Hicks realized that his health was failing, and he wrote a summary account of what he felt about the conduct of the war. For the first time there is a frank weariness in what he writes going beyond saying he feels tired from sheer overwork:

> *During the War, & especially in these later stages, all actions seem paralysed, and I see little that I can do to shape the policy of the Church or the Country. But I am tired of yielding & temporizing.*

On 15 September 1918, Hicks discussed with Jeudwine "a scheme for adding *one* or two new Archdeaconries". "I seriously think that this is the only wise method of rearranging the Diocese. It cannot satisfactorily be subdivided." Was tiredness and age beginning to blunt the man? Certainly the diary was now more heavily punctuated with comments on Hicks's state of health. He had been worried enough to go to see Sir Thomas Barlow in Wimpole Street in July 1918 and get "good advice". At the end of September he noted a "sense of malaise all day".

He could, however, still take pleasure in an interesting lecture. On 22 May 1918, he records a meeting where the dean "gave us an Exposition of his ... preferred settlement of the Religious Difficulty in schools, from which I derived profit & pleasure; despite the professional manner!" Hicks presided at a meeting in Grimsby on 30 September 1918, where he heard Edward Leach, "one of Gore's men, & a follower of Scott Holland" talk about post-war reconstruction.

Two inconsistent decisions may even suggest that his moral compass became less reliable as he aged. Hicks wrote cagily in his diary for 13 July 1918 about what appears to have been a cleric who seems to have made a young maidservant pregnant:

> *The enormity of the offence ... lay in the circumstances of its commission – her age, & relation to the household, his age, & character & station.*

Always humane, Hicks suggests that if there are indeed no "consequences" it may be possible to arrange for the priest to leave the parish quietly. "But my conviction – *of which I have no evidence* – is that the matter has been whispered about along the countryside, & is no secret by this time."

In a case involving the seduction of a parishioner of a different social class, his response was different. In mid-September 1918, Mr Hand, churchwarden of Sibsey, came to talk about the new vicar, Mr Brown, who was discovered to be "deeply in debt all round" and the subject of "ugly rumours" about a girl of eighteen who was repeatedly at the vicarage, allegedly being prepared for confirmation. The vicar's "evil designs" apparently "culminated" in "gross familiarities" in Easter week, 4, 5, and 6 April. The girl kept a diary which the mother discovered and the vicar was confronted. Hicks does not seem to have considered the possibility that the girl was fantasizing. The vicar had promised in writing that he would resign and Hicks noted, "I must write & compel him to do so." The resignation took place as was noted in the diary. "This gets rid of a villain: I must write to the Bp. of London and the Archbp. of C." In October he was signing Brown's resignation and noting his exit *immundissimus*, "utterly unclean".

He was perhaps becoming more irritable as well as occasionally more condemnatory. In September 1918, at the Board of Missions, a weary Hicks allowed himself a frank expression of irritation. "Cheney Garfit very tiresome: it is clear that the CMS friends intend to defy, if they cannot capture, the Board of Missions." He was also quite waspish about Mrs Weigall. On 15 September Hicks had tea at Petwood with Mrs Weigall and a number of leading men. "It is noteworthy how few *ladies* Mrs. Weigall ever has about her: like Queen Elizabeth?"

THE END OF THE WAR

Fighting ended on 11 November 1918, though the Treaty of Versailles which formally ended the war was not signed until June 1919. The family anxiety about the safety of the soldiers Bede, Ned, and Edmund Knox presumably eased a little, though the diary makes no comment about that.

There was a particularly lengthy stocktaking by Hicks towards the end of 1918. On 1 December he wrote an overview of the war as a whole:

> *The nervous strain of the War, the fearful slaughter, the constant fear of raids or of bereavement, the worry about daily food, the darkened streets, the heavy taxation & high prices, & the great difficulty in finding domestic servants, all these features in daily life combined to darken our homes & rob us of comfort and hope. Then came the unexpectedly early armistice on Nov. 11, followed by the outbreak of Influenza on a scale so wide & terrible as to take the features of a Plague. It was particularly bad in Nov. & Dc. In Haxey, in Barnetby le Wold,*

& smaller places like Bardney or Kirkstead. In many places it was difficult to obtain either doctoring or nursing. The Clergy were overwhelmed with sick visiting, & with funerals. In some villages it was difficult or impossible to find hands to dig the graves or bury the dead. … it was a bad time … In point of Religion … the distraction of the public mind did not make for serious thoughts: the excessive labour on Munitions, & the excessive wages, did not help matters. Familiarity with the brutalities & cynicism of War was not a wholesome influence.

The ending of the war saw no diminution of Hicks's concerns and business in the diocese, and on 14 November 1918 he had "a quiet talk with Miss Savill, on Women's Work in the Church". He notes what were evidently points she made to him in their discussion. "How the Educated Women contemn 'Church Work' & mistrust the clergy – their ignorance, & autocracy. Get some really competent woman to train them." She was opening for him an avenue to better understanding about what was now happening regarding the serious education of women, more than a decade on from Christina's time at Somerville.

The army chaplaincies were still causing difficulties which seem to have continued across the date of the war's official ending. On 12 December 1918, Hicks notes that "Clay [chaplain in France] had recently written to me a letter full of amazement at the courage, cheerfulness, & good behaviour of the troops". Hicks saw him face to face back home in his parish on 6 March 1919, where they discussed an ageing cleric, a "Curate at 60", Mr Rashleigh, who needed to move from his curacy at Halesowen. He was "a Socialist & a Pacifist". He was not the only one strangely affected by war fever even so late on. On 4 November 1918, Hicks wrote of one of his clergy, "I wish he had settled down" in his parish. Leask was asking to go to Russia as chaplain, where he had been English chaplain for five years. On 27 March

1919 Hicks met Leask again for a confirmation in his parish, and found him "strangely restless & excitable". His churchwarden said, "He is from Russia & his ways are Russian".

On his seventy-fifth birthday, 18 December 1918, Hicks wrote a further self-review. Spiritually, he hoped he was more "humble-minded" and he noted that he had to make special efforts to curb his temper and his tongue. He was feeling gloomy about the state of the nation and distinctly unenthusiastic about the influence of Lloyd George:

> *I have found the turn of political events of late very galling. Lloyd George is in the hand of Reaction & his success will be theirs. We are in for a bad time for Gt Britain & for the Empire, as regards Liberty, Sobriety, Progress. The Chief Whip is Sir Geo. Younger, the ablest & most influential Brewer in the House: I know not how many more liquor men will not be elected. Of Temperance Reformers scarcely any are likely to survive.*

Chapter 19 .

Conclusion: The End of a War and the End of a Life

THE END OF THE WAR

At the end of the war, Winston Churchill realized that suddenly the direction of all effort in preceding years had come to a halt. People wanted "the dear one back at the fireside" and ordinary life restored at once. "Putting things back" did not turn out to be easy for the nation. It was not going to happen quickly or straightforwardly in Lincolnshire. Returning to normal was not easy even for individuals. In Hicks's own family, Ned Hicks was "demobbed" (demobilized as a soldier), but found himself looking for a job. He is "much exercised in the endeavor" comments his father, though he was confident that if he tried hard enough he would succeed.

Retrieving buildings and putting them back to their former use turned out be a complicated and protracted business. Bids for the continuing use of the Old Palace for military-medical purposes did not end. Dr Webb came to ask whether the Old Palace might now be used by the Ministry of Pensions for "orthopedic" cases of officers, and massage, but this time Hicks turned the suggestion down. A captain and a colonel arrived seeking permission to quarter seventy or eighty nurses there. They too were refused. The diocese and its bishop wanted their palace back.

The business of getting the Hostel back into running order for its original purpose also proved slow and tangled, even when the use of the building had been formally retrieved for the Church of England. In September 1918, Carey the warden, Hicks, and Johnston the chancellor were conferring about future of the Hostel (the warden having gone off to St Deiniols in Wales, the library founded by Gladstone in 1889 for the promotion of "divine learning"). In November 1918, the Hostel Trustees were concerned about "Investments", and when the War Office would release the building, now housing eighty nurses. The diary records that on 28 December 1918 the Trustees held a Hostel meeting, reorganizing the constitutional structure. The War Office had instructed that the Hostel was to be vacated without delay, and repairs were to be done. A builder was organized. "It seems we are already receiving many applications from students," wrote Hicks.

But on 3 January 1919 there were still more discussions, this time with the "Quartering Committee" about removing the soldiers from the Old Palace and putting the nurses from the Hostel there. Hicks was still resisting as firmly as he could. "I said it did not lie with me, but with the War Office." More negotiations were attempted in February, with the War Office and the Red Cross fighting for priority. Hicks was now entering his final illness and experiencing "heart weakness (shortage of breath)".

As bishop he found himself facing no diminution of complex new pastoral demands in these last few months of his life. His clergy were worrying about what was to happen when they came home. If they were married men with families, they could not afford to return to parish work unless they could have the living with its income. The reactions of returning servicemen who came to see the Bishop about their futures varied. Some were traumatized. Some were fired with a sense of mission. Hicks comments on one "young Flying Man" who came to see him in February 1919. His brother had been killed by his side as they served in France – "Both are churchmen". The brothers had wanted to be missionaries and the survivor was now resolved to train for the mission field. Hicks writes, "I sent him on to Canon Foster, of Burgh College."

Life was to slowly return to normal for others as well. Of the Belgian refugees who had flooded into the country, some had already left but others were still in Lincolnshire in late February 1919. Then the "Major" came to say goodbye to the Bishop before leaving with fifty others "for Hull, & so to Antwerp".

Diocesan business went on. On 17 February 1919 Hicks wrote in his diary that "Archdeacon Wakeford today leaves for France, to lecture & talk to the troops". He was still writing robustly in his diary about the lamentable lack of adequate theological and liturgical knowledge among his clergy and people. He records a conversation with the dean in March 1919 in which they "expressed" their "pained amazement at the backwardness of knowledge about Bible & Inspiration among the Clergy & people esp. of Lincolnshire. Of this his postbag is witness".

On 17 March 1919, the Bishop was meeting Lee, a new incumbent, a "man of (say) 55, ill-educated, but very good & shrewd". He could see the desirability of the characteristics he brought to his new work, despite his lack of theological sophistication. "He is assiduous & kindly in his parish work, & in his home also. Two of his children were Confirmed today. A hospitable tea for everyone afterwards." This was a man whose curacies had been spent on the moors. "He might have been one of Charlotte Bronte's Curates of Keighley!"

In April 1919 Hicks called to see the long-term problem cleric Simmons, who was now "seriously ill with mitral disease of the heart". His response continued to be humane, but he was still helpless to remove the man from his parish:

> *He was as elusive and discursive as usual: not even his grave condition reduced him to simplicity & directness. ... he is wilful and sly. Poor creature!*

In early March 1919 he was able to hear Dorothy Giles's "account of the first meeting of the Commission on Women Workers" and to learn from the dean about the "successful proceedings of the Representative Church Council ... Women admitted to it; Baptismal Franchise".

HICKS'S DEATH

Despite some longish periods of ill-health, Edward Hicks's diary records generally good health and a great deal of energy well into his seventies; but gradually and then decisively his health failed. He resigned his See after a stroke in 1919 but the resignation did not have time to take effect before he died. He died still Bishop of Lincoln in August 1919.

Agnes added a note at the end of the diary after his last entry on Easter Day that year. She says he spent Easter Monday clearing up books and papers in his study and then the two of them left "the beloved room" for the "restful holiday" on the South Coast which his doctors had "advised". They went to Worthing and stayed at the Beach Hotel, taking quiet walks along the front. Edward Hicks "wrote a good deal in the mornings, & read in the evenings". On 27 April he had a stroke while taking a bath. On 13 May he was moved to a nursing home, where he asked to be read to and was able to dictate letters. By July it had been possible to take a house and "to his great joy" they moved in on the 30th – "Then the presence of his children & grandchildren cheered him". Bede, who became a Major and survived the war, had arrived in England on 17 July which was "a matter of great thanksgiving to the Bishop".

On the evening of 14 August he was very quiet and rather breathless. Prayers were said as usual at 6 p.m. His family came and stood round his bed:

> *Then just before 8.30 he uttered a cry – long & wondering – an expression of great joy & triumph came over his face: & he sighed & passed away.*

EDWARD HICKS'S OWN STOCKTAKING OF HIS LIFE

Agnes went through his diaries after he died; but although she "suppressed" some of what he records about the family, she left all the rest as he had written it, risky remarks included. She also left in his own assessments of his work and achievements.

When Edward Hicks became a bishop and began his diary, he wrote – increasingly frankly as he gained confidence – about his first tentative responses and feelings about his new position and the difficulty of working out what manner to adopt. Should he be dignified? Should he just be himself? Which of his habits should change with episcopal office? Should he drop unsuitable friends? Should he abandon some of his enthusiasms as being unfitting for a bishop? In the end he stuck to his guns, kept up the campaigning he profoundly believed in, and emerged in his diaries as the man he was, spiritual and practical; hardworking, but with an immense capacity for enjoyment.

WAS HIS OWN ASSESSMENT RIGHT?

Did Edward Hicks feel at the end of his life he had failed, or that he had made the best of things? In normal health and in his prime he was not given to gloom. He tackled what came his way with humanity and humour. His spiritual life was not marked by dark nights of the soul or agonizing wrestlings. In his "annual summaries" he sometimes writes regretfully about his failures and inadequacies on his personal "journey to God", but these are not the words of a man profoundly disturbed. He told his diary that he was enjoying his life. He seems to have had a quiet confidence about meeting his God.

Hicks was a man of principle and would stand up for what he believed in, though he disliked confrontation and disagreement and preferred to be "merry and happy and in a loving atmosphere", his daughter Christina wrote.

> *He always found it hard to work in an atmosphere of disapproval and disagreement. … But his principles came first always. … "I believe in freedom," he said to me countless times; and the sight of a tyranny, either an individual, a class, or a trade, never failed to rouse him.*

A gentle but firm and a moderate man may not cut swathes, but he can make a difference. "It will do good" was a characteristic note of satisfaction. He favoured "undogmatic and humanitarian religion", and that is what he lived by.

Perhaps he wrote his most important sentence of self-assessment on 18 December 1917, his seventy-fourth birthday: "being a poor lad, & without any influence to push me, I just did what I could, & here I am. *Deo gratias* [thanks be to God]."

Timeline

23 December 1843 Edward Lee Hicks born in Oxford

1855–61 at Magdalen College School, Oxford

1862–66 undergraduate at Brasenose College, Oxford

1866–73 Corpus Christi College, Oxford as a Fellow and Tutor

1871 Hicks is ordained deacon

1872 Hicks is ordained priest

1873 Hicks becomes vicar of Fenny Compton

1876 Hicks marries Agnes Mary Trevelyan Smith

1886 Hicks goes to Hulme Hall, Manchester

1892 Hicks becomes a canon of Manchester Cathedral and vicar of Salford

1910 Hicks becomes Bishop of Lincoln

14 August 1919 Hicks dies

Further Background to the Story

Lucie Savill (1878–1970) had been appointed as headmistress by the governors of the Lincoln High School for Girls in March 1910, so Hicks had had no hand in her appointment. It seems that there had been over a hundred applications and she was chosen from a shortlist of seven. She had previously been teaching at the Girls' Grammar School in Bradford. Her own education had been at the Girls' High School in Berkhamstead and the Cambridge Training College for teachers. Then she taught in Cheshire for two years before going to Somerville College, Oxford 1900–03, to read History. She had left just before Christina arrived there in 1904. She remained headmistress at Lincoln until 1943, greatly expanded the numbers there and set standards comparable with those expected of boys.

Such educated women seem to have been congenial to Hicks, though he found they were not all as easy to deal with as his own beloved daughter. It is not easy now to recapture the flavour of the transformation of education for girls which was going on in the last decades of the nineteenth century and the first decades of the twentieth. For girls of working-class families aspiring to a career, there had usually been only apprenticeship to one of the trades in which women traditionally worked, such as making hats or being a seamstress. A girl with some education who had to earn her living might become a governess. For girls from middle and upper-class families it was common to see their brothers sent to school and then to Oxford or Cambridge, while they made do with a governess and learned music, drawing, French, and other ladylike accomplishments. When they left the schoolroom their next task was to find a husband. So a girl who sought serious educational equality with her brother was still something of a pioneer, and if she wanted a university education, she was still more unusual. Miss Savill was ploughing a furrow in a still very recently tilled field. Educated women were emerging in a tradition given a strong impetus by Dorothea Beale and Frances Buss. Lucie Savill was now working in a growing tradition which was to transform education and career opportunities for girls. The girls' high schools had much to aspire to academically. Under Lucie Savill the one at Lincoln did, and successfully.

HENRY SCOTT HOLLAND, HASTINGS RASHDALL AND THE CHRISTIAN SOCIAL UNION

One of the Christian Social Union's principal leaders was Henry Scott Holland (1847–1918). He was Regius Professor of Divinity at Oxford from 1910 to 1918 during most of Hicks's time as bishop. Hastings Rashdall became involved with the CSU's work, along with the hymn-writer Percy Dearmer (1867–1936) and others in Hicks's wider circle of friends and acquaintances. Rashdall had become active in the CSU on his return to Oxford as a Fellow of Hertford College in 1889. He maintained his interest. He wrote a letter in early December 1896 in which he described the "enormous" CSU meeting he had been to in Bristol "as one of the Oxford representatives on the C.S.U. Council". He said he had heard "exceptionally good addresses by the Bishop of Durham, Scott Holland, [Charles] Gore, and Alderman Philips".

Rashdall collaborated with Henry Scott Holland in producing a handbook for the CSU which describes what might now be called its "mission" in a double sense of the word. Its very title *Our Neighbours* deliberately set the organization's work in the Christian context of "loving one's neighbour ... The Christian Social Union aims at producing citizens inspired by spiritual convictions and equipped by patient and thorough study", its preface says. It claims that it is not enough, as the economists argue, to let the forces of change work themselves out. Men of conscience must put in some work. "If you leave forces to work blindly, you are sure to back the strong, at cruel cost to the weak". It quotes the autodidact scientist T. H. Huxley:

> *In place of ruthless self-assertion, ... self-restraint; in place of thrusting aside, or treading down, all competitors, it requires that the individual shall ... help his fellows; its influence is directed, not so much to the survival of the fittest, as to the fitting of as many as possible to survive.*

The *Handbook* suggests that what first brought the CSU together is the emerging question, "What ... constitutes true Christian Citizenship?" The membership responded by setting out to do research ("study"), each branch choosing a topic. Only then should they turn their minds to "direct application" of their findings locally. A drawback to this approach was a tendency for its publications to be too theoretical and sometimes overidealistic.

Nevertheless, the Christian Social Union was concerned with practicalities and detail as well as with theorizing. It published many leaflets, especially on wages, produced by individual branches, as London, Oxford, Cambridge. The London branch secretary – the liturgist and hymnographer Percy Dearmer –

included in some June 1897 *Notices* of the Research Committee
the information that

> *the Committee is now actively engaged upon the investigation of*
> *the conditions of work of the Artificial Flower Makers. The next*
> *meeting will be at the Women's Trade Union League Offices …*
> *Any members of the C.S.U. who care to come will be welcome.*
> *The Report of the Committee on Laundries, which was sent to the*
> *Home Secretary, is printed in the June Commonwealth.*

In the Christian Social Union, *The Wages Problem*, Plan of Study,
1912–13 (apparently for the London branch) is included a long
booklist, and the stricture:

> *It will be found very desirable to have some acquaintance with*
> *the history of the theory of wages, and branches are strongly*
> *advised to arrange at least one or two lectures on the general*
> *theory of wages.*

By the end of the First World War, concern was to move to the
post-war housing problem, shortage of housing, high rents,
"question of the provision of houses for the working classes at the
conclusion of the war". The intention was always, as Scott Holland
put it, that once the CSU had mastered its subject, there should be
"direct application" locally.

Scott Holland was respected for the usefulness of his
contributions to improving the style and content of the leaflets
the CSU issued on a wide range of subjects, including Christian
approaches to investments, wages, and individual rights. "His
well-balanced mind was of great service in criticising and revising
the leaflets", and so on.

Scott Holland was well connected in contemporary politics.
His correspondence with Mrs Drew – born Mary Gladstone, a
daughter of William Ewart Gladstone – went on for many years.

She worked unofficially for her father as a secretary and political hostess and had many correspondents, including John Ruskin, some of whom were perhaps anxious to use her as a gateway to influence with her father. Forms of collective action seem to have been attractive to the CSU. Holland – though he had no experience of working life except as an academic and clergyman – was optimistic about trade unions working collaboratively with the state and also operating through the law for the common good. But above all, he thought, the Church of England could be a force for good by working collectively – "our parochial organisation carries our workers everywhere" and that meant the Church of England was peculiarly well placed to have its effect:

> *How far-reaching could be the effect, if all our hosts of Church workers, going in and out amongst the poor, could carry with them, wherever they went, the illuminating knowledge of all the care and privilege and security with which the Law of the State has already encompassed the workers ... to mediate between the Legislation and the weak and unbefriended labourers whom, without intelligent mediation, it cannot reach.*

NURSING: VERA BRITTAIN, DAISY DOBBS, AND THE VADS

The nursing career of his sister Katherine gave Edward Hicks an informed interest in nursing as a career for able women, and it must have provided a useful background during the war when women's nursing became important in a diocese full of wounded soldiers come home to convalesce.

Nursing seems to have been more or less universally a female profession at this date. Its social standing was another question. In early Victorian times it had attracted working-class women and there were plenty of tales of dirt and drunkenness. The work of Florence Nightingale had begun to open a respectable career in nursing to well-born women. Nevertheless, Victorian nursing still had its horror stories of uneducated and unsuitable women. Nursing training, even where it was undertaken in mid-Victorian decades, lasted only about a year and one of the reasons for the pressure for regulation was the conviction that something closer to three years was what was really needed. The hospitals employed both "trained" and untrained nurses.

Was Katherine to be regarded as a "lady" or a "woman" entrant? Katherine had to earn her living and was not brought up to be a lady. The family was of modest origins but her brother was a clergyman. We can see something of the complexity of this question from the story told by Vera Brittain in her letters and her autobiographical *Testament of Youth*.

In April 1915, the middle-class Vera Brittain went to her local Buxton hospital hoping to become a Voluntary Aid Detachment nurse, a "VAD". The hospital had been extended to take 150 wounded, she said in a letter. It took her until July to obtain leave to break off her studies at Somerville College, Oxford, to which she hoped to return after the war (and did). Then she began in earnest at Buxton as a probationer. Most of her work was general, tidying up, dusting, some bandaging, and watching the experienced nurses in order to learn from them.

The VADs were a recent invention, founded with support from the Red Cross and the Order of St John in 1909 and officially recognized by the Red Cross in 1915. More than half of the volunteers were women, and they tended to come from the leisured classes. There were concerns that they would not be able to cope with hard and unpleasant work. The armed forces were sceptical about their usefulness and initially refused to let them serve in hospitals at the Front. That objection was overturned after Katharine Furse (1875–1952), a widow who had been involved with the VAD "movement" from its first attachment to the Territorial Army, introduced VADs into the roles of catering workers in the camps in France. It took only the emergency need arising in battle to bring them into the wards, where they so impressed the military authorities that experienced nurses – at least in their mid-twenties – began to be allowed to nurse in France.

So Vera Brittain faced the task of equipping herself to be accepted. She wrote in late July that she was hoping to get a place in "a large London Hospital as a V.A.D." nurse. This hospital was expanding and needed more nurses. "I should love to go there as they get all the wounded straight from the trenches". "Fully trained nurses are rather scarce just now".

At first Vera Brittain idealized nurses.

> *No female figure in the whole of this War has such a glamour as a hospital nurse, or such dignity. No one else so much looks down into the depths, which is a privilege, as it means a corresponding ability to look up into the heights ... I had no idea what a capable person a fully trained nurse was until I went to the [Buxton] Hospital.*

These are striking observations given the still uncertain status and standards of nursing training in a field which had only been an upper or middle-class profession for a few decades.

Still at Buxton in early August she was beginning to recognize that nursing was not glamorous and exciting. "The more intimate you become with a nurse's duties, the harder it is to see the beauty in them," she wrote. She got her post in London and from there she wrote with increasing disillusion in October. "I hate it. There is something so starved & dry about hospital nurses – as if they had to force all the warmth out of themselves before they could be fit to be really good nurses." And she was learning that wounded men fresh from the trenches were not simply more interesting. "There are some pretty ghastly things in my ward." She began to learn why the nurses had to become unemotional.

The orderlies won't do one or two of the dressings I have to help with – or rather, the Sisters won't have them, because they seem to be made sick so easily, & one of them who was holding a basin the other night fainted right on top of the patient.

She enjoyed the contact with the wounded soldier patients, especially the lower "ranks" ("I would rather look after Tommies than officers"). Most of the patients she encountered were suffering from "rheumatism" caused by their wounds. The freshly wounded were not coming to Buxton because it was too far from where they could be landed in Britain, so the hospital was dealing with transfers from these frontline receiving hospitals.

For the professional nurses the experience was, on one level, the same. They too had to deal with unimaginable horrors. One of the Territorial Force nurses from the Wragby Road hospital in the grammar school buildings was Daisy Dobbs, eventually awarded a military medal for her courage. A trained nurse, she joined the Territorial Force Nursing Service on 3 February 1915, and worked at first at the 4th Northern General Hospital, Lincoln. Then, like Vera Brittain, she saw service overseas. In October 1916, Daisy Dobbs was sent to serve in Salonica. She was wounded in an air raid on her hospital. On her way back – still technically on active service – the ship, which was an ambulance transport, was torpedoed in the English Channel and 117 lives were lost. Daisy survived and went home for some leave before going back to her hospital in Lincoln.

Miss Sidney Browne, matron-in-chief of her Territorial Force Nursing Service, wrote her a letter combining sympathy and respect for her courage, and asking for

any further particulars, and … the name of the Sisters who were with you. It is very sad to think that so many of the poor wounded men were lost. Did they rescue them first of all, or did they put the women first? I hope they took the wounded.

Wounded first, women second because they were nurses, was evidently her professional view of the priorities. Daisy replied with a detailed account in the same spirit:

When we arrived on board we found out that two V.A.Ds were making their way home from France, and Mrs Long, Commander of the W.A.A.Cs and her orderly. We consisted of two sisters of the T.F.N.S. and myself, making a number of seven altogether. After dinner we went to see the wounded officers and men to help them talk, oh … What an interesting time we had, the thrilling adventures which made us glow with admiration and filled us with a longing to do more for these men who willingly gave their lives for us. How time flies, we helped fix life belts until the signal for "lights out" made us seek our cabin.

She commented that when it came to rescue, the nurses did not make a fuss about who should go first:

Being seven women we did not delay the rescue work which went on around us as. We got into our boat, but I soon lost sight of my friends as the boat became full of wounded men.

THE BLOOMSBURY SET TRIES NOT TO GO TO WAR

Hicks's diaries reflect the problems experienced by conscientious objectors, some of which came home closely in the diocese. It is helpful to set this experience in the wider context of the behaviour of those with money and influence. Some with the necessary social standing and some intellectuals simply set about getting exemption with no apparent sense of duty to the nation. Virginia Woolf certainly had no ethical objection to using all means available to keep her husband and friends out of the army. The rest of the "Bloomsbury set" seem to have agreed. Woolf wrote, "the whole of our world does nothing but talk about conscription, and their chances of getting off … and wire pulling". Her husband Leonard

> *lunched with the Sidney Webbs, who of course professed to be behind the scenes; and according to them, the War Office has already too many men, and will connive at any gentleman getting off; so the thing to do is produce letters from Harley St. doctors, or the peerage.*

Virginia Woolf could be waspish about the Webbs. She wrote in her diary on 23 January 1915 about a meeting with Mrs Webb, who was "seated like an industrious spider at the table" … "the hall was full of earnest drab women, who are thought 'queer' at home, & rejoice in it". Leonard's own version of this link with the notorious socialist Webbs throws a more favourable light in the motivation for his own draft-dodging. He says that in 1915 Sidney Webb had asked him to "undertake research" for the Fabian Society and write a report "on the causes of the 1914 war and of war in general and … finding ways, if possible, of making war less likely in the future".

Leonard's friends were discouraging. Many thought, like Edward Hicks, that when war threatened the dispute could and should all be settled by "arbitration". There was a general sense that it was a long time since England had been invaded and, in recent experience with South Africa, wars were something which happened at a safe distance. But he did tackle the subject and "worked like a fanatical or dedicated mole" from 1915 to 1916. Then he published his report which promptly appeared in *The New Statesman*. "This was the first detailed study of a League of Nations to be published". He carried on and burrowed deeper, with Sidney Webb's encouragement, and published more, and others began to think along similar lines, until a "League of Nations Union" emerged.

The friendship with the Webbs and other left-wing leaders of opinion was balanced by the Woolfs' social contact with the Asquith family. Herbert Asquith remained Prime Minister until 1916 and that gave his social circle a direct route into contact with government. Virginia Woolf describes how members of the Bloomsbury set tried to use this advantage. Her story, incidentally, provides glimpses of the way the conscientious objector tribunals actually worked.

The painter Duncan Grant and his lover David Garnett had been refused exemption by the local tribunal. Virginia wrote to her sister Vanessa, married to Clive Bell, but already in an intimate relationship of her own with Duncan Grant, on 14 May 1916. "I know nothing about the Tribunal beyond what I saw in the Daily News ... What steps will they take now? Do they mean to go to prison?" The two appealed and were eventually awarded non-combatant service.

In support of Duncan Grant and David Garnett, Virginia began a campaign of getting letters from important people. That was an activity in which Edward Hicks had agreed to engage when he wrote on behalf of Mr Sharpe and Mr Effield. On 3 June 1916, she wrote to Lady Robert Cecil. Duncan Grant would be coming before the central tribunal "in a week or two". She asks her friend to write to Lord Salisbury who chaired the tribunal to tell him that Grant

> *is perfectly honest in his objections, and also remarkable as a painter ... I am told that the Central Tribunal enquires into the good faith of applicants – and I've known Duncan many years and very well, and could testify to his honesty – .*

She was gently warned that this was not the right way to go about it, and told that Lord Salisbury had said she should write herself to the secretary of the central tribunal. She had, she commented, "no wish to do anything underhand". Duncan and David Garnett got off on condition they did farm work till the war ended. It was arranged that they would do this at Charleston, which was rented by Vanessa and her husband partly for the purpose.

Virginia's husband, Leonard, had decided to get a doctor's letter, she told Vanessa. Virginia says he was promised

> *a certificate of unfitness on his own account, as well as mine ...*
> *He thinks they ought to give L. complete exemption on these*
> *grounds, and strongly advises him not to put in anything about*
> *conscience, which annoys them. It is rather difficult to know*
> *what to do, as the Tribunals are so erratic.*

Leonard gives his own account in his autobiography. He did have a problem with trembling hands, about which he had consulted a doctor when he came back from Ceylon shortly before he married Virginia. His doctor wrote a strong letter on his behalf for the tribunal – though Leonard notes that he "did not entirely (medically) agree" with its contents:

> *Mr. L. S. Woolf is in my opinion entirely unfit for Military*
> *Service and would inevitably break down under conditions of*
> *active service. Mr. L. S. Woolf has definite nervous disabilities,*
> *and in addition an Inherited Nervous Tremor which is quite*
> *uncontrollable.*

Leonard was called up and went for his "medical" on 30 May 1916. When he was examined he was shaking with cold after waiting with no clothes on in a draught, and he had left the letter in his pocket so he did not have it to show the examining doctor. The doctor noticed the conspicuous trembling of his hands, and took him to a more senior doctor "in the uniform of a Captain. 'Here's a fellow with chorea, Sir,'" he said. Leonard mentioned his doctor's letter and was sent to fetch it. Leonard got his exemption.

Virginia wrote about it – rather tactlessly perhaps – to Ka Cox, whose lover, the "war poet" Rupert Brooke, had died of an infected mosquito bite while serving with the navy a few months earlier:

> *Leonard has been completely exempted from serving the Country in any capacity. He went before the military doctors trembling like an aspen leaf, with certificates to say that he would tremble and has trembled and will never cease from trembling.*

Leonard was surprised that even in "the great comb-out of 1917" – when the government, facing huge losses on the battlefield, made a further effort to bring men into the armed forces – he was again given the same "complete exemption". In her diary Woolf records how on 14 October 1917 she waited outside while Leonard got his exemption certificate, and saw "soldiers crossing, coming out of staircases, & going into others; but gravel & no grass. A disagreeable impression of control & senseless determination".

Women's suffrage: The key issues

In the nineteenth century battle for the extension of the franchise, the starting-point had been the idea that only those who owned property in the form of land should be entitled to vote. The vote, it was argued, should be restricted to those who had a "stake". The Third Reform Act of 1884 had given the vote to men in town and countryside who paid a rent of £10 a year or owned property to that value.

The fundamental question in the debates about giving more of the population the vote – and especially women – was still whether the prospective new voters had a sufficient "stake" in the affairs of the nation to be entitled to a say in the way it was run. The position of women changed greatly during Hicks's lifetime, especially in the last few years while he was Bishop of Lincoln and the country was at war. That was partly a consequence of the demands of wartime, when the shortage of men who were required for active service, and who were dying in such numbers, opened activities to women they would normally not have been allowed. Many were reluctant to see this as an irreversible change. It was not until 1918 that the Representation of the People Act gave the vote to men over the age of twenty-one and women over the age of thirty. Women over twenty-one were not to get the vote until 1928.

EDITH PICTON-TURBERVILL AND THE ORDINATION OF WOMEN

Like other able women who appear in active roles in Hicks's life, Miss Edith Picton-Turbervill (1872–1960) came from a gentry or minor aristocratic background and involved herself in several of the same "causes" as he embraced. She had been drawn into the labour movement because of concerns about the navvies working on the Vale of Glamorgan railway near her parents' home. She began to be involved with the YWCA through her friendship with Emily Kinnaird and worked for them in India from 1900 to 1908. Back in England, she became a suffragist. She worked with the YWCA in England during the war to provide canteens and accommodation for women munitions workers.

In 1917, she published a book, *Woman and the Church*, with the Oxford don and cleric Burnett Hillman Streeter (1874–1937), who specialized in New Testament studies but ran a theological discussion group and published on a wide range of topics. Their joint introduction stressed that:

The purpose of this book is not to promote an agitation for the throwing open to women of the priesthood and other offices in the existing hierarchy of the Church. It is rather an attempt to demonstrate and to emphasize the position that a wider employment in some way or other of women in the preaching and pastoral work of the Church cannot but make for the Church's spiritual welfare.

The Bishop of Durham provided a preface.

The chapter on "Woman and the Ministry" was contributed by Streeter, who began by asserting that women's ministry was "not merely a question of woman's rights". Christian ministry is not about "rights", he said. Women and men have their "typical excellences", but these are cultural, a result of different educational objectives, and each sex can and should be encouraged to develop the best characteristics normally attributed to the other. Christ himself embodied both. So what is the first step, practically speaking, he asks.

Licences should be given to properly qualified women to preach and exercise the other functions entrusted to lay readers ... on exactly the same terms and conditions as those on which they are at present given to men. This would add immensely to the resources available to the Church where busy parish clergy have to write more sermons than they can possibly have time to do properly.

Women would also be an invaluable pastoral resource, he thought. They could explain about sex to women and girls, and that might help diminish society's problems with venereal diseases. They could even, if not actually hear confessions, which is traditionally a priestly function, "give help and advice to persons who are troubled with moral, spiritual and intellectual difficulties".

He mentioned the revival of the Order of Deaconesses but he thought their role confusing to many people. "There is considerable haziness in the general mind as to what is the exact position and function" of deaconesses. On the controversial question of making women priests, Streeter was restrained. It "ought to be indefinitely postponed". It could not be tackled until "the great majority of members of the Church, both men and women, are convinced that it is desirable". Nevertheless, he allowed himself some discussion of the theological and ecclesiological issues. And in any case, the governance of the church would need to be reformed. "The autocracy of the incumbent is one of the great weaknesses of the incumbent in a democratic age." He ends with "an appeal to the Bishops … to act courageously and to act at once".

CANON FOSTER AND THE LINCOLN RECORD SOCIETY

The Lincoln Cathedral Chapter seems to have become increasingly active from the 1890s. As well as attending to the fabric of the cathedral, it began to consider putting the cathedral archives in better order. Charles Wilmer Foster (1866–1935), one of the canons, became a leader in this enterprise. He had graduated from Oxford in 1887, but with only a Pass Degree (a degree requiring a lower level of attainment than an Honours degree, with special easier examination papers set for the candidates). This poor performance has been put down to ill-health, but it is also likely that his father's death in 1886, two years after Charles had become a student at St John's College, left the family in financial and other difficulties. This was a clerical family and Charles wanted to go into the church too.

He took the slightly unusual step of going to the Clergy School at Leeds. This was a relatively new venture. It had been founded in 1876 as a small theological college, possibly with a special aim of preparing students for urban ministry. In 1890, soon after his ordination, he found himself with a curacy in the diocese of Lincoln. In that diocese he remained, and from 1902 until his death he was vicar of Timberland.

He was soon appointed to administrative roles in the diocese. He became secretary to the Diocesan Board of Education (1904–10) and then, in 1908, of the Lincoln Diocesan Trust and the Board of Finance. It was as one of the Lincoln Cathedral's canons that he was able to promote the idea of creating a Record Society. He was keenly interested in the archives. Foster was actively studying the records himself and was still working on the early Chapter Acts in 1919. He was a determined man. Frank Stenton, writing a memorial note, said of Foster that "few men have surpassed him in imperturbable consistency of will".

So Canon Foster wrote in the *Lincoln Diocesan Magazine* to propose the formation of a local Record Society. It would have the same sort of purpose as many such local record societies, to "provide for the printing of unedited documents relating to the Diocese and County of Lincoln". Would-be members were invited to send in their names. In late Victorian England, people all over the country began to realize that there were vast treasure troves of historical evidence going back many centuries, much of it held in the archives of cathedrals, which needed sorting and cataloguing and publishing so that it could all be more widely read. (This was the equivalent of more modern work which has been putting "family history" evidence online.) Lincoln's records had come out in a few specimen volumes from 1866, but it began to be felt that the task needed tackling more systematically. This Lincoln venture was the fruit of the work of a Records Committee which had been formed in 1906, chaired by the then Bishop Edward King, with Canon Foster acting as the secretary. King had commented that the documents which could be studied if published contained, among other things, this history "of families in the Diocese".

The proposed society which was to undertake the actual printing, funded by member-subscribers, did not have universal support. The rector of Maltby-le-Marsh thought "the past was often best left undisturbed". There is a snapshot of this rector, Mr Duke, in a diary entry of 25 June 1914, when Hicks consecrated a new piece of graveyard and preached in the open air. The rector had provided a generous tea in a tent. "Mr. Duke is an odd man, but a Xtian & a gentleman: great nephew of W. S. Landor, of whom he has an interesting oil portrait & other relics".

Hicks was one of the founder members of the resulting new Lincolnshire Record Society which eventually published his diary. We see him at the meetings which discussed how to organize this enormous task for Lincolnshire. Hicks saw Foster's faults: "Foster – over flowery & over polite etc as usual: but a clever, good, & suitable man". Nevertheless, he liked him and approved of his work in launching the society.

On 21 July 1911, Hicks wrote that the council of the Lincolnshire Record Society had met in his room. On 15 October 1913, there was an "Annual Meeting of the Record Society at O.P. a very interesting & pleasant gathering. A nice conversazione later. Mrs. Brockhouse played lustily: & Foster sang". On 30 October 1914, Canon Foster "motored [Hicks] into Lincoln with him" from the village of Martin. "He came to luncheon later, & made great friends with Miss Jones, & showed over his muniments." On 4 December 1914, Hicks records "At 12.15 a good meeting of the Record Society: which is doing excellently – except in regard of the Register section".

The war was eventually to have its effects on the society. On 28 November 1917, Hicks records the "Record Society Annual meeting, which went off with spirit, tho' few there, by reason of this horrid war". On 20 December 1918, his note of the annual meeting is less optimistic still. "We are doing good work, but feel the results of the War in the cost of Paper & labour!'"

More About Some of the Characters

The work of Henry Bazely which helped to win Hicks over to an enthusiasm for open-air missionary preaching was not without precedent. Hugh Stowell Brown (1823–86), a convinced teetotaller, was a vicar's son, though after some experimentation on the way to becoming ordained himself, he realized that his beliefs were closer to those of the Baptists. He became a popular preacher in Liverpool late in the 1840s and never looked back. He reached working-class people through the directness of his expressions and illustrations. He gave sermon-lectures on Sunday afternoons to large attendances and he preached to thousands in the open air.

WILL CROOKS

Will Crooks (1852–1921) was a trade unionist and one of the first Labour MPs. He became a Fabian at a time when the left-wing Fabian Society envisaged transforming the very structure of the social order. In 1906 deals were negotiated with the Liberals, who wanted to avoid dividing their support. The Conservative government was unpopular, and by agreeing to share out the constituencies and not stand against one another, the Liberals and Labour got the Conservatives out of seats which had been "safe" for them. The Liberals won a landslide victory and a majority, and the new Labour Party gained twenty-nine seats and became a force to be reckoned with.

RANDALL DAVIDSON, ARCHBISHOP OF CANTERBURY, 1903–28

Randall Davidson (1848–1930) had been chaplain to two previous Archbishops of Canterbury, Tait and Benson, before he became archbishop in his turn in 1903. He had held two bishoprics, Rochester (1891–95) and Winchester (1895–1903). He was a very politically engaged bishop at the level of the innermost and highest levels. He was not a strong supporter of Hicks's appointment.

CHARLES GORE

Hicks's friend Charles Gore (1853–1932) was vice-principal of Cuddesdon Theological College from 1880 to 1883, then principal of Pusey House, Oxford (1884–93). He resigned after giving some controversial Bampton Lectures and became vicar of Radley. By 1894 he had become a canon of Westminster Abbey, where his preaching made him famous. He was offered the bishopric of Worcester, where he served from 1901 to 1905, when he became Bishop of Birmingham. He was made Bishop of Oxford from 1911.

Until he became a bishop, he led the life of a celibate, in the Community of the Resurrection which he had founded at Cuddesdon. This he saw as the nearest approximation to the ideal of a Christlike community life possible in modern times. Gore was also an Anglo-Irish aristocrat by birth, so that it was from that perspective that he behaved as an eager social reformer.

MARGARET HAIG

Others pushed much harder at the boundaries of what was socially permitted than Christina Hicks did as a young woman with an Oxford education. Margaret Haig Thomas (1883–1958), though she abandoned Somerville early for marriage in 1908 to Sir Humphrey Mackman before she took her degree, soon found marriage dull and looked about her for occupation. In the very year of her marriage she joined the Women's Social and Political Union and during the next few years she was campaigning actively in South Wales for votes for women. That enthusiasm had begun before she married. Her mother had accompanied her on her first march, partly as a chaperone, but partly because she supported the cause herself. At first the attraction to this cause was emotional, but then Margaret did her homework. "My intellectual assent was complete, but it came second, not first."

It came when she realized how restricted women's lives still were, in different ways for "ladies" than for women of lower social classes, but limited nonetheless. She says she met a neighbour by chance one day, "setting off to play bridge". It was a lovely April day. Margaret asked her why she was spending such a beautiful afternoon playing cards. "A shadow crossed her face and a queer, discontented inflection came into her voice. 'One must do something,' she said."

For Margaret, once she discovered the suffrage movement,

*militant suffrage was the very salt of life. The knowledge of
it had come like a draught of fresh air into our padded, stifled
lives. It gave us release of energy, it gave us that sense of being
of some use in the scheme of things.*

Her approach was highly activist and it even landed her in prison. Her husband proved surprisingly willing to let her be a militant and even brought the odd flask of hot soup to meet a train back from a demonstration, when it arrived in the early hours.

Her father, a Welsh MP, "turning about for someone who should be a cross between a confidential secretary and a right-hand man whom he could completely trust, was induced by my mother to try me". Here she was adopting a role similar to that in which we find Christina when her father became a bishop. She was an able woman assisting a grateful professional parent.

Her success in a man's world was of a different order, however, and was probably a result of her father's influence and the doors it opened, as much as a reward for her own abilities and determination. Once her father became a minister, Margaret

*got onto a good many new and more important Boards than I
had ever been on before, Boards of which he, formerly had been
a member. I was acting really as a kind of unofficial liaison
officer to report to him how things were going and to give the
board his view on any line of policy.*

She had to negotiate being accepted, speaking, smoking, swearing. She loved it. "The feeling of tackling interesting problems, concentrating on them, getting things done, was exhilarating." Her confidence encouraged her to try to take her father's seat in the House of Lords on his death, though she was far before her time in trying.

JOHN EDWARD HINE

John Edward Hine (1857–1934), who was an emergency appointment as suffragan bishop at the end of Hicks's life, was medically qualified and had served as a missionary as well as a doctor in Africa. His obituary in the *British Medical Journal*, 14 April 1934, gives more details of his early medical career and explains that he had gone to Central Africa with the Universities Mission in 1888, two years after his ordination and five years after qualifying as a doctor. In Africa he had been made bishop in 1896 and served in that role in Zanzibar and in Northern Rhodesia (1909–14). He wrote his own life story, which he called *Days Gone By*.

A. S. DUNCAN-JONES

Duncan-Jones (1879–1955) was well known to Hicks and they appear to have been good friends over a number of years. He first appears in the diary as Examining Chaplain. In July 1912 he brought a pupil of his, who had been a Methodist and was a recent graduate, to be confirmed on the day of a jovial YMCA garden party; he brought a party of "his soldiers (Scottish Horse)" for confirmation in January 1916.

Hicks spent the afternoon of 10 June 1917 "reading Duncan Jones' new book on 'Ordered Liberty' which is very clever, & full of literary knowledge. It will do good". By now Duncan-Jones had accepted the living at Primrose Hill, but Hicks kept up with him and his wife in London. He made a visit in November 1917, at which he regretted in his diary that the "charming" women present "outshone" Mrs Duncan-Jones who was "pretty but silent". He did not like to see her put at such a disadvantage. He took the Duncan-Joneses to the theatre a few days later. "I treated DJ & Mrs. DJ to 'Dear Brutus' (Barries) at Wyndham's Theatre. They were so nice."

LEIFCHILD LEIF JONES

Leif Jones (1862–1939) eventually became Baron Rhayader. As a student at Oxford he had been appointed tutor to the children of the future Earl of Carlisle and his wife. She was a vociferous prohibitionist and she encouraged him to make speeches at temperance meetings locally. This connection had provided Leif Jones with a job as personal assistant for a time. From there he went on to become an MP.

RONNIE KNOX

Ronnie Knox (1888–1957), who influenced Ned in his decision to become a Roman Catholic, wrote two descriptions of the way he himself later came to the decision to become a Roman Catholic. One of these accounts he called *Apologia*, a choice of title which must have evoked John Henry Newman and been particularly painful for his father. This was a brief work of a mere four printed pages, which he wrote at the wish of the Society of SS Peter and Paul. The society was concerned about the stories which had been spread about Knox's "connexion" with it. It published various of his writings with his name on them, and two tracts without his name, published anonymously. He said he had never had any "financial interest" in the society.

The other self-explanatory publication was Knox's *Spiritual Aeneid*, which he describes in the preface as a "religious autobiography." He explains the Aeneid-motif he has adopted. "Troy is undisturbed and in a sense unreflective religion; in most lives it is overthrown, either to be rebuilt or to be replaced."

Ronnie also published, under the title *Naboth's Vineyard in Pawn*, three sermons on the Church of England which he had preached at Plymouth. In the first he presents the Church of England as the result of emergency measures at the time of the

Reformation. This bishop's son is scathing about the episcopate as it was set up then (Queen Elizabeth's "henchmen"; "a kind of ecclesiastical body of policemen spying on their clergy"), (p. 7). In the second sermon he considered not the history but the present state of the Church of England and the lack of wisdom in believing that "if we would only trust the bishops", all would be well with the church (p. 16). In the third he spoke of reunion, mentioning Canon Scott Holland as one of the "Churchmen of different schools" who would be forced to seek "Reunion of some sort" in an age when rivals to the Christian faith were beginning to win their supporters as "toys of the upper or leisured classes" and could soon be expected "to make a wider appeal" (p. 18). "It is Peter who beckons us" (p. 21).

Reunion All Round, a pamphlet by Knox (London, 1915) suggested that the old reasons for division "can no longer be thought to place any Obstacle" in the way of reunion (p. 9). He even though Moslems might be brought to accept the Athanasian Creed after some sensible discussion (p. 12). He has less hope of the Jews but "would not despair, even here, of some better understanding" (p. 20).

HASTINGS RASHDALL

Hastings Rashdall (1858–1924) remained in some respects more of a lifelong scholar and less of a pastoral cleric than Hicks. There was a mutual high regard between the two men. Their interests were not identical, however. They found different solutions to the dilemma which faced numerous former Fellows of Oxford and Cambridge colleges who were ordained and moved on to live as clergyman scholars. Which should come first, scholarship or priestly priorities? As a boy, Rashdall wrote a letter home about his new undergraduate life in Oxford on 21 October 1877 which suggests (unless he was just trying to impress his parents) that he was already a serious-minded student:

As you like to know about Lectures, &c., I have 11 per week –
i.e. 2 per morning (at 10 & 11 or 12) except one mg., viz. 3
Virgil (Papillon), 2 Gk. Test: (Spooner), 3 Logic (Robinson),
2 Unseen Translation. I can't say exactly what I do per day,
as it is not necessary to do the same every day. Chapel 8–8.25
a.m. Breakfast and read till 10: 10–1 Lectures & Reading. So
far regular. Then as a minimum I consider 1 hour in the Aft.
(gen. before hall) and 2 in the Ev. Dinner in hall at 6.15. A
charge in my battels of 1d per day for napkin at dinner in hall
is amusing.

Rashdall realized that there were choices to be made. In 1894 he
wrote to W. J. Ferrar, one of his pupils who was now wondering
whether to seek a move to a parish where he would have more time
for his intellectual work and perhaps "have rather more to do with
educated people":

I quite understand your feelings about "a great piece of you
being wasted". I have felt something of the other side of the
matter – of another piece of me, if it exists, being undeveloped.

Rashdall meant that he did not think he would have been good at
pastoral parish work. As to scholarship:

I believe it does make all the different to a man's work in the
long run, and that there are people who are looking out for help
of the kind which only thoughtful men who have kept up their
contact with serious thinking can give them.

Hicks does not seem to have gone in for such soul-searching,
adapting himself cheerfully to the demands of new work in new
places and giving each all his energies, and keeping up his work on
inscriptions in any odd moments he had.

Maude Royden

Maude Royden (1876–1956) was a baronet's daughter. She had been educated at Cheltenham Ladies' College, another of the girls' schools which were setting out to provide girls with education comparable with that of their brothers. This was also the old school of Miss Todhunter, her close contemporary, so Maude Royden and Winifred Todhunter must have known one another. Then she went to Oxford, to Lady Margaret Hall. She did some university lecturing for the University Extension movement, which was to play a part both in providing (often chiefly economic and socialist) higher education for the workers and in promoting higher education for women. By 1912 she had become a committee member of the National Union of Women's Suffrage Societies.

But Maude Royden was also a committed pacifist and when war began and the Union offered its support, she separated herself from the CSU and gave her energies to the Fellowship of Reconciliation and the Women's International League for Peace and Freedom.

Frederick Tryon

The obituary of Frederick Tryon (1813–1903) published in *The Gospel Magazine* in 1904 claimed that "nearly the entire period of his lengthened ministry was unconnected with any particular denomination" and gives more of the context in which the Bishop of Worcester's brother had left the Church of England but had lingered as something of an embarrassment in the diocese of Lincoln. Tryon had been ordained and obtained the curacy of Wirksworth, but that was before his "conversion". Once he felt himself to be converted, he began to preach passionately to large crowds, using a disused malting shed. Tryon's angry vicar had him removed from the curacy by the bishop, but he was licensed to another curacy by another bishop.

In 1834 he had been offered the living of Deeping St James. He was still too young to hold it, but once he began to serve there he found his conscience "uneasy about many things in connection with the Church Service ... He finally wrote to his bishop severing his official relations with the Establishment". This was in 1839, when the bishop was John Kaye. After Tryon had joined forces with Philpott and Tipton, they "conferred together on their common action"; "A chapel was soon built in Deeping St. James, and many persons who had sat under Mr. Tryon's ministry in the parish church joined his new congregation". The "pastorate of this flock" continued for over sixty years. The "Memento" of Tryon prepared by his son immediately after his death includes extracts from his diary and some letters.

Tryon came to feel that he "must serve the Lord Christ in his members without reference to other preachers"; "I believe that the fear of the reproach of professors has weakened me, and that the more I yield to this the weaker I shall be."

ARCHDEACON WAKEFORD

Archdeacon Wakeford became the source of a famous scandal. He was in the end "deprived" of his orders when he was charged under the Clergy Discipline Act of 1892 of having committed adultery with a young woman at the Bull Hotel in Peterborough on two occasions in 1920. *The Times*, 7 December 1921, p. 14, reported the finding of guilt by Lincoln Consistory Court. The Chancellor of the Diocese presided (Mr G. J. Talbot, King's Counsel) with five assessors, including Hicks's colleague, Jeudwine. Canon Woolley gave "character" evidence; he had known the archdeacon for fifteen years and found the accusation "monstrous".

The affair had another dimension. The Reverend Thomas Moore had been prosecuted in the Consistory Court in 1915, at the instigation of the Archdeacon of Stow, but had been found not guilty. He was alleged to have said that "at any cost and however long he had to wait he would wreck the Archdeacon who brought him there". The bishop had given Kirkstead to Wakeford because Moore, as the patron of the living, had not made a presentation to the living. On 26 February 1914, Hicks says, he saw Jourdain "about my right to present to Kirkstead". He did present to the living, choosing Wakeford, and Wakeford got on with rebuilding and improvement work which had been neglected there.

Wakeford said in his evidence at his trial as reported by *The Times* that he was a lecturer at King's College, London as well as Archdeacon of Stow and Precentor of the cathedral. He had been at that hotel on 17 March and had accidentally been given a double-bedded room, but he had slept there alone. He had encountered the girl in question in Peterborough Cathedral where he had gone to make notes for a sermon. She was wet through and looking miserable and he had some conversation with her during the next half-hour but never saw her again. Eight witnesses had been ready to say differently. He was found guilty, but he appealed.

During the appeal, Herbert Edward Worthington, rector of Nether Seale, Ashby-de-la-Zouche, the archdeacon's wife's brother, giving evidence as a witness, said that "the late Bishop Hicks had told him in 1915 that there was a scandal in connection with the Archdeacon but he (the witness) took no steps: the matter was distasteful to him". This affair of 1915 is not mentioned in the diary. But according to *The Times's* account of the appeal hearing on 9 April 1921 Sir Edward Carson KC elicited a lot of detail about Moore's involvement in stitching up Wakeford. Having exhausted his avenues of appeal, and condemned, Wakeford became bankrupt in 1924 and he died at Barming Heath Asylum, according to the obituary published in *The Times* on 14 February 1930.

Places to Visit

Lincoln Cathedral
The Old Palace, Lincoln is now a hotel
Petwood is also now a hotel

Further Reading

Adams, Pauline, *Somerville for Women: An Oxford College 1879–1993*, Oxford: OUP, 1996.

Bennett, Nicholas, *Lincolnshire Parish Clergy c. 1214–1968: A Biographical Register*, The Lincoln Record Society, 103, 2013.

Bennett, Nicholas, *The Lincoln Record Society, News Review*, 1, 2012.

Brittain, Vera, *Testament of Youth*, London: Little, Brown, 1978.

Brittain, Vera, *Letters from a Lost Generation: First World War Letters of Vera Brittain and Four Friends*, ed. Alan Bishop and Mark Bostridge, London: Abacus, 1999.

Carpenter, S. C., *Winnington-Ingram: The Biography of Arthur Foley Winnington-Ingram, Bishop of London 1901–1939*, London: Hodder & Stoughton, 1949.

Ceadel, Martin, *Pacifism in Britain 1914–45: The Defining of a Faith*, Oxford: Clarendon Press, 1980.

Christianity and Industrial Problems, London: SPCK, 1918; reissued in 1927, unchanged, with a preface by Edward S. Talbot, formerly Bishop of Winchester.

Churchill, Randolph, *Winston S. Churchill*, London: Houghton Mifflin, 1966–88.

Clark, G. B., *The Transvaal and Bechuanaland*, London: 1883.

Condell, Diana, and Jean Liddiard, *Working for Victory: Images of Women in the First World War, 1914–18*, London: Routledge Kegan and Paul, 1987.

Davey, Arthur, *The British pro-Boers, 1877–1902*, Cape Town: Tafelberg, 1978.

Dowland, David A., *Nineteenth-Century Anglican Theological Training: The Redbrick Challenge*, Oxford: OUP, 1997.

Elton, Lord, *Edward King and Our Times*, London: G. Bles, 1958.

Fowler, J. H., *The Life and Letters of Edward Lee Hicks*, London: Christophers, 1922.

Gore, Charles, *Bishop Latimer as a Christian Socialist*, Christian Social Union, Oxford: 1905.

Gore, Charles, ed., *Essays in Aid of the Reform of the Church*, London, 1898.

Graham, John W., *War From a Quaker Point of View*, London: Headley Bros, 1915.

Grier, R. M., *Church and State*, Rugeley, after 1873.

Haig, Margaret, Viscountess Rhondda, *This Was My World*, London: Macmillan, 1933.

Harrison, M., "T. C. Horsfall and the Manchester Art Museum", in K. W. Roberts, *City, Class, and Culture: Studies of Social Policy and Cultural Production in Victorian Manchester*, ed. A. J. Kidd, Manchester: MUP, 1985, pp. 120–47.

Hayler, Mark H. C., *The Vision of a Century: The United Kingdom Alliance in Historical Retrospect*, London: United Kingdom Alliance, 1953.

Heeney, B., *The Women's Movement in the Church of England, 1850–1930*, Clarendon Press: 1988.

Hesketh, Ian, *Of Apes and Ancestors: Evolution, Christianity and the Oxford Debate*, Toronto: University of Toronto Press, 2009.

Hicks, E. L., *Henry Bazely, the Oxford Evangelist: A Memoir*, London: Macmillan, 1886.

Hicks, E. L., *The Optimist*, October, 1906.

Hicks, E. L., *Building in Troublous Times, Charge to the Clergy of the Lincoln Diocese at his Primary Visitation*, London: Longmans, 1912.

Hine, John Edward, *Days Gone By*, London: J. Murray, 1924.

Holland, H. S., *A Forty Years' Friendship: Letters from the Late Henry Scott Holland to Mrs Drew*, ed. S. L. Ollard, London, 1919.

Horsfall, Thomas, *National Service and the Welfare of the Community*, London, 1906.

Marson, Charles L., *Hugh, Bishop of Lincoln: A Short Story of One of the Makers of Medieval England*, London: Edward Arnold, 1901.

Hulme Hall, "The Early Days of Hulme Hall", *Hulme Hall Magazine*, 1912.

Jowett, Benjamin, "Letter to Roundell Palmer", MP, 15 November 1847, Evelyn Abbott and Lewis Campbell, *Life and Letters of Benjamin Jowett*, Vol. I, London: 1897, p. 190.

Kaye, John, *Correspondence of John Kaye, Bishop of Lincoln, 1827–53*, ed. R. W. Ambler, The Lincoln Record Society, 94, 2006.

King, Edward, Spiritual Letters, London: A. R. Mowbray, 1910.

Knox, Edmund, *The Tractarian Movement, 1833–1845: A study of the Oxford Movement as a phase of the religious revival in Western Europe in the second quarter of the nineteenth century*, London: Putnam, 1933.

Knox, Edward, *Reminiscences of an Octogenarian, 1847 to 1934*, ed. Kevin Feltham, www.stwilfs.freeserve.co.uk/past.htm#count5.

Knox, Ronald, *A Spiritual Aeneid*, London: Longmans Green, 1918.

Laity, Paul, *The British Peace Movement 1870–1914*, Oxford: OUP, 2002.

Mansbridge, Albert, *Fellow Men*, London: J. M. Dent, 1948.

Matheson, P. E., *Life of Hastings Rashdall*, Oxford: OUP, 1928.

McGann, Susan, Anne Crowther, Rona Dougall, *A Voice for Nurses* Manchester: MUP, 2009.

Modern Medical Opinions on Alcohol, Church of England Temperance Society, London, 1911.

Neville, G., ed. *The Diaries of Edward Lee Hicks, Bishop of Lincoln, 1910–1919*, The Lincoln Record Society, 82, 1993.

Paxman, Jeremy, *Great Britain's Great War*, London: Viking, 2013.

Ragg, L., *Memoir of Charles Edward Wickham*, London: Edward Arnold, 1911.

Rowan, Edgar, *Wilson Carlile and the Church Army*, London: The Church Army Bookroom, 1926.

Ruskin, John, *A Joy For Ever*, Manchester Lectures 1855. London: George Allen edition, 1911.

Scott Holland, Henry, *Our Neighbours: A Handbook for the C.S.U.*, ed. Henry Scott Holland assisted by Hastings Rashdall, London, 1911.

Snape, M. F., and Edward Madigan, eds, *The Clergy in Khaki: New Perspectives on British Army Chaplaincy in the First World War*, Farnham: Ashgate, 2013.

Southern, R.W., *Robert Grosseteste*, Oxford: OUP, 1986.

Streeter, B. H., and Edith Picton-Turbervill, *Woman and the Church*, London, 1917.

Thompson, David, "Historical Survey, 1750–1949", in *A History of Lincoln Minster*, ed. Dorothy Owen, Cambridge: CUP, 1994, pp. 210–318.

Trollope, Anthony, *Barchester Towers*, London, 1845.

Tryon, M. J., *A Small Memento of Frederick Tryon*, London, 1904.

Waugh, Evelyn, *The Life of the Right Reverend Ronald Knox*, London: Chapman and Hall, 1959.

Wilkinson, A., *The Church of England and the First World War*, London: SCM, 1978.

Woolf, Leonard, *Beginning Again: An Autobiography of the Years 1911–18*, London: Hogarth Press, 1968.

Woolf, Virginia, *Letters*, ed. Nigel Nicholson, Vol. II, London: Hogarth Press, 1976.

Debates in Parliament are quoted from the official record, Hansard, http://hansard.millbanksystems.com.

Index